Seeing Jefferson Anew

Seeing Jefferson Anew

In His Time and Ours

Edited by John B. Boles and Randal L. Hall

UNIVERSITY OF VIRGINIA PRESS
CHARLOTTESVILLE AND LONDON

University of Virginia Press

Printed in the United States of America on acid-free paper

First published 2010

9 8 7 6 5 4 3 2 1

LIBRARY OF CONGRESS CATALOGING-IN-PUBLICATION DATA
Seeing Jefferson anew : in his time and ours / John B. Boles and Randal L. Hall, editors.
p. cm.
"The essays in this volume were originally presented at a symposium held at Rice University on February 23–25, 2007"—Introd.
Includes bibliographical references and index.
ISBN 978-0-8139-2993-4 (cloth : alk. paper)
ISBN 978-0-8139-2997-2 (e-book)
1. Jefferson, Thomas, 1743-1826—Political and social views— Congresses. 2. Jefferson, Thomas, 1743-1826—Influence—Congresses. 3. Jefferson, Thomas, 1743-1826—Historiography—Congresses. 4. Presidents—United States—Biography—Congresses. I. Boles, John B. II. Hall, Randal L., 1971–
E332.2.S44 2010
973.4'6092—dc22
2009048480

Contents

Acknowledgments

These essays were originally presented at a conference held at Rice University on February 23–25, 2007, and entitled "Thomas Jefferson: In His Time and Ours." Funded by a grant from Lisa Simon of Southern National Bank and matched by an anonymous contribution, the symposium was one of an ongoing series of biennial symposia dedicated to different aspects of Southern history. Our colleagues at the *Journal of Southern History,* Patricia Dunn Burgess and Francelle L. Blum, were indispensable assistants, as were a large number of our graduate students, who helped in a variety of ways to make the symposium a success. We would also like to thank Ira D. Gruber, Rebecca A. Goetz, and Melissa Kean. Rhonda Ragsdale helped with fact-checking several of the essays. Any significant event on a university campus depends on the assistance of a number of people, and we appreciate the staff of the Rice Memorial Center, Rice Catering, and others who helped. Paula Platt, administrator of the Department of History, took care of all the disbursements and accounting and made hotel and flight arrangements, a major contribution to the event. Richard Holway of the University of Virginia Press has been an enthusiastic supporter of the book project since the moment we approached him about it. In fact, every person involved with the book's production was wonderfully cooperative and helpful: project editor Ruth Steinberg, acquisitions assistant Raennah L. Mitchell, copyeditor Beth Ina, indexer Carolyn C. Sherayko, and designer Chris Harrison. And the presenters at the conference—the authors of the essays here collected—have been an absolute delight to work with. They were amenable to our suggestions (which always endears authors to editors), met all deadlines (mirabile dictu), and proved by their essays that there is still something new to say about Thomas Jefferson.

Introduction

In a readily understandable way, history is—as one definition has it—a conversation between the present and the past. Such a definition suggests that as present concerns and issues change, then the nature of the conversation will change too. New questions will be asked, old assumptions will be reexamined, and current perspectives will shed fresh light on what once were considered settled opinions. For that reason, revisionism, much maligned in the popular mind, is the meat and potatoes of history. Every topic, person, and event of significance is subject to constant restudy: new methodologies are employed, recently discovered evidence is brought to bear, different questions are asked, and contemporary assessments and attitudes toward a variety of issues often render previously accepted historical judgments problematical. All historical interpretations become more complex as new ones are not so much overlaid on older interpretations as placed beside them.

Surely no one in American history has been subjected to a greater range of interpretations than has Thomas Jefferson. Merrill D. Peterson's brilliant study, *The Jefferson Image in the American Mind,* now fifty years old, showed how history had treated Jefferson over the past generations and how different he had looked to different observers at different times. Jefferson has been, in Peterson's words, "a sensitive reflector, through several generations, of America's troubled search for the image of itself." "More than any other

American," Peterson concludes, Jefferson "impressed himself on the nation's future."[1]

Jefferson's image has been on a historical roller-coaster ride since Peterson's book appeared. When that book came out in 1960, scholars as well as the general public were laying aside critical older studies of Jefferson by Henry Adams and others and were instead reading the equally magnificent series of respectful volumes that Dumas Malone was turning out. Two volumes of this biography had been published by 1960, and over the next two decades four additional hefty volumes were published.[2] Malone took Jefferson's greatness as a given and wrote life-and-times biography in the grand tradition. Very much in the same tradition would be Peterson's own one-volume (but over a thousand pages) study, *Thomas Jefferson and the New Nation: A Biography.*[3] But 1960, with Malone's ongoing biographical project looming definitively over the field of Jefferson studies—or so it seemed—was the last period of calm before the storm. Over the next four decades, Jefferson would take a historiographical beating, with many claiming that he should be toppled from the American pantheon and wishing, if it were possible, for him to be cleaved from Mount Rushmore. No longer was Jefferson almost automatically praised.

In such criticism, Leonard Levy describes Jefferson as an enemy of civil liberties, Fawn Brodie renews the charges that he had a long-time sexual affair with a slave woman he owned, Michael Zuckerman emphasizes his "negrophobia," Michael Lind labels him a Southern reactionary and racist morally equivalent to Theodore Bilbo, Pauline Maier strips him of sole authorship of the Declaration of Independence, Joseph J. Ellis diminishes him systematically, Roger G. Kennedy essentially blames Jefferson for the Civil War, Paul Finkelman relentlessly focuses on the discrepancies between Jefferson's noble-sounding words and both his ownership of slaves and his refusal to forthrightly attack or work to end the institution, and Conor Cruise O'Brien—in the most intemperate attack of all—conjectures that "the twentieth century statesman whom the Thomas Jefferson of January 1793 would have most admired is Pol Pot." O'Brien even imagines Jefferson approving of the bombing of the federal office building in Oklahoma City.[4] Yet despite all this, as John Adams legendarily said on his deathbed, "Thomas Jefferson still survives."[5]

Much of the new scholarship has been insightful, thorough, and salutary, though some of the attacks are ahistorical, uncontextualized, and exaggerated. Our understanding of Jefferson and his time is little enhanced by renewed attention to the facts that, over his long life, his views changed; that holding office required deviation from purely theoretical formulations; and that, in the exigency of opportunity, a higher principle might take precedence over a lesser—in the case, for example, of the Louisiana Purchase, in which Jefferson deemed doubling the size of the nation more important than being consistent on the matter of strict construction of the Constitution. Now we are more aware than ever that mindless devotion to every principle even as circumstances change is not always a virtue.

The essays in this volume were originally presented at a symposium held at Rice University on February 23–25, 2007. The symposium was entitled "Thomas Jefferson: In His Time and Ours" both because we wanted to examine the relevance for today of Jefferson's ideas and practices and because we wanted to use the latest scholarly discoveries to better place him in his historical context. We sought not to settle Jefferson's reputation so much as to present a more complex, nuanced interpretation of it. Jefferson's ideals are so elevating and his rhetoric so soaring that his inability to fully live up to his promise can cause disappointed latter-day observers to lament his imperfections. Yet as many have said, critics use Jefferson's own democratic principles to judge him, and over the course of history, and in ways he could have hardly understood, his principles have often triumphed and beckon us yet as a nation. Jefferson's failures are more pronounced in retrospect.

If one considers Jefferson's ideas and actions in comparison with those that preceded him, he may look far more progressive. For instance, racism has been the issue driving many recent critiques of Jefferson. Looking back at Jefferson from today, his continuing ownership of slaves even as some Virginia planters freed their bond-people, and his unwillingness to condemn slavery more forthrightly in his later years and to work actively to end slaveholding can lead one to question the depth of his commitment to liberty and freedom. But looking from the vantage of 1776, Jefferson's antislavery words in his draft of the Declaration of Independence, his involvement in the Northwest Ordinance's prohibition of slavery in the Northwest Territory, and his proclamation to Congress in November 1806 that the new Congress in the spring of 1807 should forthwith make illegal the importation of slaves effective January 1, 1808—the moment the Constitution allowed but did not require the ending of the international slave trade to the nation—make his an effective and prophetic voice against slavery.

We asked our contributors to examine seven aspects of Jefferson by looking forward from his era and by looking backward from ours. We knew that they would be careful to place Jefferson in the context of his own times, and that while they would be alert to those occasions when he did not live up to his own highest standards, they would seek to explain and understand these deviations instead of merely criticizing from a presentist position. We wanted subtlety, not moralizing. We wanted careful attention to context, to language, to nuance. Jefferson was involved in the public realm for more than fifty years, and he held a string of elective and appointive positions and faced a daunting set of shifting domestic and international situations. No armchair philosopher but rather a philosopher statesman, he had to adjust, tack against adversity, compromise; he changed his mind—for example on the merits of the Constitution—and struggled tenaciously against political opponents. Having fought to achieve independence and create the new nation, for the rest of his life he worried about its continuation and was quick—often overly quick—to see political opponents as threats to the survival of the nation. Dedicated to the ultimate cause of the nation, he at times was prone to identify his own positions with the best interests of the United States and to fight unremittingly against political enemies whom he saw as more than just personal threats. Hence, if one chooses quotations indiscriminately from fifty years of political controversy, Jefferson can be made to look shamelessly contradictory and even hypocritical. Given the long years he was involved in the political fray and that he wrote more than nineteen thousand letters, proof-texting can seem to shred his putative reputation as a friend of liberty and the apostle of freedom. But Jefferson deserves better than that kind of cherry-picking of quotes and examples. He should be subjected to criticism but not demonization, and our contributors lived up to that responsibility. Here is neither reverential praise nor self-righteous condemnation. We sought not to produce a full-blown defense of Jefferson but rather a more complicated portrait. Jefferson was a human with human failings, but he articulated a set of ideals that still inspire most people, even his severest critics. Nonetheless, at the end of the day many people—considering Jefferson's full career—will remain ambivalent about him, perhaps even hostile.[6]

While most general readers are aware of Jefferson's elegance on behalf of political and religious freedom and his support of a free press and public education, what makes him equally attractive to many—even though on occasion he can be so disappointing—is his astounding breadth of interests. Born wealthy but philosophically democratic, Jefferson's birthright (and later his wife's fortune) allowed him the leisure of pursuing his intellectual, scientific, medical, agricultural, and other interests with almost all-consuming diligence. Jefferson was a bibliophile and prolific reader; he was fascinated with paleontology, ethnography, and natural history; he loved music and art; he enjoyed listening to and performing music; he was an oenophile and gourmet and became more so after his service as American minister to France; he dedicated himself to agricultural improvements with regard to implements, seeds, and breeds of livestock; he was an extraordinarily accomplished amateur architect; he was an educational reformer; he developed the manual for conducting the business of the U.S. Congress that shaped that institution for two centuries. Jefferson had, as John Adams said in 1776, "a peculiar felicity of expression," which partially explains why Jefferson's articulations of his principles have had such international appeal. His private letters often display his literary flair, and unlike modern presidents, Jefferson wrote nearly all the papers and resolutions that issued from his office. Reading Jefferson's correspondence and state papers, one gets a sense of the real man, not the prose by committee produced by a writing staff.

Jefferson's multiplicity of interests and talents make him attractive to many readers, and the result of a number of his interests—for example, the design of Monticello—themselves offer insight into the working of his mind. But Jefferson lives today because of what he wrote about and achieved on behalf of political and religious freedom. There were limitations to his imagination, so he did not comprehend the gendered, racial, and geopolitical blinders that restricted his advocacy and the implementation of his own principles. For the symposium and in this volume, we chose not to have sessions and essays on Jefferson and music, or Jefferson and the mastodons, or Jefferson the traveler, and so on, as fascinating as such topics would have been. Rather, we solicited authors who would probe the applications and implications of Jefferson's key principles to modern life with full attention to the context out of which those principles emerged. We wanted to recapture both the eighteenth-century world from which he came and the present-day world he helped to produce. Here we encounter Thomas Jefferson in his time and ours.

Peter S. Onuf opens the volume with a powerful, subtle reflection on the ongoing importance of Jefferson's political ideas in this multiracial, multicultural, globally potent nation. With idealized notions of Jefferson chastened by near-certain confirmation of his long relationship with Sally Hemings, we can plunge anew into the documents to find a more complicated Jefferson. Onuf teases out the dynamism of Jefferson's thoughts on democracy, and what he finds is perhaps disconcerting and cautionary. According to Onuf, Jefferson looked to "the progressive enlightenment of public opinion" to draw Americans together behind the Revolutionary republicanism he cherished above all else. But everywhere in the young republic Jefferson saw threats to the national unity he longed for: public opinion was not so easily shaped. He and his like-minded allies redefined aristocracy to include their factious opponents at home and abroad, while reserving the label of "democrat" for Jeffersonians. The U.S. conception of democracy thus relies heavily on a notion born of a singular time and place. The uneasy relationship between national self-determination and mediation of dissent within the nation during the early nineteenth century grew until the outbreak of disastrous civil war, but nonetheless Americans have long failed to historicize this often-unthinking sense that individualistic democracy was the founding principle of a strong nation.

Every student of Jefferson must strike a balance between analyzing Jefferson's ideas and emphasizing his actions. Eva Sheppard Wolf explicitly seeks the Jefferson of democratic political action, but inevitably his ideas enter the picture as well. Reflecting the mid-eighteenth-century ideal of hierarchy and deference, the young Jefferson's view of politicking was to take little or no action, i.e., to allow his social and economic eminence naturally to bring political power. Concern for the people's wishes entered his political outlook with the Revolution, but the link between citizens' desires and politicians' actions still was indirect in the political structures Jefferson worked toward. For a politician to seek votes would be to burden his good judgment with unseemly dependence on his supporters. But just as Onuf emphasizes democracy's time-bound birth in the Jeffersonian fight against so-called aristocracy, so Wolf describes Jefferson's partisan battles to preserve his Republican ideas as pushing Jefferson to, reluctantly, ease more directly into the fight for popular support. With his power secure after 1800, however, he willingly returned to passively receiving the people's endorsement. Onuf and Wolf would surely agree: democracy is hard to pin down.

So is geography. Peter J. Kastor also dwells productively on the interplay of ideas and action in looking at Jefferson's relationship with one of his major political and intellectual problems—the West. Kastor usefully defines a Near West between the Appalachians and the Mississippi and a Far West beyond that great river. By tying Jefferson's writings on these Wests to the context of his life at the moment of writing, Kastor traces a Jefferson capable of inspiring Americans with idealistic prose about Indians and vast new territories yet also able to take on the mundane task of overseeing America's administrative incorporation of both slave states in the Old Southwest and free states in the Old Northwest, all of them on lands from which Indians were being pushed. Fascinated by the native inhabitants and the potential of both Wests to strengthen the nation, Jefferson changed his focus depending on his day-to-day imperatives. As delegate to Congress or secretary of state or president, Jefferson had to take a different view than he did as a planter and retired politician. Ironically, the aging Jefferson who feared slavery would split the nation had had much to do with forming both sides of that divide in the Near West.

Slavery more exclusively occupies Adam Rothman's essay, and like the other contributors, he turns to primary sources to illuminate old questions. Newly assembled databases on the slaves of Monticello reveal men and women who over generations, in Rothman's words, "had sunk deep roots into the ground" and "spun sticky webs of kinship and community." Rothman contrasts the slaves' attachment to the soil with Jefferson's insistence that the slaves whom he hoped in the future would be emancipated would have to be colonized outside America. Jefferson's refusal to see clearly and understand the black people surrounding him raises questions about the morality of his time and the proper way for historians to evaluate it today, questions with which Rothman wrestles vigorously.

In our time the topic of gender oppression, like racism, has led extensively to rigorous and passionate analysis. Jefferson's relationship with Sally Hemings mingles these two flashpoints. Jan Ellen Lewis leads up to that relationship by tracing Jefferson's evolving understanding of women and gender. Jefferson's casual youthful misogyny reflected gender norms of his time and place, and marriage likewise tempered those views in conventional ways. But his anxious misogyny resurfaced when Jefferson, a widower, found women abroad to hold values that contrasted with the womanly virtue he expected to underpin the emerging American nation. The most virtuous role for a woman was, in his view, to be busily engaged in orderly household manufacture. Lewis raises the provocative possibility that in assigning Sally Hemings to do just such work, Jefferson was reconciling the gendered and racial arrangements of his life after returning from France.

If any subjects other than race and gender more readily grab the attention of Americans today, then surely those topics would be religion and sex. The volume's final two essayists deftly cover these themes in Jefferson's life.

Thomas E. Buckley, S.J., shows that the interaction of church and state incited controversy just as fiercely in Jefferson's time as in ours. With his fresh look at Jefferson's education in the home of the Reverend James Maury, Buckley identifies within the church a source of Jefferson's later emphasis on the need for religion and reason to fit together. The pursuit of such harmony required the religious freedom with which we identify Jefferson and which so enraged many of his contemporary political enemies, most notably during the campaign preceding the election of 1800. But as Buckley astutely demonstrates, the separation of church and state did not mean the separation of religion and government, for Jefferson often invoked religion in a political context, approved federal aid to missionaries, and attended church while president.

Andrew Burstein looks to some even older sources—scientific and medical writing reaching all the way to the Greeks—to understand the earthier side of Jefferson. For Burstein, explaining Jefferson's sexuality necessarily involves forays into race, gender, health, emotions, and politics. The medical literature of the time would have guided the widower Jefferson to find sexual release without guilt, just as he bathed his feet in cold water and avoided overindulgence in food. His science led Jefferson to see women and blacks and Indians in certain ways, and the parallels between a healthy body and a healthy body politic, guided by proper "sensibility," appear throughout Jefferson's writings. Likewise, passion not properly channeled could wreak havoc—on either an individual or a harmonious nation.

In reviving and dissecting so many facets of Jefferson's mind,

Burstein's essay fittingly stands as the final full-length chapter. Although even the prolific Merrill Peterson once wrote that Jefferson "is one of those men about whom the last word can never be said," for this volume, we are giving the last word to Andrew Jackson O'Shaughnessy.[7] Who better to have had in the audience for the entire symposium than the director of the Robert H. Smith International Center for Jefferson Studies at the Thomas Jefferson Foundation! We are honored that O'Shaughnessy accepted our invitation to offer closing insights on these collected papers and on Thomas Jefferson in his time and ours.

Notes

1. Merrill D. Peterson, *The Jefferson Image in the American Mind* (New York, 1960), [vii], 14. Peterson's book now must be supplemented by Francis D. Cogliano, *Thomas Jefferson: Reputation and Legacy* (Edinburgh, 2006).

2. Dumas Malone, *Jefferson and His Time,* 6 vols. (Boston, 1948–81). Henry Adams, *History of the United States,* 9 vols. (New York, 1889–91), is, of course, one of the great classics of American history.

3. Merrill D. Peterson, *Thomas Jefferson and the New Nation: A Biography* (New York, 1970).

4. Leonard Levy, *Jefferson and Civil Liberties: The Darker Side* (Cambridge, Mass., 1963); Fawn Brodie, *Thomas Jefferson: An Intimate History* (New York, 1974); Michael Zuckerman, *Almost Chosen People: Oblique Biographies in the American Grain* (Berkeley, Calif., 1993), 196; Michael Lind, *The Next American Nation: The New Nationalism and the Fourth American Revolution* (New York, 1995); Pauline Maier, *American Scripture: Making the Declaration of Independence* (New York, 1997); Joseph J. Ellis, *American Sphinx: The Character of Thomas Jefferson* (New York, 1997); Roger G. Kennedy, *Mr. Jefferson's Lost Cause: Land, Farmers, Slavery, and the Louisiana Purchase* (New York, 2003); Paul Finkelman, ed., *Slavery and the Founders: Race and Liberty in the Age of Jefferson,* 2nd ed. (Armonk, N.Y., 2001); Paul Finkelman, "Jefferson and Slavery: 'Treason against the Hopes of the World,' " in *Jeffersonian Legacies,* ed. Peter S. Onuf (Charlottesville, Va., 1993), 181–221; Conor Cruise O'Brien, *The Long Affair: Thomas Jefferson and the French Revolution, 1785–1800* (Chicago, 1996), 150, 310, 317. See also the briefer version of O'Brien's diatribe: "Thomas Jefferson: Radical and Racist," *Atlantic Monthly,* October 1996, 53–74. On the more critical turn in Jefferson scholarship, see Jeffrey L. Pasley, "Politics and the

Misadventures of Thomas Jefferson's Modern Reputation: A Review Essay," *Journal of Southern History* 72 (November 2006): 871–908; and Cogliano, *Thomas Jefferson.*

5. For a debunking of the legend that these were in fact John Adams's final words, see Andrew Burstein, "Jefferson Still Survives," *History News Network,* March 18, 2002, http://historynewsnetwork.org/articles/article.html?id=634 (accessed July 15, 2008).

6. Jefferson's principles are at the forefront of, for example, Bernard Bailyn, "Jefferson and the Ambiguities of Freedom," in Bailyn, *To Begin the World Anew: The Genius and Ambiguities of the American Founders* (New York, 2003), 37–59; Pasley, "Politics and the Misadventures of Thomas Jefferson's Modern Reputation," 871–908, esp. p. 908; and Douglas L. Wilson, "Thomas Jefferson and the Character Issue," *Atlantic Monthly,* November 1992, 57–74.

7. Peterson, *Thomas Jefferson and the New Nation,* viii.

Peter S. Onuf

Thomas Jefferson and American Democracy

The continuing cascade of scholarship on Thomas Jefferson suggests that the third president retains his exalted standing in the American pantheon, notwithstanding iconoclastic assaults from both right and left.[1] In the wake of the civil rights movement, Jefferson's ownership of large numbers of slaves represented the biggest threat to his reputation. Yet even his bitterest critics invoked the natural rights principles of Jefferson's Declaration of Independence in their assaults on Jefferson. Failing to free his slaves, Jefferson may have fallen far short of his own lofty standard, but few commentators concluded that the standard itself was thus compromised. Jefferson promised freedom for all, and as successive generations of Americans have redeemed that promise, they have also refurbished Jefferson's iconic standing in the American pantheon.

The democratic Jefferson has emerged with new force in recent scholarship, both because of the way we now think about race and therefore slavery and because of persistent doubts about the future of American democracy. The challenge for historians now is to extricate Jefferson from mythic, exceptionalist narratives of democracy's inexorable ascent. The mythic Jefferson is a mirror for self-admiring Americans; a properly historicized Jefferson can illuminate the world he sought—and failed—to transform. The American Revolution did not initiate the republican millennium and therefore lead to the "end of history." Instead, it gave rise to a new nation that would play a leading role, for better and worse, in shaping the history of the modern world.

Over the last generation, Jefferson's equivocal stance on slavery and his endorsement of proto-racist "suspicions" of black inferiority have been subject to blistering criticism, culminating in the recent uproar over his relationship with Sally Hemings and their children. Given long-standing efforts of the "Jefferson establishment" to stifle discussion of the Hemings liaison, we might have expected that his image would have been terminally tarnished by Annette Gordon-Reed's exhaustive and compelling review of the evidence in *Thomas Jefferson and Sally Hemings* in 1997 and the publication the next year of DNA test results that made Jefferson the only plausible candidate for fatherhood of Hemings's children.[2] Of course, a few die-hard defenders resisted the charges, appointing themselves to a "scholar's commission" that was reduced finally to raising pseudo-profound questions about whether *anything* in the past could be definitively proven.[3] But the big news was that most scholars and interested laypeople were unfazed by the revelations. If anything, Jefferson's stock rebounded. Was this the darkness before the dawn, with Jefferson's image shining more brightly than ever?

Historians have trouble enough making sense of the past and are probably best advised to leave the present day to better equipped social scientists and cultural commentators. But we might suggest that changing contemporary attitudes toward race generally and race-mixing particularly have something to do with the response to the Hemings affair. We might further suggest that this focus on race deflects attention from slavery, mitigating—or at least complicating—the absolute moral clarity of our judgment on the peculiar institution. If most scholars resist the temptation to sentimentalize the Jefferson-Hemings relationship as a "plantation marriage" or transgressive love match, very few are willing to call it rape.[4] To do so would be to deny Hemings agency, and thus to be complicit in her erasure from history.

Recovering Sally Hemings is by no means forgiving Thomas Jefferson, but Jefferson as lover—however unequal the lovers' power—is a more sympathetic character than Jefferson the owner and exploiter of his fellow human beings. In the classic antislavery account, masters' sexual exploitation of female slaves was a particularly extreme instance of their despotic rule, the most devastating and demoralizing possible assault on the manhood of male slaves. Now, as we acknowledge the agency of slaves (however limited), we distinguish the domains of race and gender relations, granting them some degree of autonomy (however limited). All slaves were not created equal, nor did they occupy equal positions, notwithstanding the totalizing imperatives of the institution and the binary logic of racial hierarchy.

As Sally Hemings rises into history, Jefferson descends from his mythological pedestal. For beleaguered defenders of his stainless character, this might seem like a disastrous demotion; for disenchanted modern Americans who know more than they want to know about presidential sex lives, the convergent trajectories of master and slave make Jefferson more "human." In any case, it seems hardly surprising that Jefferson would exercise his sexual prerogatives over a female slave. After all, Jefferson himself acknowledged the irresistible temptation for the master class in general, though he never applied the generalization to himself. "[A] lover of natural history" should not be a lover of his slaves, if he would keep the races of man, like "the races of animals . . . as distinct as nature has formed them." The inability of masters—including Jefferson—to respect "nature's" distinctions made the colonization of freedpeople a moral imperative.[5]

Re-envisioning Jefferson through the prism of race proves not to be the last chapter in a deconstructive chronicle but rather a preface to a broad reconstruction of a humanized, if not fully rehabilitated, Jefferson who speaks to us more eloquently than ever about our fundamental values. My contrarian goal in the pages that follow is to call the reconstructed Jefferson who has again ascended to the national pantheon (if, indeed, he was ever demoted) back to the bar of historiographical judgment. The "real" Jefferson and his role in our national history will remain obscure as long as we keep struggling to define ourselves in—or against—his image.

Indictments of the slave-owning racist are always framed in Jeffersonian terms: Jefferson is condemned for not living up to his own natural rights philosophy and democratic vision. Because historians have been obsessed with the alleged discrepancy between his words and deeds, the "character issue" continues to command their attention. Yet, whether, with Paul Finkelman and Conor Cruise O'Brien, they conclude that the hypocritical Jefferson is hopelessly compromised or, following Jack N. Rakove's lead, they insist that "our Jefferson's" fundamental commitments transcend his acknowledged, all-too-human flaws, historians nonetheless all rally around the democratic flag, reaffirming their own Jeffersonian values. "Jefferson lives" because the "good" Jefferson is the best antidote for the very pathologies that his most virulent critics trace back to Jefferson himself.[6]

As the culture wars subside, Jefferson's sins seem less damning, or perhaps simply more banal. By contrast, historians' concerns about the future of democracy have been increasingly pronounced in recent years. The net result has been to secure Jefferson's primary position in the grand sweep of American history, notwithstanding the serious reservations many writers have about him. Pauline Maier's *American Scripture,* a superb account of the drafting and reception of Jefferson's Declaration of Independence, brings a plethora of "other" declarations to the fore and emphasizes the critical role of the Virginian's congressional editors. Maier's clear intention is to empower present-day citizens by democratizing the founding, showing that ordinary folk across the continent could grasp and articulate the fundamental values that we now celebrate in the Jeffersonian "scripture" and reflexively impute to his soaring genius. By confusing "democracy" with the new regime the Revolutionaries created, by transforming those Revolutionaries into "Founders" and then worshipping them and their works, we implicitly acknowledge our own civic impotence.[7]

More self-consciously radical young historians stalk the same prey in their campaign against what they contemptuously call "Founders chic."[8] A broad general readership, with its insatiable appetite for biographies of Jefferson and the other Founders, and the authors who pander to it, remain in thrall to a long-dead generation of white men (now accompanied by a select company of white women) and therefore subject to the dead hand of the past that Jefferson himself so eloquently denounced. Democracy will die if we revere the fathers too much and therefore fail to fulfill our own democratic potential. After all, as Jefferson famously wrote to James Madison in 1789, *"the earth belongs in usufruct to the living,"* not to a departed generation that had no legitimate claim over its successors.[9]

Whether they acknowledge or resist his influence, modern democratic theorists and fellow-traveling historians are pulled irresistibly in Jefferson's direction. Yet again, Jefferson is both the problem, as an object of disempowering ancestor worship, and the solution, as the theorist of revolutionary renewal. One of the most impressive recent efforts to reinvigorate a moribund American democracy, Mark Hulliung's *The Social Contract in America,* prescribes a strong dose of undiluted Jeffersonianism, giving equal weight to the Lockean premises of the Declaration and the Revolutionary doctrine of "the earth belongs to the living." Jefferson's anxieties about counterrevolutionary tendencies have proven prophetic, not only because conservatives have retrospectively transformed *Revolutionaries* into *Founders* but also because *progressives* have themselves jettisoned Jeffersonian first principles in their pursuit of rights and entitlements. The long reign of contract theory and therefore of democracy is what once made America *exceptional,* but this fundamental difference from other modern nations is fast disappearing. Yet the very fact that he can appeal so effectively to Jefferson suggests that Hulliung's dire conclusions may overshoot the mark. Successive generations of reformers have turned, and—with Hulliung—will continue to turn to the Revolutionary democrat for inspiration. And as long as the Declaration remains *American Scripture,* "Jefferson lives."[10]

Just as efforts to banish Jefferson from the pantheon or deny his authorship of the Declaration draw attention to him in his "absence," any historical discussion of democracy inevitably reverts to Jefferson and his legacy. Recent syntheses of the Revolutionary era underscore Jefferson's central importance, even when they criticize him for his failures to live up to his ideals. The triumph and travails of democracy provide the main narrative thrust of the two most influential narratives, Gordon S. Wood's *The Radicalism of the American Revolution* (1992) and Sean Wilentz's *The Rise of American Democracy* (2005), as well as a host of specialized studies.[11] Gary B. Nash's *The Unknown American Revolution,* an ambitious attempt to construct a national historical narrative that marginalizes the Founders and celebrates marginal groups, also tells a Jeffersonian story. Democracy's promise was only finally fulfilled when the "rivulets" of dissent that Nash traces across the Revolutionary landscape were at last channeled into the national mainstream. The distance between the Revolution we "know" and Nash's "unknown" Revolution is the distance between Jefferson's world and the world he envisioned. The cast of characters may differ, but the plotline is comfortingly familiar in Nash's inspiring narrative of progressive inclusion.[12]

Jefferson the visionary democrat is consolidating his position in the national pantheon, overshadowing the slaveholding racist who seemed, briefly, to be toppling from his pedestal only a few short years ago. The scholarly focus on Jefferson's character-cum-personality, however damaging its particular revelations and implications, has facilitated this rehabilitation. Not only has Jefferson been "humanized" and thus made more familiar and accessible to modern Americans, but the sharp edge of neo-abolitionist criticism has been blunted: the slave-owning hypocrite is now, thanks to the Hemings controversy, relocated in his plantation home where he has relations *with* as well as power *over* his slaves. In its diversity, this newly recovered Monticello looks much more like modern America than the republic of white males that Jefferson and his fellow Virginians established in 1776.[13] The stark juxtaposition of a racially exclusive Virginian polity to a capacious conception of a multiracial, multicultural Virginian society suggests yet another version of our democratic saga. After great, sometimes bloody struggles, the universal values Jefferson so eloquently articulated are finally brought home to his own Monticello: it is, after all, the perfect alignment of society and polity, the people and their government, that constitutes the fulfillment of democracy's promise.

It is ironic that "democracy" in this demographic and cultural sense should be in the ascendant, seemingly triumphant, at precisely the moment when historians and political theorists are expressing so much concern about democracy's *political* future. Yet again, our incoherence focuses on the iconic figure of Jefferson. Perhaps the oft-quoted proposition of the early Jefferson biographer James Parton is truer than we would like to admit: "If Jefferson was wrong, America is wrong. If America is right, Jefferson was right."[14] At the very least, whenever we think about the meaning of American history, we cannot escape Jefferson. But we might be able to make more sense of him—and of ourselves—if we let go of "our Jefferson" for a moment and imagine him in his own time and place.[15]

The image of a multiracial, multicultural nation that can embrace the Hemings-Jefferson relationship stands in sharp contrast to the nation that Jefferson and his fellow revolutionaries actually created. But Jefferson's democratic followers insist that he envisioned a progressive expansion of the electorate and would have welcomed successive "declarations of independence" by excluded groups. Focusing on Jefferson's natural rights philosophy, Abraham Lincoln congratulated his predecessor for having "the coolness, forecast, and capacity to introduce into a merely revolutionary document, an abstract truth, applicable to all men and all times."[16] That Jefferson was a slaveholder throughout his life did not trouble Lincoln or other self-professed Jeffersonians who recognized the enormous obstacles to emancipation in Jefferson's time. Reformers needed a high standard. Jefferson provided it.

But does Jefferson really deserve credit for what has been done in his name? Does the modern American republic really represent the fulfillment of Jefferson's vision? There are no definitive answers to these questions, for our mythic Jefferson is a protean character, constantly refashioned to suit our needs. We can ask more specific questions, however, about Jefferson's expectations for the new American republics. Certainly they would one day be freed from the incubus of slavery, whether "with the consent of the masters" or "their extirpation" in a bloody servile insurrection. But Virginia would *not* be racially mixed. Either it would become all white, as enlightened masters following the counsels of reason emancipated and expatriated their slaves, "declar[ing] them a free and independant people" in some other country—or, in the horrific alternative, the face of the commonwealth would blacken as slaves extirpated (or, still more horribly, enslaved) their former masters. "[A] revolution of the wheel of fortune, an exchange of situation, is among possible events" all the more likely, Jefferson acknowledged, "when I reflect that God is just."[17]

Jefferson's vision of racial homogeneity was not simply an aberrant, pathological response to an intractable social problem.[18] Quite to the contrary, Jefferson looked forward to a growing ideological and moral convergence, a "union of sentiment . . . auguring harmony and happiness."[19] The Americans' "experiment" in republican government constituted an epochal moment in the history of mankind precisely because it enabled subjects to become citizens who recognized in themselves and each other a capacity for moral improvement.[20] Progress was predicated on transcending diversity and so creating a New World in the negative image of the corrupt Old World. For Jefferson, the old regime—the "abandoned confederacy" of "kings, nobles and priests" that waged war "against the happiness of the mass of the people"—institutionalized diversity, mystified inequality, and stunted the progress of the human mind.[21] But if Jefferson's vision of equality, "harmony and happiness" was juxtaposed to Old World inequality and despotism, its deeper source was in anxieties about anarchy and disorder in America itself.

Jefferson characteristically condemned homegrown "aristocrats" and "monocrats" as alien and un-American, witting or unwitting pawns of their British masters: they represented a persisting and ominously resilient Europe-in-America that must be purged if the American experiment were to succeed. Of course, Jefferson did not have to look to Federalist New England for the more immanent and dangerous threat to the republic that the potentially hostile, captive nation of enslaved Africans represented. Perhaps Jefferson displaced doubts about Virginia's republican future by conjuring up imaginary foreign threats—or by imagining that fellow Americans were foreigners. But whatever the psychological or ideological logic involved, Jefferson cherished a vision of a broadening and deepening American union, of a New World that finally escaped thralldom to the Old.

The shaky foundation of Jefferson's hopes was in the progressive enlightenment of public opinion. Given the failure of the state legislature to support comprehensive public education, the destruction of the Anglican establishment and the free competition of the various Christian sects in the religious marketplace provided the most likely impetus toward enlightenment. As Jefferson began to think of himself as a "Christian" in his later years, he viewed the extraordinary expansion of evangelical Christianity known by historians as the "Second Great Awakening" in an increasingly positive light.[22] Baptists and other dissenters celebrated Jefferson's role in dismantling Virginia's Anglican establishment; for his part, Jefferson admired the evangelicals' democratic theology and ecclesiology, practical, this-worldly morality, and rejection of priestly privilege. When Jefferson wrote in 1822 that "there is not a *young man* now living in the United States who will not die an Unitarian," he was celebrating the Awakening's progressive, enlightening tendencies. Rather than supposing a fundamental opposition between the Unitarians' reasonable religion and the revivalists' heartfelt faith, Jefferson envisioned their ultimate convergence.[23]

Jefferson's belief in the ultimate triumph of reason and a "reasonable" Christianity was profound, leading him to envision the emergence of an enlightened Christian nation within a generation. Of course, most faithful Christians of Jefferson's day would have questioned Jefferson's Christian faith. But Jefferson insisted that doctrinal differences were increasingly unimportant to practical-minded, democratic Christians. "[O]ceans of human blood have been spilt, & whole regions of the earth have been desolated by wars & persecutions" over "unimportant" and "mischievous" doctrinal questions.[24] In America, by contrast, Christians had learned not only to respect the autonomy of individual conscience but also to recognize the common principles that animated followers of different sects. Americans understood that it was not necessary "that we should all think alike," that it would "usurp the throne of God" to impose uniformity of belief.[25] Sectarian differences were ultimately inconsequential in a free republic where one sect could not impose its will over others. "Were I to be a founder of a new sect," Jefferson playfully wrote in 1819, "I would call them Apriarians, and, after the example of the bee, advise them to extract the honey of every sect." In America, the competition of proliferating sects would simultaneously reveal the insignificance of theological differences and the harmonizing principles of a common republican Christianity. "My fundamental principle would be the reverse of Calvin's, that we are to be saved by our good works which are within our power, and not by our faith which is not within our power."[26] Unity would emerge from diversity, binding patriotic Americans ever more closely to their nation.

As the somewhat reluctant champion of the emerging Republican opposition to the Federalist administrations of the 1790s, Jefferson also imagined a glorious future in which trivial differences of "opinion" that enflamed self-seeking partisans would give way to the reaffirmation of shared "Federal and Republican principles."[27] And just as he considered the priestly power of the state-supported churches of New England (not coincidentally, the leading advocates of the mystifications of Calvinist theology) as an alien excrescence that threatened freedom of thought and republican government, Jefferson reflexively denominated his Federalist foes as foreigners. These "Anglomen and monocrats" had never been fully weaned from their attachments to the "mother" country or to the monarchical principles that had justified British rule in America.[28] Jefferson acknowledged that there might be honest differences of political opinion among Americans, and even that party divisions might be "natural," but he always suspected that his political enemies were *America's* enemies.[29] If he expected sectarian competition in the religious marketplace to lead to the ultimate emergence of a thoroughly republicanized popular Christianity, he was less sanguine about the nation's political prospects, for reactionary elements would constantly seek to exploit popular ignorance, incredulity, and indifference to reverse the Revolution's outcome. Only two decades after independence, Americans again stood on the brink, Jefferson told Philip Mazzei: "In place of that noble love of liberty, & republican government which carried us triumphantly thro' the war, an Anglican monarchical, & aristocratical party has sprung up, whose avowed object is to draw over us the substance, as they have already done the forms, of the British government." Happily, "the main body of our citizens . . . remain true to their republican principles" and could yet again be rallied to the Republican—that is, to their own—cause. The counter-revolutionary threat would recur repeatedly through Jefferson's career, and patriotic Republicans would mobilize to meet it.[30]

In the religious realm, theological diversity progressively diminished the significance of doctrinal differences; in the realm of the political, the tendency of partisan strife was regressive and reductive, juxtaposing the counter-revolutionary tendencies of would-be aristocrats to the patriotism of Republican custodians of the Revolutionary faith. In moments of crisis, Jeffersonians would reenact the Revolution, repelling Federalist foes at the ballot box or even, if necessary, on the battlefield. For, as Jefferson warned the Republican editor William Duane in 1811, we must not "schismatize on either men or measures" but must "act in phalanx," as we did in the election of 1800 when "we rescued" the nation "from the satellites of monarchism," "[f]or the republicans are the *nation*."[31] Partisan conflict might contain and sublimate belligerent impulses, but those impulses were never far below the surface—as successive generations of post-Revolutionary Americans implicitly recognized in their celebration of the union the Founding Fathers had created—until they finally erupted in the Civil War.

Jefferson believed that progress toward racial, religious, and political homogeneity would strengthen the bonds of nationhood and fulfill the promise of the American Revolution. The spread of white settlement and republican institutions across the continent—and the obliteration or absorption of its indigenous peoples—sustained his faith in the progress of American civilization.[32] His election to the presidency did not initiate the promised new republican millennium: counter-revolutionary forces, no longer "avowing" their "monarchical, & aristocratical" principles, would mount new, more insidious and subversive challenges to republicanism and union through John Marshall's "consolidationist" jurisprudence and through their cynical manipulation of sectional differences over slavery in the Missouri controversy. But, in his penultimate letter, Jefferson testified to his undying faith in the ultimately irreversible worldwide progress of republicanism. His Declaration would remain "the signal of arousing men to burst the chains under which monkish ignorance and superstition had persuaded them to bind themselves, and to assume the blessings and security of self-government." And it would continue to be an inspiration for Americans themselves, "after half a century of experience and prosperity," as they renewed their republican faith.[33]

Jefferson's vision for America depended on his own enduring faith in the enlightenment of a self-governing people. The people could not be forced to embrace progressive policy prescriptions, for then they would cease to govern themselves, and their capacity for moral improvement would diminish accordingly. Only when "public opinion" had advanced sufficiently to see and act on the injustice of slavery was there any hope for Jefferson's emancipation scheme. He recognized that he would not live to see his proposals for emancipation and colonization "consummated, they will not die with me; but living or dying, they will ever be in my most fervent prayer."[34] This is why Jefferson urged his young neighbor Edward Coles not to free his slaves and take them to Illinois, lest "[y]our solitary but welcome voice" be lost to Virginia and the "progress of public sentiment" on the slavery question be retarded or reversed. The emancipation cause "shall have all my prayers," Jefferson promised; his letter to Coles was itself a kind of prayer, an appeal to the conscientious reason on which moral development was predicated. Coles must "come forward in the public councils, become the missionary of this doctrine truly christian; insinuate & inculcate it softly but steadily, through the medium of writing and conversation; associate others in your labors, and when the phalanx is formed, bring on and press the proposition perseveringly until its accomplishment."[35]

Jefferson prayed that Virginians would see the light on slavery. When he stepped down from the presidency, he enjoined Caesar Rodney and his fellow Republicans to sustain their united phalanx, offering "daily prayers that ye love one another, as I love you. God bless you."[36] Given his growing preoccupation with religion, such language came naturally to Jefferson. But it also reflected the imperatives of Jefferson's republicanism, for the sacrifices of the Revolution would only be justified if the people fulfilled its ultimate promise, uniting with "one heart and one mind."[37] Republican government depended on a union of sentiment that religious freedom fostered. "Adhering to this expression of the supreme will of the nation in behalf of the rights of conscience," Jefferson told the Danbury Baptists that "I shall see with sincere satisfaction the progress of those sentiments which tend to restore to man all his natural rights, convinced he has no natural right in opposition to his social duties."[38]

Jefferson's faith in the future now seems hopelessly misplaced. The revivals of the Second Great Awakening did not lead to the ascendancy of an enlightened, democratic Christianity; blind faith did not give way to enlightened reason and moral progress. Few voices were raised against slavery, and those few were drowned out in the rising tide of the proslavery movement.[39] Virginians grew increasingly dependent on and comfortable with their "peculiar institution": Jefferson's vision of a white republic, purged of slavery and slaves, was delusional—as he must have known by the time of his death.

A progressively more perfect republican government would secure the peace and prosperity of a free people. In optimistic moments, Jefferson could assert that the republican millennium had already arrived. As he wrote a European friend in 1807, America was a "blest . . . nation, whose silent course of happiness furnishes nothing for history to say"; meanwhile, "Europe has been in constant volcanic eruption," suffering from a surfeit of history.[40] Yet Jefferson could not suppress persistent anxieties about the failure of America's republican experiment and powerfully regressive tendencies that would draw Americans back into history's savage vortex, unleashing the dogs of war and obliterating the distinction between New World and Old. "Oceans of human blood" would flow in America as in Europe if religious sects competed for control of the state, or if the captive nation of enslaved Africans rose up in revolt, or if a crypto-aristocratic faction, aided and abetted by America's foreign enemies, sought to reverse the Revolution's outcome. It was a measure both of Jefferson's growing desperation and of his abiding faith in republicanism's regenerative capacity that he increasingly turned to prayer in his later years. The prospects for his colonization scheme might be dwindling, but Jefferson still prayed for a "revolution in public opinion" that would make emancipation possible—and vindicate his faith in the people.[41]

Jefferson's interest in religion in his later years is indicative of the increasing discrepancy between the young revolutionary's hopes for the republic's future and the sordid realities of everyday life in slaveholding Virginia. The democratization of American Christianity did not, as Jefferson so fervently prayed, lead to popular enlightenment, moral improvement, and social peace. To the contrary, faithful Christians divided bitterly over slavery and then, in a frenzy of pious patriotism, rushed into a devastating Civil War that destroyed the union that Jefferson and his fellow Founders had created at such cost, thus perpetrating an "act of suicide on themselves, and of treason against the hopes of the world," as Jefferson would say in another context of the dissolution of the republic.[42] Yet it is all too easy to read the Civil War as a bloody epitaph to Jefferson's tragically bankrupt vision of the American future and therefore to locate "our Jefferson"—the one Lincoln played such a key role in inventing—in an entirely different world from his own lost one. There are vitally important links between these two worlds that are manifest in—but at the same time obscured by—the perpetual refashioning of Jefferson's image. The interpretative problems pivot on the ways we think about "democracy."

The Founders worried obsessively about the "character" of the American people, about whether they were virtuous and vigilant enough to sustain free government. The Founders were acutely aware of the cultural determinants of forms of rule: as Montesquieu taught, stable regimes depended on a proper fit between the constitution of a ruling class, environmental conditions, and the prevailing principle or ethos (honor in aristocracies, virtue in republics).[43] Jefferson eventually rejected Montesquieu's neoclassical typology of regimes, embracing instead the "modern" political science of the ideologist Destutt de Tracy, with its Jeffersonian juxtaposition of the illegitimate, class-based ("partial"), and despotic forms of government that supposedly characterized the European old regime to new, postrevolutionary nation-states (the United States and France) that were based on popular sovereignty and dedicated to the general welfare.[44] But a more dynamic, protean conception of "national character" remained crucially important to Jefferson. Simply put, the survival of the American republic (or democracy) ultimately depended on the emergence of a truly republican (or democratic) people. That implicitly cultural—and, for Jefferson, explicitly racial—definition of American nationhood never took on the more inventively exceptionalist, sometimes virulent forms of romantic European nineteenth-century nationalism but was always in tension with the universalistic, social contractarian premises of the first paragraphs of his Declaration of Independence.[45]

For patriotic Americans, the idea of "democracy" resolves or disguises the tension between universal regime principles and the unique and exceptional "character" of the American people. The conflation of constitution and character was most influentially captured by Alexis de Tocqueville, who discovered democracy in the daily life and political culture of a restless and enterprising people dedicated to the master principle of equality.[46] Americans were democrats less because their revolution made them so than because they had fewer obstacles to overcome in enacting the immanent logic of modernity: Europeans therefore should look to America for an image of their own future. The United States was the exemplar for peoples elsewhere (for better or, as Tocqueville suspected, for worse), because they were a precociously modern, democratic people. This is the story Americans have always told themselves; their democratic character became so well established that they could absorb new streams of immigrants and even the marginalized and exploited groups—Indians and slaves—that were so conspicuously excluded from the democracy Tocqueville encountered.

Democracy is so central to our national self-understanding that Americans reflexively attribute it to a bountiful landscape ("the land of the free"), or to the "genius" of the "chosen people" who tapped its extraordinary potential, or to divine providence, "manifest destiny," or some more acceptably secular equivalent. In these accounts, Americans have *always* been democrats, practically speaking, whether or not they have been conscious of the fact. The American Revolution thus constituted a massive recognition of the facts on the ground, articulating the implicit premises of a long colonial apprenticeship and clearing the way for subsequent generations to fulfill their new land's infinite promise.

Jefferson would have embraced the progressive spirit of this celebratory narrative. Indeed, I would argue that Jefferson in his First Inaugural Address and other key texts is one of that narrative's leading authors.[47] But he would have been troubled by our failure to recognize the Revolution's world-historical significance, the daunting obstacles that revolutionaries faced at home and abroad, and the challenges subsequent generations faced in preserving their legacy —not to mention the ultimate failure of the Americans' federal and republican experiment in the Civil War. In short, Jefferson had a better sense of history, of the contingencies that threatened to disappoint his vaulting hopes, than most historians who have attempted to make sense of him and his time.

A good place for a fresh start would be to historicize the idea of democracy. Robert R. Palmer pointed the way many years ago in his magisterial *Age of the Democratic Revolution*.[48] Palmer persuasively argued that the term in its modern (nonpejorative) sense emerged in response to an "aristocratic resurgence" of privileged corporate bodies (including the colonial Anglo-American assemblies) against the modernizing and centralizing designs of modern monarchies.[49] In their struggle against monarchical power, American elites mobilized the masses by elaborating or inventing a more capacious corporate identity—that of the "people"—and thus sublimating or universalizing their class identity. The distinctive shape of early American politics resulted from the often uneasy convergence of "aristocratic," corporate impulses—expressed in American constitutionalism, the vindication of provincial liberties in American federalism, and in the apotheosis of private property rights (including property in human beings)—with broadly "democratic" participation in a vastly expanded electorate. That alliance proved much less tenable in the French Revolution, where aristocrats found themselves increasingly at odds with "democratic" elements determined to centralize authority and destroy traditional privilege. The binary opposition of "democracy" and "aristocracy" was exported to the rest of the Western world, even to the new United States, where elites could plausibly assert their fealty to republican principles. The bizarre result was that great slaveholding planters such as Jefferson could lead an ostentatiously "democratic" opposition to a Federalist administration that they saw tilting ominously toward Britain and away from the French "sister republic."[50]

My intention is not to give the lie to Jefferson's political sociology, to show once again that this aristocratic democrat was a hypocrite. Instead, I would argue, Jefferson's "democracy" represented a redefinition of the "republic" that emerged *from* the worldwide struggle for national self-determination. The French Revolution thus taught Jefferson and his followers to think of their opposition to the Washington and Adams administrations as a "democratic" challenge to "aristocracy," radically simplifying an extraordinarily complicated political landscape. This was the same binary opposition that had clarified an equally complicated landscape when Americans were forced to decide for or against independent nationhood in 1776. For Jefferson, the mobilization of a democratic opposition party was a return to patriotic first principles and reaffirmation of American nationhood. "Democracy" was a synonym for the "nation." Federalists who sought to consolidate power and subvert popular government were "aristocrats," the nation's most insidious enemies: they were traitors to the Revolutionary cause they so ostentatiously professed to support. Not surprisingly, these "Anglomen" cultivated closer connections with Britain, the new nation's original, inveterate, inevitable enemy.

Party divisions in the 1790s pivoted on polarized responses to the French Revolution. Alienated oppositionists insisted that American independence had been betrayed when the Washington administration negotiated a diplomatic rapprochement with Britain in the controversial Jay Treaty of 1795. As they impugned Federalists' patriotism, Jeffersonians overcame their antipartisan scruples and mobilized popular resistance to administration policy. The premise of this mobilization was that the "people" were no longer truly represented by a government with increasingly conspicuous "aristocratic" tendencies. Jefferson and his allies were thus forced to rekindle the "Spirit of 1776," reenacting the American Revolution even as they imaginatively aligned themselves with the great French Revolutionary struggle against the British-led "conspiracy of kings."[51]

Jeffersonians came to think of themselves as democrats as they mobilized to overthrow the aristocrats who dominated the new federal government. The Antifederalists who had opposed ratification of the Constitution provided the conceptual framework for identifying abuses of federal power, analogizing the Federalists' "imperial" ambitions to those of their British predecessors. Reinforcing the fundamental opposition of Britain and America, Antifederalists elaborated their analogy by describing their foes as aristocrats, thus setting the stage for the ideological polarization of the first party system.[52] Antifederalists thus *invented* an American aristocracy, imagining that surviving fragments of the old provincial elites and ambitious new allies were coalescing into a monolithic class united by their determination to reverse the Revolution's outcome and give rule to the continent.

Thrown on the defensive by such charges, defenders of the Constitution proclaimed their fealty to republican principles, insisting that the new regime would secure the fundamental rights and interests of all Americans. But their strongest argument was that the union would fall apart without a more energetic central government, leaving Americans in a dangerously anarchic state of nature. In effect, the Federalists' "anarchy" trumped the Antifederalists' "aristocracy."[53] Only when the new government was successfully launched could its opponents begin to talk about "democracy"—now valorized by revolutionary struggles in Europe—without evoking its usual pejorative connotations of anarchy, licentiousness, or mob rule. Deploying the Antifederalist language of aristocracy, the Jeffersonian opposition could now embrace democracy, its newly minted opposite term.

The persisting caricature of Jefferson is that he was an antistatist libertarian with a naïve faith in the capacity of free citizens for self-government. But geopolitical considerations were always of paramount concern to Jefferson, as David Armitage's recent book on the Declaration of Independence demonstrates.[54] The Declaration was self-evidently designed to gain international recognition for the United States and through this recognition to make rebellious colonies into a "nation." Resistance to British tyranny in the various provinces was tenuously coordinated through the continental congresses but could only succeed under a more powerful and authoritative central government. As Jefferson insisted late in life, the Declaration was "the fundamental act of union of these States."[55] Securing the union would enable patriotic Americans to act as a nation, with "full Power to levy War, conclude Peace, contract Alliances, establish Commerce, and to do all other Acts and Things which Independent States may of right do."[56] The vindication of American pretensions to nationhood through war and diplomacy was the necessary precondition for the enjoyment of the natural rights Jefferson so eloquently articulated in the Declaration's first paragraphs. The contemporaneous significance of those famously "self-evident" "truths" was to counter the British government's presumption of legitimacy and so persuade a "candid world"—and Americans themselves—that the patriots had a right to govern themselves.

Jefferson understood that the world-historical significance of the American Revolution was to articulate and implement the fundamental principle of national self-determination. That meant thinking of the people or nation not only as the ultimate source of legitimate authority but also, in some meaningfully continuous capacity, as active participants in their own government. Nation came first; what we, following the mature Jefferson's lead, now call "democracy," followed. It is more than coincidental that as he embraced democracy and its implications and moved perceptibly away from the more circumspect—sometimes even antidemocratic—republican constitutionalism of his Revolutionary years, Jefferson began to celebrate the people's power.[57] "[T]his Government" was not only "the world's best hope," as he told his countrymen in his First Inaugural Address, but "the strongest Government on earth," "the only one where every man, at the call of the law, would fly to the standard of the law, and would meet invasions of the public order as his own personal concern."[58]

The libertarian fantasy, which Bernard Bailyn describes as the animating principle of the resistance movement before the Revolution, is that liberty can check, even transcend power; in the modern democratic ideal of an irresistibly empowered people—made manifest on the battlefields of revolutionary Europe and, in retrospect, of Revolutionary America—power and liberty converge.[59] The American Revolution showed that a self-governing people would act as one in time of crisis: patriotic Americans were "prepared to meet even the most powerful . . . foreign invasion," even "that of a Bonaparte."[60] Jefferson's conception of what the political scientist Jeremy D. Bailey calls democratic "prerogative" doubtless reflected his transformation from opposition leader to commander-in-chief but also grew out of his new understanding of what democracy meant in a war-torn revolutionary age.[61] Embattled democratic movements in France and other European countries sought to create "a unitary, homogenous, and juridically centralized republic," Palmer notes, while "in America the democratic movement was suspicious of centralized, homogenous, or unitary government, and strongly insistent on local liberties and state rights." But when the threat of war crossed the Atlantic, as it did during the Louisiana crisis of 1803, or when Americans found themselves drawn into the French Revolutionary and Napoleonic wars, the imperatives of strengthening the union, energizing the executive, and encroaching "on local liberties and state rights" became manifest.[62] Jefferson's exchange with Destutt about the translation and publication of the latter's *Commentary and Review of Montesquieu's Spirit of the Laws* in 1811 shows how Jefferson's ideas about democracy and nationhood developed in tandem. A modern great nation must protect itself, for self-preservation was the first law of nature; it must secure the welfare of its people; it must also project itself across space and through time until history's end, when enemies at home and abroad were finally vanquished.[63]

Situating Jefferson in the nation's history as the apostle of national self-determination rather than of "democracy" enables us to escape the solipsistic exceptionalism of our mythology. For our understanding of ourselves as a uniquely free, democratic people is a *national* myth, perhaps useful for "peoples" elsewhere who would overthrow the shackles of foreign rule but useless as a model for how those peoples should in fact govern themselves. In its original, modern conception, Palmer shows us, democracy was a belligerent, anti-aristocratic creed, designed to liberate nations from the dead hand of corporate privilege. The dialectical juxtaposition of aristocracy and democracy reflected deep cleavages in early modern political societies that demanded explanation and resolution. That "revolutionary" moment has passed—though Americans persisted in calling their enemies "aristocrats" throughout the antebellum decades—and one of its two terms, "democracy," emerged as the foundational premise of modern nationhood.

The Jefferson who helped conceive and create the American nation has something to tell us about the history of the modern world. But we must first look through and past our national mythology, historicizing democracy and recognizing that its limits and exclusions are our own. Jefferson's paradoxes and contradictions seem less conspicuous when we lift him out of his mythmaking role as democracy's presiding genius. This does not mean that we cannot—or should not—find the liberal and democratic ideals that Jefferson invoked compelling or inspiring. But we also need to understand how these ideas have been harnessed to national purposes in a confusing and rapidly changing world. Republics are not naturally peaceful, as the founding generation recognized, nor, finally, were the Founders' efforts to construct a durable federal union or "peace pact" for the new United States successful.[64]

In the end, democracy destroyed the union, for the two nations that struggled for supremacy in the Civil War expressed the belligerent will of their respective peoples with extraordinary fidelity. Thomas Jefferson prayed that it would not be so; he prayed for peace and prosperity, popular enlightenment, moral improvement, and the emancipation and expatriation of the captive nation of slaves. What he left us instead was a prophetic vision of the United States as a great nation that would wield enormous power, for better or worse, in democracy's name.

NOTES

1. On the icon theme, see Jan Ellen Lewis and Peter S. Onuf, "American Synecdoche: Thomas Jefferson as Image, Icon, Character, and Self," reprinted in Onuf, *The Mind of Thomas Jefferson* (Charlottesville, Va., 2007), 50–64. For a comprehensive and authoritative review of the literature, see Francis D.

Cogliano, *Thomas Jefferson: Reputation and Legacy* (Charlottesville, Va., 2006). Cogliano's fine book belongs on the short shelf of essential Jefferson titles with Merrill D. Peterson, *The Jefferson Image in the American Mind* (New York, 1960). Thanks to Mark Hulliung and Frank Cogliano for helpful comments.

2. Annette Gordon-Reed, *Thomas Jefferson and Sally Hemings: An American Controversy* (Charlottesville, Va., 1997); Jan Ellen Lewis and Peter S. Onuf, eds., *Sally Hemings and Thomas Jefferson: History, Memory, and Civic Culture* (Charlottesville, Va., 1999). See also the excellent review of the Hemings affair in Cogliano, *Thomas Jefferson*, 170–229.

3. Cogliano, *Thomas Jefferson*, 180–84.

4. Rhys Isaac, "Monticello Stories Old and New," in Lewis and Onuf, eds., *Sally Hemings and Thomas Jefferson*, 114–26.

5. Jefferson, *Notes on the State of Virginia*, ed. William Peden (Chapel Hill, N.C., 1954), Query XIV, 143. See the discussion in my "Every Generation Is an 'Independent Nation': Colonization, Miscegenation, and the Fate of Jefferson's Children," in *Mind of Thomas Jefferson*, 213–35.

6. Paul Finkelman, "Jefferson and Slavery: 'Treason Against the Hopes of the World,'" in Peter S. Onuf, ed., *Jeffersonian Legacies* (Charlottesville, Va., 1993), 181–221; Conor Cruise O'Brien, *The Long Affair: Thomas Jefferson and the French Revolution, 1785–1800* (Chicago, 1996); Jack N. Rakove, "Our Jefferson," in Lewis and Onuf, eds., *Sally Hemings and Thomas Jefferson*, 210–35.

7. Pauline Maier, *American Scripture: Making the Declaration of Independence* (New York, 1997).

8. Jeffrey L. Pasley, Andrew W. Robertson, and David Waldstreicher, eds., *Beyond the Founders: New Approaches to the Political History of the Early American Republic* (Chapel Hill, N.C., 2004), introduction; David Waldstreicher, "Founders Chic as Culture War," *Radical History Review* 84 (Fall 2002): 185–94.

9. TJ to James Madison, September 6, 1789, in Jefferson, *Papers*, 15:392.

10. Mark Hulliung, *The Social Contract in America: From the Revolution to the Present Age* (Lawrence, Kans., 2007). The most influential previous account of Jefferson as a democratic theorist is Richard K. Matthews, *The Radical Politics of Thomas Jefferson: A Revisionist View* (Lawrence, Kans., 1984).

11. Gordon S. Wood, *The Radicalism of the American Revolution* (New York, 1992); Sean Wilentz, *The Rise of American Democracy: Jefferson to Lincoln* (New York, 2005). For a review of recent writings that foregrounds the democracy theme, see Jeffrey L. Pasley, "Politics and the Misadventures of Thomas Jefferson's Modern Reputation: A Review Essay," *Journal of Southern History* 72 (November 2006): 871–908. Pasley concludes that "Jefferson's democratic political ideals . . . are the reason to study him, a fact that has been easy to lose sight of over the course of the long effort to personalize our history" (908).

12. Gary B. Nash, *The Unknown American Revolution: The Unruly Birth of*

Democracy and the Struggle to Create America (New York, 2005), 79. But notice Nash's favorable account of Jefferson's natural rights philosophy, offsetting his censure of Jefferson and Washington for not deploying their "huge funds of moral and political capital" in behalf of emancipation. Ibid., 211, 432.

13. Annette Gordon-Reed's work has been crucial in this transformation of the Jefferson image. See her *Thomas Jefferson and Sally Hemings* and the more recent *The Hemingses of Monticello: An American Family* (New York, 2008). Clarence Walker develops the diversity theme in his *Mongrel Nation: The America Begotten by Thomas Jefferson and Sally Hemings* (Charlottesville, Va., 2009).

14. Parton, quoted in Peterson, *Jefferson Image in the American Mind,* 234.

15. For my previous efforts to historicize Jefferson, see *Jefferson's Empire: The Language of American Nationhood* (Charlottesville, Va., 2000) and the essays collected in *Mind of Jefferson,* including a historiographical essay, "Making Sense of Jefferson," at 19–49.

16. Lincoln to Henry L. Pierce et al., April 6, 1859, in Roy P. Basler, ed., *The Collected Works of Abraham Lincoln,* 8 vols. (New Brunswick, N.J., 1953), 3:376.

17. Jefferson, *Notes on the State of Virginia,* Query XVIII, 163; Query XIV, 138; Query XVIII, 163.

18. The best study on the topic is Eva Sheppard Wolf, *Race and Liberty in the New Nation: Emancipation in Virginia from the Revolution to Nat Turner's Rebellion* (Baton Rouge, La., 2006).

19. Jefferson, Second Inaugural Address, March 4, 1805, in Jefferson, *Writings* [Peterson], 522.

20. For a discussion of Jefferson's conception of moral progress, see Ari Helo and Peter Onuf, "Jefferson, Morality, and the Problem of Slavery," in Onuf, *Mind of Thomas Jefferson,* 236–70.

21. TJ to George Wythe, August 13, 1786, in Jefferson, *Papers,* 10: 244–45.

22. Nathan O. Hatch, *The Democratization of American Christianity* (New Haven, Conn., 1989). See also Eugene R. Sheridan, *Jefferson and Religion* (Charlottesville, Va., 1998); Charles B. Sanford, *The Religious Life of Thomas Jefferson* (Charlottesville, Va., 1984); Paul K. Conkin, "The Religious Pilgrimage of Thomas Jefferson," in Onuf, ed., *Jeffersonian Legacies,* 19–49; Edwin S. Gaustad, *Sworn on the Altar of God: A Religious Biography of Thomas Jefferson* (Grand Rapids, Mich., 1996); and Onuf, "Jefferson's Religion: Priestcraft, Enlightenment, and the Republican Revolution," in *Mind of Jefferson,* 139–68.

23. TJ to Dr. Benjamin Waterhouse, June 26, 1822, Thomas Jefferson Papers, Manuscript Division, Library of Congress, Washington D.C. Jefferson subsequently wrote Waterhouse, "I am in hopes that some of the disciples of your institution [Harvard] will become missionaries to us, of these doctrines truly evangelical, and open our eyes to what has been so long hidden from them. A bold and eloquent preacher would be no where listened to with more freedom than in this state, nor with more firmness of mind." Such a preacher

"would be attended in the fields by whole acres of hearers and thinkers." TJ to Waterhouse, July 19, 1822, ibid.

24. TJ to James Fishback, September 27, 1809, in J. Jefferson Looney, ed., *The Papers of Thomas Jefferson, Retirement Series* (5 vols. to date; Princeton, N.J., 2004–), 1:564.

25. TJ to Charles Thomson, January 29, 1817, in Jefferson, *Works* 12:51–53. See also TJ to John Adams, January 11, 1817, in Lester J. Cappon, ed., *The Adams-Jefferson Letters: The Complete Correspondence between Thomas Jefferson and Abigail and John Adams,* 2 vols. (Chapel Hill, N.C., 1959), 2:506.

26. TJ to Thomas B. Parker, May 15, 1819, in Dickinson W. Adams, ed., *Jefferson's Extracts from the Gospels: "The Philosophy of Jesus" and "The Life and Morals of Jesus." The Papers of Thomas Jefferson,* 2nd. ser. (Princeton, N.J., 1983), 386.

27. Jefferson, First Inaugural Address, March 4, 1801, in Jefferson, *Writings* [Peterson], 494.

28. TJ to Thomas Lomax, March 12, 1799, ibid., 1063.

29. For placatory comments on party differences, see TJ to Abigail Adams, September 11, 1804, and TJ to John F. Mercer, October 9, 1804, in Jefferson, *Writings* [L&B], 11:52, 54.

30. TJ to Mazzei, April 24, 1796, in Jefferson, *Writings* [Peterson], 1036–37. For further discussion, see Onuf, *Jefferson's Empire,* chap. 3–4.

31. TJ to Col. William Duane, March 28, 1811, in Jefferson, *Writings* [L&B], 13:25–31 (quotations at 28–29).

32. Bernard W. Sheehan, *Seeds of Extinction: Jeffersonian Philanthropy and the American Indian* (Chapel Hill, N.C., 1973).

33. TJ to Roger C. Weightman, June 24, 1826, in Jefferson, *Writings* [Peterson], 1517.

34. TJ to James Heaton, May 20, 1826, ibid., 1516.

35. TJ to Edward Coles, August 25, 1814, ibid., 1344–46. See the excellent discussion of Jefferson's correspondence with Coles in Alan Pell Crawford, *Twilight at Monticello: The Final Years of Thomas Jefferson* (New York, 2008).

36. TJ to Caesar A. Rodney, February 10, 1810, in Jefferson, *Writings* [Peterson], 1218.

37. Jefferson, First Inaugural Address, March 4, 1801, ibid., 493.

38. TJ to Messrs. Nehemiah Dodge and Others, a Committee of the Danbury Baptist Association, January 1, 1802, ibid., 510.

39. Wolf, *Race and Liberty in the New Nation;* Charles F. Irons, *The Origins of Proslavery Christianity: White and Black Evangelicals in Colonial and Antebellum Virginia* (Chapel Hill, N.C., 2008); Irons, "The Spiritual Fruits of Revolution: Disestablishment and the Rise of the Virginia Baptists," *Virginia Magazine of History and Biography* 109, no. 2 (2001): 159–86.

40. TJ to Monsieur Le Comte Diodati, March 29, 1807, in Jefferson, *Writ-*

ings [L&B], 11:181–83. See my "Nations, Revolutions, and the End of History," in *Revolutionary Currents: Nation Building in the Transatlantic World,* ed. Michael A. Morrison and Melinda Zook (Lanham, Md., 2004), 173–88.

41. TJ to James Heaton, May 20, 1826, in Jefferson, *Writings* [Peterson], 1516.

42. TJ to John Holmes, April 22, 1820, ibid., 1435. Jefferson is referring to the horrific prospect of disunion during the Missouri Crisis.

43. Montesquieu (Charles Secondat), *The Spirit of the Laws,* trans. and ed. Anne M. Cohler, Basia Carolyn Miller, and Harold Samuel Stone (Cambridge, 1989), book 3, 21–30.

44. Antoine Claude Destutt de Tracy, *A Commentary and Review of Montesquieu's Spirit of the Laws. Prepared for the Press From the Original Manuscript, in the Hands of the Publisher* (Philadelphia, 1811; rpt., New York, 1969). See the discussion in Nicholas Onuf and Peter Onuf, *Nations, Markets, and War: Modern History and the American Civil War* (Charlottesville, Va., 2006), chap. 7.

45. This issue is most fully explored in Rogers M. Smith, *Civic Ideals: Conflicting Visions of Citizenship in U.S. History* (New Haven, Conn., 1997). See also James H. Kettner, *The Development of American Citizenship, 1608–1870* (Chapel Hill, N.C., 1978); and Douglas Bradburn, *The Citizenship Revolution: Politics and the Creation of the American Union, 1774–1804* (Charlottesville, Va., 2009).

46. Alexis de Tocqueville, *Democracy in America,* 2 vols., trans. Phillips Bradley (New York, 1945).

47. Onuf, *Jefferson's Empire.*

48. Robert R. Palmer, *The Age of the Democratic Revolution: A Political History of Europe and America, 1760–1800,* vol. I, *The Challenge;* vol. II, *The Struggle* (Princeton, N.J., 1959, 1964).

49. Ibid., 1:13–20.

50. For suggestive commentary on Jefferson and this viewpoint, see ibid., 2:521–25, 570–71, and passim.

51. Lance Banning, *The Jeffersonian Persuasion: Evolution of a Party Ideology* (Ithaca, N.Y., 1978); Onuf, *Jefferson's Empire,* chap. 4.

52. Onuf, "Federalism, Republicanism, and the Origins of American Sectionalism," in Edward L. Ayers et al., *All Over the Map: Rethinking American Regions* (Baltimore, 1996), 11–37. Gordon S. Wood, in *The Creation of the American Republic, 1776–1787* (Chapel Hill, N.C., 1969), 483–98, discusses the pervasiveness of anti-aristocratic rhetoric in the ratification debates but is less persuasive in depicting Antifederalists as "democrats."

53. Onuf, "Anarchy and the Crisis of the Union," in *To Form a More Perfect Union: The Critical Ideas of the Constitution,* ed. Herman Belz, Ronald Hoffman, and Peter J. Albert (Charlottesville, Va., 1992), 272–302.

54. David Armitage, *The Declaration of Independence: A Global History* (Cambridge, Mass., 2007). See also my "A Declaration of Independence for Diplomatic Historians," in *Mind of Jefferson,* 65–80, and Peter Onuf and Nicholas Onuf, *Federal Union, Modern World: The Law of Nations in an Age of Revolutions, 1776–1814* (Madison, Wisc., 1993).

55. Jefferson, Resolution of the Board of Visitors, March 4, 1825, in Jefferson, *Writings* [Peterson], 479.

56. Final Draft of the Declaration, July 4, 1776, in Jefferson, *Papers,* 1:432.

57. David N. Mayer, *The Constitutional Thought of Thomas Jefferson* (Charlottesville, Va., 1994).

58. Jefferson, First Inaugural Address, March 4, 1801, in Jefferson, *Writings* [Peterson], 493.

59. Bailyn, *The Ideological Origins of the American Revolution* (Cambridge, Mass., 1967), 55–93.

60. TJ to Dr. James Brown, October 27, 1808, in Jefferson, *Writings* [L&B], 12:184–85. For further discussion, see my "Jefferson, Louisiana, and American Nationhood," *Tocqueville Review* 25 (2004): 23–34.

61. Jeremy D. Bailey, *Thomas Jefferson and Executive Power* (New York, 2007).

62. Palmer, *Age of the Democratic Revolution,* 2:27.

63. Onuf and Onuf, *Nations, Markets, and War,* chap. 7.

64. David C. Hendrickson, *Peace Pact: The Lost World of the American Founding* (Lawrence, Kans., 2003); Daniel Deudney, "Publius before Kant: Federal-Republican Security and Democratic Peace," *European Journal of International Relations* 10 (September 2004): 315–56.

Eva Sheppard Wolf

Natural Politics

Jefferson, Elections, and the People

In January 2007 at the ceremonial opening of the 110th Congress, the first to be led by a female Speaker of the House, minority leader John Boehner and the incoming Speaker Nancy Pelosi referred repeatedly to the nation's Founders when trying to put the historic event in context. Boehner acknowledged the significance of electing the first woman Speaker of the House and commented graciously that he thought the Founders would approve of the innovation. Pelosi invoked the Founders frequently in her speech as she called on the members of Congress to fulfill the Founders' vision of a "new America driven by optimism, opportunity, and strength." With one exception, the Founders made their appearance that day as a group, a single symbol of the American past and the glory of the American political system. The exception was Thomas Jefferson, whom Nancy Pelosi quoted in an effort to reach out to her colleagues across the aisle after years of bitter partisan struggle. Jefferson, she reminded them, had said that "every difference of opinion is not a difference of principle."[1]

Thomas Jefferson emerged that day from the group of Founders because, in spite of the controversy he generates, we remember Jefferson above all others as a champion of democracy and government by the people. As Pelosi and Boehner both emphasized, the

House of Representatives is the "people's house"; Jefferson, then, served as an appropriate figure to invoke in its chambers.[2] Jefferson proved useful in the particular moment, too, because what Pelosi quoted, Jefferson's First Inaugural Address given in March 1801, was designed similarly to heal wounds after a period of bitter partisan strife. We think of Jefferson as a partisan, and we still call his party "the Jeffersonian Republicans," at the same time that we think of him as a democratic theorist in whose philosophy the people cohere as an undivided, not partisan, body.

These two views of Jefferson, as active politician and as democratic champion and theoretician, seem at first to stand in great tension with one another. On the one hand, Jefferson was a successful political actor and party leader. That success can be measured in part by how often and easily he got himself elected to public office. Jefferson served as an elected official for twenty-eight of the forty years between his election to the House of Burgesses in 1769 and his retirement from the presidency in 1809, and he served in public office the entire period except for 1794–96, when he briefly lived in retirement at Monticello. He was always a popular candidate and never lost an election in his home state starting with that first election in 1769. A few years later, the people of his county elected him to the Revolutionary body that replaced the House of Burgesses. Virginia's Revolutionary leaders then chose him from among themselves to serve as a delegate to the Continental Congress. Jefferson's Albemarle County neighbors elected him to the new House of Delegates as soon as it began to meet, and the Virginia Assembly elected him in 1779 to serve as governor. After the governorship, Virginia's leaders again sent him to Congress (1783–84). Nationally, voters chose electors or state legislators who supported him in 1796, a close election he lost by only a small margin, leaving him as vice president. And then the "people" chose him in 1800 and 1804 to be their president.

Historians have likewise given Jefferson a great deal of credit for his role in creating and leading a modern political party. He was "the father of the first truly national Republican party"[3]; a man whose party was in the 1790s "a new political engine, the first of its kind in modern history"[4]; and a "politician" who was "unsurpassed in ancient or in modern times" in "guiding and controlling public opinion."[5]

On the other hand, Jefferson was a thinker and writer who eschewed the strife and conflict inherent in party politics, who displayed almost no traditional politician-like qualities, avoided large social gatherings, and never made a single campaign speech or wrote a political broadside or pamphlet. Instead, his importance to many observers lay, and still lies, primarily in his role as the author of the Declaration of Independence and as the "Friend of the People," a sobriquet used as early as the 1790s. Thomas Jefferson as champion of the people and their self-evident rights seems to stand above the fray, well removed from the tussle and jockeying of day-to-day politics and politicking.

But precisely because the people so frequently elected him to public office, Jefferson's engagement with them was more than theoretical. It was actual. Through the process of elections, Jefferson entered into a direct relationship with the people. In fact, to the Revolutionary generation it was the most important political relationship that existed—that between representative and represented—since it was representation that linked people to their government and leaders. "No taxation without representation" could serve as a powerful and catchy revolutionary slogan only because it pointed to the deep political issues at the heart of the Revolution. After independence the question of representation remained central as Americans created new state and national governments; it was, for instance, the compromise over representation—that the Senate should represent states and the House the people—that made agreement on the Constitution possible.

Bringing together Jefferson's ideas about the people, elections, and representation with Jefferson's actual behavior in the elections through which he became a representative of the people can help tie the philosophical Jefferson to the political Jefferson, yielding a fuller understanding of his political thought and behavior. Further, the changes over time in Jefferson's ideas and actions signal important shifts in our nation's early political history, and examining those changes helps us both understand and bridge the gap between Jefferson's time and ours.

Even before first being elected to the House of Burgesses in 1769, Jefferson had begun to form ideas about government, politics, and the people. Jefferson was a perpetual student, always seeking new information, deeper understanding. That was especially true in the early 1760s when he was formally a student at the College of William and Mary, located in the colonial capital of Williamsburg, and when he read law with George Wythe, who lived just down the block from the capitol building. During his time in Williamsburg, the student Jefferson sat in on sessions of the Assembly so that he could learn about the law and government in preparation for his own career as a lawyer, and also so that as one of the wealthiest and best educated men in Albemarle County, he could prepare himself to take the place for which he seemed destined—a seat in the Assembly.[6]

The specific characteristics of the mid-eighteenth-century House of Burgesses that Jefferson observed shaped his ideas about how government should operate and how representatives of the people should behave. Although some democratizing influences were at work in the Virginia legislature of the era, particularly an increase in the number of burgesses who served on the standing committees of the House, the House of Burgesses remained the province of a small group of leaders, about one-sixth of the whole.[7] Most important among them was the speaker, who generally retained his post for a long period of time. When Jefferson was at William and Mary, John Robinson served as speaker and had done so for decades. By the early 1760s Robinson controlled the burgesses through what has been likened to a "modern political machine."[8] After Robinson's death in 1766, the "tall and stately" Peyton Randolph was elected speaker, and he served through the Revolution.[9]

In his 1764 comments on the proceedings at another colonial capital, Annapolis, we can see how much the young Jefferson valued the model of government he saw in his home colony of Virginia.

"The assembly," he wrote to his good friend John Page, "happens to be sitting at this time."

> Their upper and lower house, as they call them, sit in different houses. I went into the lower, sitting in an old courthouse, which, judging from it's [*sic*] form and appearance, was built in the year one. I was surprised on approaching it to hear as great a noise and hubbub as you will usually observe at a publick meeting of the planters in Virginia. The first object which struck me after my entrance was the figure of a little old man dressed but indifferently, with a yellow queue wig on, and mounted in the judge's chair. This the gentleman who walked with me informed me was the speaker, a man of a very fair character, but who by the bye has very little the air of a speaker. At one end of the justices' bench stood a man . . . reading a bill then before the house with a schoolboy tone and an abrupt pause at every half dozen words. This I found to be the clerk of the assembly. The mob (for such was their appearance) sat covered on the justices' and lawyers' benches, and were divided into little clubs amusing themselves in the common chit chat way. I was surprised to see them address the speaker without rising from their seats, and three, four, and five at a time without being checked.[10]

Jefferson, then a mere twenty-one years old, clearly knew how legislating *ought* to be done and saw that they were *not* doing things correctly in Annapolis. His arch description revealed more than youthful confidence in what is right. It also demonstrated how much the young Jefferson's ideas typified those of his time and place. The Jefferson of the pre-Revolutionary years expected inferiors—the "common" legislators, the "mob"—to act with proper respect for their superior, the speaker. They ought to rise from their chairs to speak rather than remain seated as they did in Annapolis. They ought not engage in "chit chat." Jefferson further expected the speaker, like John Robinson, to have about him a certain "air," which the Maryland speaker, with his indifferent dress and unimposing physical presence, clearly lacked.

In his description of the Maryland legislature, Jefferson, the future hero of American populists, sounds much the snob. Indeed, his entire world and education prepared him to be an elitist, to value those things that were not common, that were not mobbish, but were instead refined and rare.

One wonders what this well-educated colonial Virginian thought upon his own entry into government when he was first elected to the House of Burgesses at the age of twenty-six. Jefferson ran against an incumbent in that first election, but his opponent had failed to attend the previous legislative session. It was perhaps not surprising, then, that the voters—the landholding, adult white men of the county—instead chose Jefferson. Jefferson was by then a lawyer and gentleman of some local repute, particularly for the leadership role he had recently taken in improving navigation on the Rivanna River. That activity suggested he would dutifully and responsibly represent his neighbors' farming and business interests.[11]

Unfortunately, the only apparent record Jefferson left regarding that first election was the notation in his account book of the drinks and cakes he purchased for the occasion.[12] The delectables were not, as one might guess, for him to enjoy as he celebrated his victory with his supporters. Rather, in the style of colonial Virginia, they were to serve as treats for the voters at the polls, where the men gathered on election day to proclaim publicly their choice for representative. It was, as one Virginian famously summarized it, "swilling the planters with bumbo."[13] The election itself probably looked a lot like the "publick meeting of planters" with its "great noise and hubbub" that Jefferson had in mind when, somewhat derogatorily, he had compared the Maryland legislature to such a meeting. One imagines that the rum offered by the candidates would soon lubricate multiple conversations, voices would rise, and the men would tell stories, laugh, shout, and swear.[14]

Jefferson's relationship to those who elected him was not as a peer. He was not one of the "people" chosen from among them to carry out their wishes. He was a person in a position to lead in a society that clearly distinguished its leaders from its followers. As a slaveholder and head of household—once he turned twenty-one he was in charge of his mother's and siblings' affairs—Jefferson was used to being in charge of and making decisions for others. Though he wrote nothing, at least nothing that has survived, about how he understood his new role as a burgess, it probably seemed to him only an extension of an already established identity as a manager and caretaker of others.

Despite his reticence, Jefferson's behavior as a burgess does yield some clues about his thoughts and self-perception. First, Jefferson did not rise immediately to a leadership position within the House of Burgesses. For several years he remained unremarkable, a typical burgess with nothing so important to fight for or do that he stood out from the rest, although he did align himself with the radical wing leading the struggle against the imperial government.[15]

Jefferson's notes on the legislative events that interested him reveal a bit more. In 1774, for example, Jefferson followed the progress of a bill he referred to as "Entail bill (my own)" as well as one he called a "General Entail bill." But this did not mean that Jefferson, who just two years later would staunchly oppose the colonial inheritance laws, was acting already against entail, a legal restriction on breaking up inherited land. Rather, the parenthetical "my own" referred to the fact that the bill regarded land *he* had inherited, or, more precisely, land his wife Martha had inherited and that by law was therefore his; and the "General Entail bill" had a similarly narrow scope, designed to "empower certain persons [in Albemarle County] to convey away their lands" and not to change the general laws concerning entail. The other two bills he tracked that year concerned a road and a ferry that would have improved transportation in his county of Albemarle. (Of the four bills, only his own entail bill passed.) At this point in his life, and during the last years of the colonial era, Thomas Jefferson served "the people" as an extension of his role as patriarch, and he was most interested in those things that pertained directly to himself and his Albemarle neighbors, not to the polity at large.[16]

The American Revolution marked a watershed in American history not only because of the obvious—the making of an independent nation—but also because it changed the way so many Americans thought about their place in the world. That was true for Jefferson. In particular it was true in respect to his thoughts about politics and the people. Until the Revolution his extant writings betrayed very little concern or respect for the people, but during the course of the imperial conflict, he began to think more carefully about the people at large and his relationship to them and to reflect more generally on the relationship between people and their government.

Specifically, it was around the time of the formal break with England, spring and early summer 1776, that Jefferson focused his attention on the people. This makes sense, for the logic of revolution, even more than the logic of colonial rebellion, necessitated the argument that the people willed it. The American attachment to "the people" was, if not invented during the Revolution, certainly consecrated then, and thus it was the Revolution that modernized American politics and made Jeffersonian politics possible.

Jefferson first mentioned the people in his (surviving) correspondence in the very process of moving toward independence. He wrote from the Continental Congress in Philadelphia in May 1776, "When at home I took great pains to enquire into the sentiments of the people on" the "subject of independence."[17]

His new concern for the people played a central role in the Declaration of Independence, which is why we remember that document so dearly. Jefferson proclaimed, in what was for the time considered universal language, "*all* men are created equal." And, having written those words, Jefferson subsequently turned his attention more toward the people than he previously had done.

As he thought about the proper relationship between people and their government, the first project he focused on—in fact, he probably was working on it at the same time that he was writing the Declaration—was drafting a new constitution for Virginia. In the spring of 1776 Jefferson viewed the Virginia Constitution as of more consequence than the Declaration. Establishing a new Virginia constitution was "the whole object of the present controversy," he said, and he yearned to return home from Philadelphia so that he might participate in that crucial venture.[18] Jefferson was not released from his duties to the Continental Congress, however, and instead forwarded copies of his draft constitution by mail to George Wythe and Edmund Pendleton, who were to introduce it to the delegates gathering in Williamsburg. Jefferson was very disappointed that his "outline" arrived in Williamsburg too late to be utilized as a basis for the new Virginia constitution, although Jefferson's preamble and several of his ideas *did* enter the Virginia Constitution as amendments to late drafts.[19] More important for our purposes than how Jefferson's ideas influenced the 1776 Virginia Constitution are Jefferson's draft constitutions—a very sketchy first draft, a fuller second draft, and the reorganized third draft apparently sent to Williamsburg—which together form one of the most coherent summaries of Jefferson's thoughts on government and the people.

In Jefferson's drafts of a new Virginia constitution we see a distinctive philosophy of the people and of their relationship to government. It was a philosophy simultaneously conservative and radical, aristocratic and democratic, rooted in Jefferson's colonial upbringing and looking forward to the egalitarian (for white men) politics of the nineteenth century. The thoughts Jefferson developed in that generative spring of 1776 remained important well beyond that season because they guided him and his politics for decades after. Much of what he fought for in the bitter partisan struggles of the 1790s was, as he put it, the "spirit of 1776."

Several provisions of Jefferson's draft Virginia constitutions dealt directly with the relationship between people and their government. One insisted that elected officials take an "oath to govmt., that [they] shall not have been bribed."[20] Elected officials, in other words, ought to serve free of undue influence. Further, they ought not profit from office. Here Jefferson may have been thinking especially of the Robinson scandal, in which it was found out upon John Robinson's death that the speaker of the House of Burgesses, who also served as its treasurer, had for years been embezzling funds from the treasury in order to give his friends illegal loans. The paper money he turned over to about 240 of Virginia's gentlemen had been slated to be destroyed, so Robinson was guilty not only of corruption but of harming the colony's fiscal health.[21]

Another provision advised that "the house of representatives when met shall be free to act according to their own judgments."[22] Surely this statement seems to reflect how Jefferson had understood his relationship to the planters who elected him as a burgess: by consenting to his service in the House of Burgesses, they empowered him to act for what he perceived to be the good of his county and the colony. Their selection of him legitimized his power, but it was *his* power to act, to judge—to "act on [his] own judgments." As much as he valued government by the people, Jefferson did not trust the people to make decisions about governance.

These provisions regarding the legislature championed freedom, a concept that ruled the day in 1776 and that then as now held multiple meanings. The provision that government officers should not be bribed or profit from office emphasized that elections ought to operate freely, without corruption, and that government officers ought to serve for free, without profiting personally. The statement that representatives should be free to act on their own judgments, unbound by instructions from their constituents, also indicated a concern that representatives act independently of influence. Indeed, Revolutionary-era conceptions of independence and freedom were closely linked. Freedom from influence or control made people, and nations, independent. (Of course, the only people in Revolutionary society who could ordinarily achieve this sort of independence in their personal lives were adult white men.) A free, independent government, a new kind of republican, American government, had in Jefferson's view to ensure that its citizens and representatives were themselves free and independent.[23]

Jefferson's constitutional provisions concerning voting and landholding sought to create the very sort of free, independent people who could sustain a free, independent country. The provisions are especially interesting because they were for the time so unusual and so far-reaching. In Revolutionary America voting was a privilege of the landed, since only they, it was felt, had an interest, a stake (literally), in society. In order to cast a ballot in Virginia elections, one needed one hundred acres of uncultivated land, twenty-five acres with a house on it, or a house and lot in a town. In his draft constitutions for Virginia, Jefferson extended the franchise to taxpayers, not only landholders, broadening the category of those who had an interest in society to anyone who contributed to it with taxes. Extending the franchise to landless taxpayers put Jefferson well in advance of most of his contemporaries. Indeed, Virginia did not abandon landholding as a basis for voting until 1851.

Although Jefferson wanted to extend the franchise to those who did not own land, holding land still seemed to him to be requisite for achieving the personal freedom and independence one needed to participate in a free, independent nation. So Jefferson went even further and provided for sweeping change: unappropriated or forfeited land would be distributed to every adult who had never held fifty acres of land in order that all adults—save for those who had already squandered their holdings and thus rendered themselves unfit—should hold a minimum of fifty acres. This fifty-acre minimum was to be held "in full and absolute dominion."[24] Although Jefferson and others surely knew of the early colonial practice of granting land to settlers, the land-distribution provision would have struck contemporaries as wild and perhaps foolhardy since Americans—even in their most potentially radical moments during the Revolution and Civil War—have generally avoided distributing land to the landless.

Indeed here was Jefferson at his most radical, for not only did he propose giving land to the landless or land-poor, but Jefferson also seems to have allowed for the possibility that women could be counted among those landholders and could, therefore, potentially be included as full participants in the polity. In his second draft he had inserted the word *male* so that the text read, "Every male person of full age neither owning nor having owned [50] acres"; but in his subsequent third draft, he simply wrote, "Every person of full age."[25] Perhaps Jefferson simply slipped when he dropped the qualifier *male,* although that seems unlike the careful Jefferson we know. On the other hand, if Jefferson intentionally omitted the word *male* in his third draft, that act would also stand very much at odds with Jefferson as we have understood him, particularly given the strong evidence both for his youthful misogyny and his later ideas that women ought to remain outside of politics. Perhaps, as Jan Lewis suggests in this volume, Jefferson found himself much more comfortable with women and with the *idea* of women when he was himself attached to one.[26] His marriage to Martha Wayles Skelton a few years earlier may have helped him, in the heady days of June 1776, to imagine women as among those who made up "the people"—not just metaphorically but in terms as real as those of real estate.

However poorly Jefferson's far-reaching ideas regarding landholding might have been received by his contemporaries, Jefferson nevertheless advanced them because they seemed to him the best way to achieve a broad, landholding electorate, a group of people who, Jefferson thought, could protect liberty better than could any subset of society. As he put it to Pendleton, "In general I beleive [*sic*] the decisions of the people, in a body, will be more honest and more disinterested than those of wealthy men."[27]

Jefferson's conception of the political enfranchisement reverted to a male one as he considered the question of interest, or disinterest. It was a crucial question because self-interest tended toward corruption and tyranny, which those of the Revolutionary generation saw as the great evils threatening liberty. Evidence of the evil of corruption lay close at hand in the example of John Robinson, who had turned the Virginia government toward his own selfish ends. More generally, Jefferson and his generation found examples of corruption and tyranny in the king and Parliament, who, from the revolutionaries' perspective, sought from selfish motives to "enslave" the colonists and reduce them to utterly dependent peoples.

The people, as a body, could never act as Robinson, or the king, or even Parliament had done. A broad electorate, the people, would act to protect their interests, but almost by definition their main interest would be to fend off corruption, undue influence, and tyranny. An interest in liberty could be redefined as *disinterest,* the quality good republican leaders sought most to obtain. Since Jefferson "believe[d]" in the honesty and disinterestedness of the people—

and the concept of belief here lends a quasi-religious quality to his formulation—he saw them as the best protectors of liberty.[28]

Jefferson's genuine faith in the people's ability to protect liberty coexisted with an aristocratic, elitist sensibility evident in his ideas about how to form the upper house of the legislature. In his draft constitutions, Jefferson provided that the legislature's lower house, which he called the House of Representatives, choose members of the upper house, the Senate. As he edited the constitution, Jefferson changed his mind about the precise details of how long senators should serve, but in his final draft the senators were to serve for nine years without the ability to be reappointed. To maintain continuity while enforcing a strict term limit, Jefferson provided that one third of the group would be rotated out of office every three years. In addition, senators had to be at least thirty-one years old.[29]

In a letter to Edmund Pendleton, Jefferson explained the thoughts behind these constitutional provisions. "I had two things in view," he wrote: "to get the wisest men chosen, and to make them perfectly independent when chosen." As he had in his direction that legislators once chosen act on their own judgment, Jefferson emphasized the importance of independent governors in a way that revealed doubt about the people's capabilities. "I have ever observed," he wrote,

> that a choice by the people themselves is not generally distinguished for it's [*sic*] wisdom. This first secretion from them is usually crude and heterogeneous. But give to those so chosen by the people a second choice for themselves, and they generally will chuse wise men. For this reason it was that I proposed the representatives (and not the people) should chuse the Senate, and thought I had notwithstanding that made the Senators (when chosen) perfectly independent of their electors.

Preserving the independence of senators required isolating them from the process of election, even though elections, under Jefferson's scheme, also operated to foster independence. As Jefferson put it, "if they [senators] might be re-elected, they would be casting their eyes forward to the period of election (however distant) and be currying favor with the electors, and consequently dependent on them."[30]

Jefferson distrusted the process of vote-getting, of "currying favor." He distrusted interest and self-interest and valued independence and freedom. He sincerely believed in the power of the people to fight tyranny and to choose representatives and believed the people had a natural right to assist in the preservation of their country. But he thought their "first secretions" somewhat dubious and did not trust the people to make decisions of the moment. He understood that power stemmed from the people and ought to be channeled into legitimate government structures through free elections, but he nevertheless thought governors—and perhaps he was thinking primarily of himself here—ought to be independent-minded. Natural rights, freedom, and independence were of a piece in the year of revolution, and they all figured centrally in Jefferson's political philosophy. By the end of 1776 Jefferson had developed an American political philosophy that focused on the people, but he was not yet a "politician."

The period in Jefferson's life in which historians have most tended to focus on him as a politician has been the period in which he became so identified with a particular political party, the Republican party, that his name became attached to its members, the Jeffersonian Republicans. But during the first years of its existence, Jefferson did not head the party at all. Instead, shortly after returning in 1789 from France, where Jefferson had witnessed the opening scenes of a revolution that to him indicated that the battle between the people and tyrannical governors had become a global one, Jefferson found himself selected by his fellow Virginian George Washington to serve as America's first secretary of state. In that position, Jefferson's official attentions fell on the nation's relationship with other countries, and it was his good friend James Madison, also a

Virginian, who led what Madison soon began to call the "republican interest" in Congress.

Nor did Jefferson lead the Republican party when, after a difficult term as secretary of state often spent in battle against his fellow cabinet member Alexander Hamilton, Jefferson retired at the end of 1793 and returned to his home at Monticello. Just a few short years into his retirement, Jefferson became a candidate again for the first time in more than a decade, this time for president in the 1796 election. Still, he was not a party leader. Indeed, as much as the election of 1796 did involve politicking—the organizing of votes and to some extent voters—that politicking was done by Republican and Federalist organizers in each state and locality, not by the principal candidates, Thomas Jefferson and John Adams. As with the question of how much Jefferson attended to "the people" when first elected as a burgess, the immediate answer to the question of how Jefferson interacted with the people during the 1796 election is that he did not.

From our perspective, Jefferson's almost complete non-involvement in the election that brought him to the executive branch as vice president seems bizarre. He gave no speeches, published nothing in the newspapers, and only mentioned the election in his correspondence *after* the votes had been cast. He was, in fact, probably privy to what was going on, and his silence can be read as a studied republican one. A true republican leader, as George Washington demonstrated, did not seek power. Indeed, members of the Revolutionary generation thought, quite wisely, that those who most desired power were the ones who least deserved it. It would have been personally unbecoming as well as unrepublican to advance himself as a candidate.

In republican style, then, when Jefferson did discuss the 1796 election in a letter to his son-in-law, Thomas Mann Randolph, he denied any desire to be elected president. He wrote that he "sincerely wishe[ed] to be the second on that vote rather than the first."[31] In another letter in which he mentioned the election and repeated that "the minor will be preferred by me to the major vote," he emphasized that he had "no ambition to govern men." He did, however, admit that he liked being liked: "I shall highly value indeed the share which I may have had in the late vote, as an evidence of the share I hold in the esteem of my countrymen."[32]

The notion that an election functioned to demonstrate how much "esteem" a person was held in by his "countrymen," combined democratic and aristocratic sensibilities just as his draft constitutions had. In referring to those who had cast ballots in his favor, Jefferson avoided the word *voters* and instead used *countrymen,* an egalitarian term that invoked a sense of the people at large, a people Jefferson himself was part of. But the people selected an obvious leader, an esteemed countryman who stood above the masses while simultaneously standing as one among them. Jefferson's words marked the political and ideological distance traveled since his first election in the 1760s when, we can safely conclude, he desired more to set himself apart from ordinary folk than to be counted as one of them. Interesting, too, is that despite his republican values and suspicion of power, Jefferson was willing to admit his desire for public esteem. The idea that the favor of his countrymen mattered fit together with Jefferson's sense that the people were the ultimate protectors of liberty—their keen judgments in elections put in place liberty-loving leaders, in this case Jefferson.

To emphasize that the new vice president was simply one of the people, Jefferson journeyed from Monticello to the capital at Philadelphia in a concertedly republican mode. Showily avoiding a showy journey, he traveled with his longtime personal slave Jupiter from Monticello to Dumfries, Virginia (located about halfway between Washington and Fredericksburg), and from there, unaccompanied, he took a simple stagecoach.

But again, democratic symbolism combined with recognition of Jefferson's status as an extraordinary citizen. The people of Philadelphia welcomed him almost royally with "a company of artillery and . . . a discharge of sixteen rounds from two twelve-pounders." The crowd displayed a flag with the words "JEFFERSON THE FRIEND OF THE PEOPLE" on it, which indicated less that they saw him as one of the people than that he was a special individual who could champion the people precisely because of his high power and station.[33]

The brief speech Jefferson made upon being sworn in as vice president followed his self-consciously simple republican style and contained another small clue to his thought about what it meant to be elected, to serve the people. After greeting the "gentlemen" of the senate, Jefferson began, "Entering on the duties of the office to which I am called . . . ."[34] He was not *elected,* or *selected,* but *called,* a word suggesting religious destiny and acclamation, a voicing from a body so general as to appear natural and right.

Just as Jefferson's "belief" in the people, expressed in his 1776 letter to Pendleton, hinted at an almost religious conception of politics, his being "called" to office echoed the religious beliefs of early Americans who saw divine office as a calling. (Even the word *election* had a religious connotation, since the Puritans and their descendants described those saved by God as the "elect.")

The use of the key words *belief* and *calling* signifies an important web of understanding. It was an Enlightenment understanding in which divine and natural forces worked through the logic and reason of individual people to put into place what ought to be. The enlightened inquisitors of the eighteenth century presumed that careful investigation could uncover Nature's divine laws and goals, and that the science of politics formed one part of that larger scientific inquiry into the character of the world.[35] Thus it was that Jefferson could declare, on behalf of America, that "the Laws" of "Nature's God" had "entitle[d]" the American colonies to political independence from Great Britain.[36] In the independent nation, investigating the natural rules of politics and developing a science of politics led to another conclusion: that it was elections that made manifest Nature's plan for the body politic. When the people in whom Thomas Jefferson believed called leaders to office, it was an act at once natural, right, and ordained.

Politics held such an important place in the natural, divine plan because the natural and correct outcome in the political sphere could ensure similar rightness in other arenas. For example, if the correct, that is to say, Republican (not Federalist), party ruled, its supporters could implement the proper commercial policies. The Republican commercial policy that Jefferson and Madison endorsed sprang, like Jefferson's draft Virginia constitutions, from principles of freedom, and would allow the free flow of American goods without monopoly or restriction. Free commerce stood as an ideological as well as economic goal, in contrast to corruption and manipulation in the form of Federalist trade policies or European mercantilist practices that would, the Republicans thought, improperly divert natural channels.[37]

Partisan politics, with its bitterness and divisiveness, seemed to violate the natural order Jefferson sought and believed in. Jefferson also had a strong personal distaste for conflict. It is odd, then, that he became the head of the Republican party in that period when the Republicans and the Federalists fought each other most fiercely, the late 1790s. Much of the rivalry played itself out in the newspapers in vicious attacks by both sides against the members and policies of the other party. Jefferson himself did not appeal to the people directly through any of these editorials or pamphlets or speeches. By contrast, others, particularly Alexander Hamilton in both his own name and by pseudonym, authored printed attacks on the Republicans. It is ironic that the Federalist leader, who was and is seen as an elitist, should have appealed more directly to the people than did the leader of the Republican party, the Friend of the People, Thomas Jefferson. Jefferson's organizational efforts came instead in the form of meetings with and letters to other leaders, such as Aaron Burr, James Madison, and Albert Gallatin. Jefferson as a politician in this period was still operating primarily in the rarefied air breathed by the elite, even if his ultimate object was to persuade the people.[38]

The partisan struggles of the late 1790s proved, like the Revolution, to mark a turning point in Jefferson's ideas about and behavior in elections. While Jefferson maintained his ideas about why elections were important—that they allowed the natural order to emerge—he altered his willingness to work personally and politically to rally support. Maybe Nature needed help. In contrast to his silence in 1796, Jefferson in 1800 wrote numerous letters regarding the upcoming presidential election and involved himself as a tactician. He weighed in, for example, on whether Virginia should adopt the winner-take-all system in voting for presidential electors or continue to choose them based on districts. He was politician enough to compromise his ideals. Jefferson thought that in order for Virginia's votes to matter, the Republican stronghold should, like ten other states, employ the winner-take-all system even though that system silenced the voice of the minority.[39]

Although Jefferson was more involved in getting elected in 1800 than ever before or after, he nevertheless remained aloof from much of the organizing that Republican party personnel engaged in during that spring, summer, and fall. His response to a letter of Philip Norborne Nicholas demonstrates Jefferson's odd mixture of engagement and distance in that election year. When Nicholas wrote to Jefferson about the Republican organization Nicholas and others were putting in place in Virginia in order to "communicate useful information to the people relative to the election," Jefferson did not respond for nearly two months. When he finally did, Jefferson confirmed that he thought he should play a more active role than he had in 1796. He told Nicholas that as soon as he could find a "private conveyance" he would send Nicholas eight dozen copies of a pamphlet he thought ought to be distributed to Republicans in each of Virginia's counties. Jefferson's suspicions were up: "I dare trust nothing this summer through the post offices," he explained. Here he was, a political plotter, an election-year strategist. But distancing himself again from that role, Jefferson instructed Nicholas to keep it a secret that the pamphlets came from Jefferson.[40]

The final indication of Jefferson's willingness to act at least partly as a candidate—in spite of protests he had made at the beginning of the election season about wishing to stay at home—came when Jefferson, Aaron Burr, and others awaited the reports of the electoral votes in December 1800. Even before the votes were in, Jefferson began to behave presidentially, rounding up cabinet members and congratulating Burr on his victory as vice president over John Adams. By the time the tie between Jefferson and Burr became apparent, Jefferson through his behavior had already established himself as the presumptive winner.[41]

After the victory in 1800, Jefferson could return to his earlier, more passive election-time behavior. In 1804, with his popularity wide and the Republicans ascendant, Jefferson needed to do little to work for his reelection beyond what he had done already as president. He had in his first term used his significant powers of persuasion at small dinner parties to urge members of Congress to implement his policies. And following the precedent he had set in 1796, he had cultivated a self-consciously simple, republican style in dress and behavior that was meant to convey his belief in equality and in the dignity of the people.[42] He had acted with attention to how the people would perceive him, and he had acted on behalf of what he thought the people wanted and needed. His easy and convincing victory in 1804 confirmed for him that, as the 1796 banner had proclaimed, the people did indeed view him as their friend.

The political success of this man who acted so little like a politician reveals several things about his time and about the relationship between his time and ours. For one thing, the professional politician, a character we have very mixed feelings about today but which we accept as an immutable reality, was just being birthed at the end of Jefferson's public career. The period of Jefferson's political life occurred before the rise of truly modern politics, which has included the professionalization of politics.

Jefferson's success as a politician tells us something else about that earlier political culture. It was a culture that valued both gentlemanly honor and republican disinterest. It had deep roots in the eighteenth-century world of hierarchy and deference in which

Jefferson, Washington, Madison, and others grew up. In that colonial world, it would have been unseemly to "run" for office, or to give a speech on one's own behalf. Leadership in that slave society had validity only to the extent that it appeared to arise naturally from the order of things—an important continuity between the worldview dominant in the colonial period and the one, based on Enlightenment faith in a natural order, that dominated during and after the Revolution. Jefferson differed from many of his contemporaries in his emphasis that the order of things ought to be based on talent rather than birth, but his words and behavior showed that he endorsed the general notion that there *was* an order of things, and that it ought to reveal itself though natural processes allowed to work themselves out freely.

Believing that the voice of the people revealed itself through the natural process of elections, Jefferson could champion the people—and mean it quite sincerely—without having any desire actually to speak to them. To do so, to speak directly to the people except when obviously called for, such as in an inaugural address, might seem to be groveling for their approval. Aside from being personally unbecoming, campaigning for the people's approval would constitute an overt interference with what was natural. Hence when Jefferson *did* interfere, when he sent pamphlets to Virginia politicos, he did so secretly.

Though a master politician, Jefferson would nevertheless fail to recognize the present-day philosophy of Alexandra Pelosi, a documentary filmmaker, who said in an interview conducted shortly after her mother became Speaker of the House, "[T]hat's what democracy is. You get enough people out there to show your point of view, and you win."[43] In the younger Pelosi's understanding, winning has nothing to do with the natural wisdom of the people. It reflects instead something much more material and less idealistic: who can get their voters to the polls. Moreover, her emphasis on winning denotes contest. And even though Jefferson spent a number of years in contest with Federalists, he did not see it as a legitimate one and was not a partisan in the modern sense. In his view the Federalist government had corrupted the spirit of 1776, and he and his party, the true inheritors of the Revolution, had to reclaim it. To Jefferson this was not a matter of simple winning or losing. Winning per se was not the object. Reclaiming the Revolution and restoring harmony—not perpetuating contest, but ending the need for partisanship—were his goals.

As much as Jefferson's ideas about democracy speak directly to us and as much as Jefferson's words still serve political purposes as they did for Nancy Pelosi in her first speech as Speaker of the House, Jefferson himself has trouble talking to us. Or, rather, we have trouble hearing him. His language is a distant one, out of a past world in which a small group of free, white men could presume there existed a natural order in which they stood on top naturally and with the assent of the "people."

Jefferson's relevance to us today, then, has much more to do with symbolism, a word used repeatedly by those who have written about him, than with how he contributed to the making of modern democracy and modern politics. Thomas Jefferson did not, in fact, intend to contribute to modern politics. But what he stood for—the wisdom of the people that emerges naturally in a free society—remains important, even central, to our notion of what America stands for.

Jefferson would not despair at having become a symbol more than an exemplar. Indeed, he cultivated his symbolic self with his dramatic embodiment of republican simplicity, such as when as president he greeted the British ambassador dressed in simple clothes and worn slippers, which the ambassador correctly interpreted as an "indifference to appearances" that was "actually studied."[44]

We should not diminish the important function Thomas Jefferson as symbol serves even as we recognize the persistent gap between Jefferson the symbol and Jefferson the eighteenth-century man. We need symbols to guide us, to remind us of who we want to be. Thomas Jefferson as an optimistic symbol of democracy and the people serves us well—better, perhaps, than he served his own political party during his life.

NOTES

1. Although the official text of her speech, as printed in "Pelosi Calls for a New America, Built on the Values that Made Our Country Great," January 4, 2007, text online at http://www.house.gov/pelosi/, reads "optimism, opportunity, and courage," the newspaper report of the speech as given substitutes "strength" for "courage." See Edward Epstein and Zachary Coile, "Madam Speaker," *San Francisco Chronicle*, January 5, 2007 [final edition], A1. For Boehner, see "Remarks by House Minority Leader Representative John Boehner (R-OH) to the House of Representatives Following a Vote on the Speaker of the House," Federal News Service, January 4, 2007, accessed online through LexisNexis.

2. Pelosi designated January 5 as "open house for the People's House," as reported in the *Washington Times*, "Pelosi ready to make history as new speaker," January 4, 2007, A.01; and Boehner in his January 4 speech referred to the "people's House." As Gordon Wood wrote, "None of the other major founding fathers was as optimistic and confident of the people as Jefferson was." And so "[t]hat is why we remember Jefferson and not Madison." Wood, *Revolutionary Characters: What Made the Founders Different* (New York, 2006), 114, 117.

3. James MacGregor Burns, "Jefferson and the Strategy of Politics," in *Thomas Jefferson and American Democracy*, ed. Henry C. Dethloff (Lexington, Mass., 1971), 119.

4. William Nesbit Chambers, "Jeffersonian Republicans and the Development of the Modern Party System," in ibid., 131.

5. Hugh Blair Grigsby, *The Virginia Convention of 1776 . . .* (Richmond, Va., 1855), 175.

6. Malone, *Jefferson and His Time*, vol. 1, chap. 4–7.

7. Jack P. Greene, "Foundations of Political Power in the Virginia House of Burgesses, 1720–1776," *William and Mary Quarterly*, 3rd ser., 16 (October 1959), 485–506.

8. Merrill D. Peterson, *Thomas Jefferson and the New Nation: A Biography* (New York, 1970), 41.

9. Grigsby, *Virginia Convention of 1776*, 11.

10. TJ to John Page, May 25, 1766, in Jefferson, *Papers*, 1:19–20.

11. Malone, *Jefferson and His Time*, 1:115, 129–30; Peterson, *Thomas Jefferson and the New Nation*, 23.

12. Malone, *Jefferson and His Time*, 1:129–30.

13. Theodorick Bland Sr., June 27, 1765, quoted in ibid., 1:129.

14. For descriptions of colonial elections, see Edmund S. Morgan, *Inventing the People: The Rise of Popular Sovereignty in England and America* (New York, 1988), chap. 8; and Rhys Isaac, *The Transformation of Virginia, 1740–1790* (Chapel Hill, N.C., 1982), 110–14.

15. Not until 1775, six years after first being elected and in the midst of a revolutionary movement, did Jefferson enter the cadre of leaders, and then only in its second tier. Greene, "Foundations of Political Power," 497.

16. Jefferson, *Papers,* 1:104–5, 105n. Although Jefferson's bill passed, the House dissolved before his bill could receive the assent of the governor and council.

17. TJ to Thomas Nelson, May 16, 1776, in Jefferson, *Papers,* 1:292.

18. Ibid.

19. Editorial notes in ibid., 335–47, 364n, 384.

20. "First Draft by Jefferson," ibid., 341. See pp. 348 and 358 for versions of the provision in the second and third drafts.

21. Peterson, *Thomas Jefferson and the New Nation,* 41; Malone, *Jefferson and His Time,* 1:95–96.

22. "Second Draft by Jefferson," in Jefferson, *Papers,* 1:348.

23. On the interrelated concepts of independence, property, and republican virtue, see Gordon S. Wood, *The Radicalism of the American Revolution* (New York, 1991), 104–6, 178–79. For a more extensive discussion, and to compare Jefferson's views described here with American practices of instructing representatives, see Wood, *The Creation of the American Republic* (Chapel Hill, N.C., 1969), chap. 2 and chap. 5. Also see Morgan, *Inventing the People,* chap. 7 and chap. 8, on eighteenth-century ideas about yeoman independence and elections.

24. "Second Draft by Jefferson," in Jefferson, *Papers,* 1:352; "Third Draft by Jefferson," ibid., 362.

25. "Second Draft by Jefferson," ibid., 352; "Third Draft by Jefferson," ibid., 362.

26. Kenneth A. Lockridge, *On the Sources of Patriarchal Rage: The Commonplace Books of William Byrd and Thomas Jefferson and the Gendering of Power in the Eighteenth Century* (New York, 1992), chap. 3; Elizabeth Wirth Marvick, "Thomas Jefferson and the Ladies of Paris," *Proceedings of the Annual Meeting of the Western Society for French History* 21 (1994): 81–94; Jan Ellen Lewis, "Jefferson and Women," in this volume; Lewis, " 'The Blessings of Domestic Society': Thomas Jefferson's Family and the Transformation of American Politics," in *Jeffersonian Legacies,* ed. Peter S. Onuf (Charlottesville, Va., 1993), 109–46.

27. TJ to Edmund Pendleton, August 26, 1776, in Jefferson, *Papers,* 1:504.

28. For elaboration of Jefferson's ideas about "the people" versus small groups, see Paul A. Rahe, "Thomas Jefferson's Machiavellian Political Science," in *Review of Politics* 57 (Summer 1995): 449–81. For an extended discussion of ideas about the people, see Morgan, *Inventing the People.* On the Revolu-

tionaries' conception of power and their fear of tyranny, see Bernard Bailyn, *The Ideological Origins of the American Revolution,* enlarged ed. (Cambridge, Mass., 1992).

29. "First Draft by Jefferson," in Jefferson, *Papers,* 1:341; "Second Draft by Jefferson," ibid., 348–49; "Third Draft by Jefferson," ibid., 358–59.

30. TJ to Edmund Pendleton, August 26, 1776, ibid., 503–4.

31. TJ to Thomas Mann Randolph, November 28, 1796, ibid., 29:211. Jefferson referred specifically to electoral votes in western Pennsylvania. See ibid., 211n.

32. TJ to Edward Rutledge, December 27, 1796, ibid., 232.

33. Malone, *Jefferson and His Time,* 3:295.

34. *Annals of Congress,* 4th Congress, 2nd session, Mar. 4, 1797, p. 1581, accessed online at memory.loc.gov. See similar language in his message accepting election as governor of Virginia, June 2, 1779, in Jefferson, *Papers,* 2:277–78. Jefferson said, "The honour which the General Assembly have been pleased to confer on me, by calling me to the high office of Governour of this commonwealth, demands my most grateful acknowledgments. . . . In a virtuous and free state, no rewards can be so pleasing to sensible minds, as those which include the approbation of our fellow citizens."

35. Gordon Wood writes of the "Whig Science of Politics" in chapter 1 of *Creation of the American Republic* and takes the word *science* from James Iredell (quoted on p. 10). On political science as a study of government, society, and moral philosophy, see Drew McCoy, *The Elusive Republic: Political Economy in Jeffersonian America* (Chapel Hill, N.C., 1980), 6.

36. Quotations from the Declaration of Independence.

37. See McCoy, *Elusive Republic,* chap. 3 and chap. 6. McCoy writes on p. 76 that the revolutionaries held a "vibrant faith that the Revolution would instigate the annihilation of a corrupting, mercantilist system of intercourse and replace it with a more natural and universally beneficent system of exchange." Similarly, Jefferson's medical-political vocabulary, recently described by Andrew Burstein, tended to focus on "convulsions" that might inhibit the "development of a natural amiability" and that disturbed the "stability and balance" he sought in the body politic as well in his own person. Andrew Burstein, *Jefferson's Secrets: Death and Desire at Monticello* (New York, 2005), 48–49.

38. For details of one example, see Dumas Malone's description of the Cabell affair in *Jefferson and His Time,* 3:334–36. Another example of Jefferson's behind-the-scenes politicking is his secret authorship of the Virginia Resolutions.

39. TJ to James Monroe, January 12, 1800, in Jefferson, *Papers,* 31:300–301.

40. Philip Norborne Nicholas to TJ, February 2, 1800, ibid., 356; TJ to Philip

Norborne Nicholas, April 7, 1800, ibid., 485 (quotation). Jefferson wrote on April 7 that he had received Nicholas's letter on February 11. The pamphlet was apparently Thomas Cooper's "Political Arithmetic"; see TJ to Joseph Priestley, January 18, 1800, ibid., 320.

41. Malone, *Jefferson and His Time,* 3:494–95.

42. For a good description of Jefferson's symbolic behavior as president, see Catherine Allgor, *Parlor Politics: In Which the Ladies of Washington Help Build a City and a Government* (Charlottesville, Va., 2000), chap. 2.

43. Joe Garofoli, "Behind the Red Curtain: Documentary Filmmaker Alexandra Pelosi, Daughter of the Speaker, Leaves the Blue States for Some Cultural Learnings of Her Own," *San Francisco Chronicle,* January 17, 2007 (quotation on p. 3 of LexisNexis version accessed online).

44. Malcolm Lester, *Anthony Merry Redivivus: A Reappraisal of the British Minister to the United States, 1803–5* (Charlottesville, Va., 1978), 31–32 (quotations at 32).

Peter J. Kastor

The Many Wests of Thomas Jefferson

"Jefferson and the West" is a phrase that rolls off the tongue. It seems familiar. It suggests continuity. After all, what account of Thomas Jefferson is complete without a discussion of his abiding interest in the West? Indeed, it is almost impossible to conceive of Jefferson without the West, for it was in the West that Jefferson found the means to understand human nature and America's future.

Jefferson's fascination with the West likewise lends itself to discussions that often seek to celebrate or to condemn Jefferson. Whether in academic or public circumstances, these discussions tend to characterize Jefferson in two ways: Jefferson the visionary who understood how to extend institutions of freedom, representative government, and individual opportunity into the West; or Jefferson the architect of conquest and misery, setting in motion the eradication and forced removal of Indians, the expansion of African American slavery, and the ethnic subjugation of the Hispanic residents of Spanish North America. The title of the symposium at which this paper was first presented is particularly appropriate. *In his time,* Thomas Jefferson helped to define how Americans conceived of the West. *In our time,* the celebration of the West remains something that Americans unquestioningly associate with Jefferson.

With that, I should be done. After all, Jefferson's commentary on the West has already been the subject of academic history, popular biography, and public commemoration. That conversation has long been in place but recently reached new heights during the bicentennial observations of the Louisiana Purchase and the Lewis and Clark Expedition. And that is the problem. How do we approach the issue of Jefferson and the West in a way that moves us beyond the most familiar of stories?

I want to engage that question by problematizing a set of assumptions about geography, narrative, and consistency that underscore much of the work on Jefferson and the West. In geographic terms, Jefferson wrote about not one West but two, both literally and figuratively. In geographic terms, he often discussed a Near West from the Appalachian Mountains to the Mississippi River and a Far West beyond the Mississippi River. Distinguishing the two is all the more difficult because Jefferson himself did not use these terms. Nonetheless, they do clarify his outlook, and as a result I use them here instead of the academic nomenclature (be it borderland or frontier or backcountry) that scholars have developed to describe conditions often (but not exclusively) associated with western North America. It was in the Near West of the eighteenth century that Jefferson saw both the greatest opportunities and the fewest threats. It was the Far West of the nineteenth century that was more troubling to Jefferson in his own time and more confusing in our time.

In the process of reconsidering the West, I also want to reconsider the ways we approach the written record and chronology itself. While Jefferson remained consistently fascinated by Western regions, his specific comments responded to a highly specific chronology. Before 1790, Jefferson began a process of theorizing a Western future. From 1790 through 1803 he grappled with the task of governing the Near West but remained generally confident about rapid settlement and federal consolidation. From 1803 to 1809 President Jefferson faced new challenges in governing the Far West that he expressed in terms far more circumspect than he had a decade earlier. From 1809 to 1819 Jefferson returned to a more theoretical and in the end a more optimistic outlook toward Western development. From 1819 to his death in 1826, new fears led Jefferson to withdraw from the West even as he sentimentalized it.

This periodization reflects the typical biographical organization of Jefferson's life (emerging leader, secretary of state and party leader, president, engaged retiree, and increasingly disengaged old man). More important, though, this periodization corresponds to major shifts in Jefferson's conception of the West, shifts that occurred not only because Jefferson's attitude changed but also because his *job* changed. I emphasize this point because Jefferson occasionally functions in the popular imagination as a figure beyond chronology. He appears bound by a set of consistent beliefs that varied more as a result of shifts in outlook or mood than as a result of the substantively different requirements of his various public offices or the profound differences between government service and private life. Ignoring that context also leads too easily in the other direction, with Jefferson becoming inconsistent or hypocritical in ways that never fully explain how and why he reached his conclusions or deployed the tools of government.[1]

How Jefferson expressed those attitudes is no less important. The notion of a singular, consistent Western vision is very much a product of selective sources. Jefferson crafted some of his most intellectually sophisticated and aesthetically elegant prose to describe the West, often in public documents or in correspondence that he intended for audiences beyond a single recipient. He described the West very differently when writing as a policymaking official to his subordinates charged with Western governance. Much of that practical correspondence is hardly sophisticated or elegant, which goes a long way toward explaining why it is so often absent from considerations of Jefferson and the West. Yet it was in this more pedestrian prose that Jefferson constructed an ongoing commentary about the West. As a result, I begin each section of this essay with three selected passages that suggest the linkages and tensions at work in Jefferson's discussion of the West, passages to which I return in the analysis that follows.

To this let me add some important caveats. Although I think we do need to examine Jefferson's approach to the West more carefully, certain things remain clear. Throughout his life, Jefferson maintained an abiding belief that the West could be the place where the United States realized its potential. The white settlers who were his primary concern would be able to preserve independence and liberty in the West, not only their own but also that of the entire nation. Western settlement might prevent the corruption and inequity that Jefferson had long associated with Europe. Jefferson became aggressively expansionistic toward territory that he considered a natural and beneficial addition to the United States. At certain moments of territorial expansion, Jefferson further believed that in the North American West, the United States was establishing a new vision of empire that would get right everything that the Europeans had gotten wrong. Meanwhile, Jefferson remained periodically sympathetic toward Indians but consistently incapable of seeing the world on Indian terms. And while Jefferson was a key figure in preventing the extension of slavery into the Northwest, he was equally effective at preserving slavery in the Southwest.[2]

I emphasize all this because in my efforts to complicate the notion of Jefferson and the West, I am not trying to overturn everything we associate with him. Instead, I want to describe a Jefferson who is not just more complex, but a Jefferson who, at the end of the day, is more satisfying as well. Such an approach makes Jefferson a more three-dimensional figure, driven less by abstract ideology than by complex thought. It also helps keep Jefferson rooted *in his time.* In the process, he becomes more revealing *in our time.*

> [We] must leave it to yourself to decide on the object of the campaign. If against these Indians, the end proposed should be their extermination, or their removal beyond the lakes or Illinois river. The same world will scarcely do for them and us.
>
> Thomas Jefferson to George Rogers Clark, January 1, 1780

> The Ohio is the most beautiful river on earth. Its current gentle, waters clear, and bosom smooth and unbroken by rocks and rapids, a single instance only excepted. . . . The Wabash is a very beautiful river. . . . The *Missisipi* will be one of the principal channels of future commerce.
>
> THOMAS JEFFERSON, *NOTES ON THE STATE OF VIRGINIA* (1781)

> An industrious farmer occupies a more dignified place in the scale of beings, whether moral or political, than a lazy lounger, valuing himself on his family, too proud to work, and drawing out a miserable existence by eating on that surplus of other men's labour which is the sacred fund of the helpless poor.
>
> THOMAS JEFFERSON, JUNE 22, 1786

By the time he wrote these passages in the 1780s, Jefferson had developed an elaborate approach to a place he called "the West."[3] Elements of that vision remained with him for the rest of his life. Nonetheless, that Western vision emerged from the specifics of the 1770s and the 1780s. Personal interest, intellectual identity, regional culture, and national chauvinism led Jefferson to develop a scientific and aesthetic outlook that celebrated the West. But Jefferson's experience as governor of Virginia during these years led him to express very different notions of the West. While in his scientific and philosophical approaches to the West Jefferson imagined amity and peaceful development, as governor, he described a landscape forged through bloody conflict. Those differences in outlook were only magnified by the way Jefferson went about describing the West, for the written genres he chose shaped his varied forms of regional representation.

Thomas Jefferson imagined himself a child of the West. Raised in Albemarle County on the western fringe of the British hold in North America, as a child Jefferson saw firsthand the process of white settlement in the Western backcountry. In his formative years as a student, attorney, and planter, Jefferson witnessed settlers situating the Western periphery at the center of their notions of what it meant to be British citizens and American colonists. Throughout the eighteenth century, British settlers concluded that the one precondition for personal and economic independence, political participation and liberty, and rough equality alongside other settlers was the acquisition of land. In the third quarter of the eighteenth century, Virginians who found themselves excluded from these opportunities increasingly looked to the trans-Appalachian West as a place where they might acquire land and all the benefits that came with it. Jefferson in turn joined Virginia's elite in recognizing that anybody with the wealth to invest in Western lands could see a quick and massive profit as the surge in white settlers fueled rising demand and, in turn, rising real estate values. This outlook was hardly limited to Virginia, as similar systems of speculation and settlement developed throughout the backcountry of the British colonies.[4]

Notes on the State of Virginia, the text that often serves as a touchstone for any consideration of Jefferson, suggests the multiple forces that came together to shape not only Jefferson's shifting understanding of the West in his time but also the seemingly immutable representation of Jefferson's West that remains in our time. While the West did not dominate *Notes,* the broad trajectory of Jefferson's ideas and even his prose style led him to celebrate the West. *Notes* reserved the West for separate praise, exemplified in his claims about the beauty of the Ohio and Wabash Rivers. Jefferson moved beyond those claims to describe a land of abundant resources, the vestiges of great Indian civilizations, and animals that were large in both size and number.[5]

It was in *Notes* that Jefferson most powerfully articulated the relationship between Western settlement and national development. Jefferson claimed that "those who labour in the earth are the chosen people of God, if ever he had a chosen people, whose breasts he has made his peculiar deposit for substantial and genuine virtue." Proclaiming the inherent virtues of labor in opposition to the corruption of luxury, Jefferson could make a virtue out of adversity, since the struggle to construct a civilization actually made Americans more civilized than the European aristocrats and urban elites who often functioned as villains in Jefferson's narratives. Jefferson was likewise seeking to correct Europeans, in this case the description of the United States in the *Encyclopédie Méthodique,* when he claimed "an industrious farmer occupies a more dignified place in the scale of beings, whether moral or political, than a lazy lounger." In neither passage did Jefferson refer exclusively to the West. Nonetheless, the West exemplified Jefferson's claims, for it was in the West that the vast majority of settlers endured the physical challenges of agriculture on a daily basis.[6]

In celebrating the West, Jefferson could celebrate America. Jefferson could also celebrate his own talents in the very process of writing about the West. In the *Notes,* the West enabled Jefferson to showcase his own ability to preserve a balance between the scientific rationalism of the Enlightenment and the emerging sentimental prose of Romanticism. The mountains, fields, and vistas of the trans-Appalachian backcountry and the Ohio and Mississippi River Valleys were ideally suited to this language. When Jefferson referred to the Ohio and Wabash Rivers as "beautiful," he did so from an eighteenth-century Enlightenment notion of resources providentially in place to support settlement, promote commerce, and serve the civilization of mankind.[7] Jefferson employed a very different set of literary tropes rooted in landscape aesthetics to proclaim "[t]he *Natural bridge,* the most sublime of Nature's work." It was not the first or last time Jefferson found an ideal subject for aesthetic description in a feature of the Western landscape.[8]

Finally, it was in *Notes* that Jefferson began articulating an inherently sentimental, almost nostalgic approach toward the Indians of North America. "What would be the melancholy sequel of their history," Jefferson explained in the section on Aborigines, "may however be augured from the census of 1669; by which we discover that the tribes therein enumerated were, in the space of 62 years, reduced to about one-third of their former numbers." He attributed this destruction to "Spirituous liquors, the small-pox, war, and an abridgment of territory, to a people who lived principally on the spontaneous productions of nature." Jefferson could celebrate Indians in part because they seemed bound for extinction, their conflict with Europeans a thing of the past.[9]

In his description of the Near West, *Notes* provided the means for Jefferson to refute European critics, establish his own identity as an intellectual on a par with those critics, and describe the collapse of Indian populations in a way that served both ends. Jefferson likewise sought numerous goals in his other great Western document of the 1780s: the March 1784 "Report on Government for Western Territory" (hereinafter "Report"). In his efforts to achieve the specific task of creating a political system that could preserve order and unity in the West, Jefferson issued a manifesto on the republican order he hoped to see throughout the United States.

In the same way that Jefferson celebrated the independence of individual settlers in *Notes,* in the "Report" Jefferson broke from every tradition of European rule—and from the suggestions of some colleagues—by proposing the trans-Appalachian West be divided into independent states rather than subordinate colonies. "[S]uch temporary government shall only continue in force in any state until it shall have acquired 20,000 free inhabitants," Jefferson explained, "when, giving due proof thereof to Congress, they shall receive from them authority with appointments of time and place to call a Convention of representatives to establish a permanent Constitution & Government for themselves." In that one passage, Jefferson recapitulated his commitment to self-government and his faith in the capacity of Western settlers. Jefferson was convinced that by enabling white settlers to own land and promoting their political development, he could guarantee not only stability in the Near West but also a Near West that would serve as the model for a republican nation.[10]

In our time, *Notes* and the "Report" often become the sole expressions of Jefferson's emerging sense of the West. Yet wedged between Jefferson's youthful upbringing in the 1760s and his expansive celebration of the Western landscape and its settlers in the 1780s was a very different Western vision that Jefferson articulated during the American Revolution. As governor of Virginia, Jefferson discussed Western Indians, Western settlers, and the relationship between them in ways very different from the world he constructed in either *Notes* or the "Report." How he governed the West was a result of his job. How he described the West in writing was a result of genre.

Jefferson understood that one of the primary reasons why the call for American independence in 1776 found traction was the belief among white settlers that British efforts to use the Appalachian Mountains as a protective boundary between whites and Indians did less to preserve racial peace than to restrict white opportunities. For public officials at the state and national level, tapping that land hunger produced an effective military force without consuming the state's limited resources. That was exactly Jefferson's goal in his 1780 letter allowing George Rogers Clark to "leave it to yourself to decide on the object of the campaign." An ambitious child of the Virginia gentry, Clark was among a cadre of Western speculators and settlers who helped spark racial violence during the 1760s and early 1770s. When the Revolution started, Clark quickly assembled an army of like-minded men. Similar movements emerged throughout the Virginia backcountry, as Western settlers found in the American Revolution an ideal opportunity to settle affairs once and for all.[11]

Virginia's government rewarded these men accordingly. To attract and reward Clark's army, Governor Jefferson recommended that Clark's enlisted men each receive three hundred acres, their officers even more. When Jefferson later had no currency to pay Clark's volunteers, he simply sent Clark a stack of additional promissory notes for Western land grants. Not only was it all he could offer, but for Clark and so many of his men, it truly did seem better than gold.[12] Jefferson was only too happy to unleash those settlers against the Indians of the Far West. In sharp contrast to *Notes* (which sentimentalized Indians en route to extinction) and the 1784 "Report" (which ignored Indians altogether), Jefferson's wartime correspondence described the Near West as a place occupied by abundant and powerful Indians.

Yet Clark's Western volunteers provided a cautionary tale for Governor Jefferson. Clark chafed at efforts—whether by Jefferson, George Washington, or the Continental Congress and the Virginia state government—to impose strategic coordination onto the military operations in the West. Jefferson and Washington quickly concluded they could no longer tell frontiersmen like Clark to "leave it to yourself" when it came to military planning.[13] As a policymaking official during the Revolution, Jefferson increasingly came to believe that Western settlement must be the subject of management, albeit with a light hand. In so doing, Jefferson sought a balance in the prevailing debate about the West in particular and frontiers in general. A long-standing European theory held that civilization collapsed on its fringes, especially when those fringes brought white settlers into contact with uncivilized peoples like the Indians of North America. Jefferson directly repudiated these theories in *Notes* and the 1784 "Report," in large part because the theories clashed with his broader goal of claiming that a great civilization could emerge from the Americas. In his management of the West, however, Jefferson saw himself and government in general as the force that could mitigate against the untrammeled development of the frontier that could only result in savagery.

What accounts for this sudden and dramatic shift in Jefferson's discussion of the West? First, there is the matter of context. Jefferson began work on *Notes* immediately after his service as governor of Virginia. Referring to that departure as a "retirement," Jefferson was eager to distance himself from the frustrations and disappointments he associated with a term in office marked by the successful British invasion of Virginia and the domestic political resistance Jefferson faced from men he had long considered his friends and allies. Jefferson threw himself into writing the *Notes* to escape that experience in Virginia as much as he did to engage a transatlantic intellectual community. Likewise, as a legislator in the Continental Congress designing a general plan for the Northwest, Jefferson left it for future government officials to address the lived reality of a complex, multiracial population.[14] He did not have to wait long. In 1787 Congress approved the Northwest Ordinance, which borrowed heavily from Jefferson's "Report," primarily in its guarantee that new jurisdictions created in the West could enter the union as states on an equal footing. But the Northwest Ordinance also concerned itself with the practical matters of governance (the subdivision of territory, the role of local officials, the relationship between the territorial leadership and the national leadership) that no longer consumed Jefferson once he was out of office.

Yet there is another, equally important explanation for the gap separating Jefferson's comments during the Revolution from his work in *Notes* and the "Report." These were fundamentally different texts intended for different audiences. In his efforts to refute European detractors of American productive capacity by writing *Notes,* Jefferson appropriated Indians in particular and the West in general as the means to proclaim America's future promise. Meanwhile, planning documents like the "Report" were by definition lean on details. The substantive tropes and aesthetic requirements of natural history, legislation, and correspondence each constructed the West in a particular way. This hardly means that Jefferson's correspondence was somehow more honest than his public writings were. To the contrary, Jefferson was often writing to men he did not wholly trust by means of a postal system in which he knew few things stayed private. Nonetheless, the rhetorical functions and the generic conventions of correspondence, natural science, and public policy imposed very different requirements. Throughout his life, Jefferson wrote in very different ways, usually with a keen awareness of gender, genre, and audience. His treatment of the West emerged accordingly.[15]

> Our news from the Westward is disagreeable. Constant murders committing by the Indians, and their combination threatens to be more and more extensive. I hope we shall give them a thorough drubbing this summer, and then change our tomahawk into a golden chain of friendship. The most economical as well as most humane conduct towards them is to bribe them into peace, and to retain them in peace by eternal bribes.
>
> THOMAS JEFFERSON TO CHARLES CARROLL, APRIL 15, 1791

> It is well known that the substratum of the country beyond the Blue Ridge is limestone, abounding with large caverns, the earthy floors of which are highly impregnated with nitre.
>
> Thomas Jefferson, Report to the American Philosophical Society, March 10, 1797

> However our present interests may restrain us within our own limits, it is impossible not to look forward to distant times, when our rapid multiplication will expand itself beyond those limits, & cover the whole northern, if not the southern continent.
>
> Thomas Jefferson to James Monroe, November 24, 1801

"A thorough drubbing," indeed. Jefferson used that phrase no less than three times in letters he wrote during April 1791.[16] He clearly liked the phrase, and it came at a moment of high pique for the nation's first secretary of state. Angered by the marauding raids of the Indians of the Ohio Country, Jefferson showed none of the magnanimous concern for a dying race that he expressed in *Notes* or in similar scientific texts he wrote throughout his adult life.[17] During the 1790s the Near West ceased to be a place of peaceful, enlightened white settlement and noble if declining Indians. Instead, the West once again became the landscape of unruly white settlers and savage Indians.

Or at least that is how things would appear. For if context and public office shaped Jefferson's outlook on the West, genre would once again shape the way he described it. In the thick of his role as a public administrator, Jefferson's official letters described the West in a way his private musing and public pronouncements did not. And that goes a long way toward explaining how Jefferson moved from the discussion of Indians and white settlers who occupied the surface of the Western landscape, in his letters to Carroll and Monroe, to his discussion of what lay beneath the surface, in his report to the American Philosophical Society.

The notion of Jefferson as a Western policymaker in the 1790s may seem odd. This situation is the result of the prevailing biographical approach to Jefferson as much as the result of structural changes in the federal government. Most treatments of Jefferson during these crucial years emphasize his role in foreign policy—especially with Great Britain and France—and the emerging political disputes that fostered a two-party system Jefferson himself helped to create. Yet Secretary Jefferson was also engaged in the daily administration of the West. The State Department had broad-reaching responsibilities that included not only foreign affairs but also territorial administration and certain facets of Indian affairs. Among Jefferson's first lessons was the gap between theory and practice, between the organized West of his imagination and the messy, confusing, often violent West of the 1790s.

After describing a neatly divided landscape in the 1784 "Report," Jefferson found that it was far more difficult to impose boundaries onto the Near West in the 1790s. Throughout his tenure as secretary of state, Jefferson tried without success to secure agreements with Spain and Great Britain that would establish clear international boundaries, guarantee American commercial privileges on inland waterways, and pledge Europeans to forswear alliances with Indians at war with the United States.[18] Only a few years after Jefferson announced Indian extinction as a sad inevitability in *Notes,* the federal government encountered an organized, effective Indian resistance in the Ohio Country that delivered a series of defeats to the United States Army that shocked white observers.[19]

Jefferson actually would have preferred to avoid Indian affairs. It was not his mandate to oversee the military conquest of Indians in the Northwest. He left that to Secretary of War Henry Knox. Likewise, it was the task of the War Department and not the State Department to negotiate treaties with Indians, a bureaucratic arrangement that reflected a broader federal policy of denying Indians any permanent status of independent sovereignty. But Indians were a powerful presence in the Northwest Territory that Jefferson governed, and their movement across the borderlands informed boundary negotiations with Spain and Great Britain. Jefferson also welcomed Knox's commitment to a formal process of civilization that would conclude with Indians adopting white manners and eventually joining white society. The policy conformed to Jefferson's vision of himself as an enlightened man of science committed to the Indians' well-being.[20]

Of course, it remains something of a false distinction to describe Jefferson as benevolent or malevolent toward Indians. Jefferson's plans for an Indian future in the 1790s rested on a system through which Indians left the most fertile lands in favor of white settlers, abandoned customs and culture in favor of white notions of civilization and settled agriculture, and surrendered political autonomy in favor of an acknowledged system of federal sovereignty. Regardless of Jefferson's intentions, the overwhelming majority of Western Indians experienced Jeffersonian principles as little more than systematized misery. Meanwhile, in his characteristic tendency to take everything personally, Jefferson had a habit of treating Indian resistance as a personal betrayal.

When push came to shove, Jefferson the policymaker recognized that his first loyalty was to white settlers, not to Indians. At the same time, these were hardly the industrious, contented farmers he had described in *Notes on the State of Virginia,* nor were they living in the sort of peaceful Western pastoral he described in the "Report." Jefferson found himself taking a hard line toward the white newcomers who fanned throughout the Northwest Territory. As Jefferson informed Territorial Governor Arthur St. Clair in August 1791, "it is the duty and determination of the Executive to see that no encroachments be made on the public Lands, yet as the settlers in this instance appear to have acted with good faith, you will be pleased to notify them that due attention will be paid to this circumstance, and in the mean time they are not to be disturbed."[21] Jefferson was committed to turning the public domain into private property as quickly as possible. Nonetheless, he wanted this process to be conducted under clear government authority, and the settlers' impulses for freedom and independence could do more harm than good.

In comparison to European imperial tradition or to the Federalist policy that emerged in the 1790s, Jefferson was striking in his endorsement of the rapid creation of new states, limited federal authority over white settlers, and ready access to cheap public lands. At the same time, the Jefferson that emerges from this correspondence is a man far less optimistic about the possibilities of rapid settlement and far less sympathetic toward Indians.[22]

Or perhaps he simply described it differently, and that remains the greatest risk in conceiving of Jefferson through his documentary record. The copious amount of written material Jefferson left in his wake has suggested the possibility of understanding him, indeed of "knowing" him, as much as any figure in American history. Jefferson's discussions of territorial governance and foreign policy took shape within specific constraints. Much of our understanding of Jefferson's attitudes toward foreign policy in the West emerges from his correspondence with the likes of George Washington, James Madison, and Alexander Hamilton. Framing his letters through the delicate calculus of diplomatic consideration, Jefferson discussed complex balances between risk and benefit, opportunities and costs.[23]

Jefferson took a different approach in writing to officials in the territorial West. There was no room for equivocation in Jefferson's correspondence with them. Writing from great distance to men whose talents and loyalties were uncertain, Jefferson opted for the detached, authoritative tone that would establish a clear hierarchy within the federal administration. Consider Jefferson's November 9, 1792, letter to George Turner, a judge in the Northwest Territory. Having received complaints that judges were failing in their joint duties as members of the territorial legislature, Jefferson informed Turner, "I am charged by the President to bring this circumstance to your notice, not doubting but that the public exigences of your Office will over-weigh in your mind any personal inconveniences." This is hardly the most eloquent prose, but it is nonetheless representative of the bureaucratic realities facing Jefferson as secretary of state.[24] Jefferson's tone also remained in place because he hardly considered officials in the Northwest Territory among his most trustworthy subordinates. He knew that many of them were interested parties in the speculative scramble for land titles. Worse still, many of them aligned with Adams and Hamilton in the dispute that split the Washington administration, and eventually, many of them emerged as ardent Federalists.[25] These concerns about supervising territorial officials may help explain why, as secretary of state, Jefferson focused his diplomatic efforts on securing federal control of the land east of the Mississippi rather than expanding to points farther west. The only major land cession he pursued was for Spanish territory east of the Mississippi. In all these efforts, Jefferson also hoped to establish federal control over waterways, especially the Mississippi.

Once Jefferson left his post as secretary in 1793, he lost touch with territorial administration. The West once again became the subject of philosophical and scientific interest, with the written record pointing more toward the interests of the American Philosophical Society than the Department of State. And so Jefferson wrote his report to the American Philosophical Society on the Megalonyx, a fossilized creature found in western Virginia. Although still fascinated by the West, Jefferson had removed himself from pragmatic concerns of its government. In 1797 he wrote about the scientific mysteries beneath the Western surface, not the human complexities above ground.

This attitude held true during his tenure as vice president from 1797 to 1801, during which John Adams excluded Jefferson from decision-making. Besides, Jefferson was too busy creating an electoral constituency in the West that would help him defeat Adams to engage in any practical Western policymaking. When Jefferson finally won his presidential victory in the bitterly contested election of 1800, he did so in no small part through support from Western settlers. Jefferson's public celebration of farmers, his vision of Western political development, and his commitment to racial supremacy resonated with the aspirations—indeed, demands—of frontier residents. The rhetoric of the Jeffersonian Republicans was all the more attractive in contrast to Federalist calls for order that many in the increasingly democratic political culture of the West interpreted as little more than an effort to preserve the power of the very elites whom many Western settlers had sought to escape.[26]

In 1801 Jefferson believed he could rescue the Near West from the dangers of Federalist policy. He was only eight months into office when he wrote to James Monroe that "it is impossible not to look forward to distant times, when our rapid multiplication will expand itself beyond those limits, & cover the whole northern, if not the southern continent." Distant indeed, for in 1801 Jefferson took no steps to realize any goals of extending the United States into the Far West. Yet this statement was also a great distance from the events of a decade earlier, when Jefferson struggled to remove the numerous hurdles to the speedy creation of a prospering republican order in the West. Jefferson would rely on the settlers themselves to achieve the goal of extending republican government to the Far West, but all in good time. For the present, Jefferson was pleased by what he saw in the Near West.

> The promotion of agriculture, therefore, and household manufacture, are essential in their preservation, and I am disposed to aid and encourage it liberally. This will enable them to live on much smaller portions of land, and indeed will render their vast forests useless but for the range of cattle; for which purpose, also, as they become better farmers, they will be found useless, and even disadvantageous.
>
> THOMAS JEFFERSON TO BENJAMIN HAWKINS, FEBRUARY 18, 1803

> [S]ettlements will gradually circumscribe and approach the Indians, and they will in time either incorporate with us as citizens of the United States, or remove beyond the Mississippi. . . . [W]e presume that our strength and their weakness is now so visible that they must see we have only to shut our hand to crush them, and that all our liberalities to them proceed from motives of pure humanity only.
>
> THOMAS JEFFERSON TO WILLIAM H. HARRISON, FEBRUARY 27, 1803

> In all your intercourse with the natives, treat them in the most friendly & conciliatory manner which their own conduct will admit; allay all jealousies as to the object of your journey, satisfy them of it's innocence.
>
> Thomas Jefferson to Meriwether Lewis, [June 20, 1803]

What had changed? What had changed within the course of nine days to make Jefferson write a letter to Hawkins celebrating the possibilities of Indian development and then write a letter to Harrison announcing the inevitability of Indian destruction? Meanwhile, what had changed within a few months to make Jefferson abandon the apparent hostility in his letter to Harrison for a more accommodating attitude in his comments to Lewis?[27]

One answer might reside in personality. After all, Jefferson was nothing if not moody. Passionate, often thin-skinned, he often moved from sentimental affection to rage in the briefest of periods. The Hawkins and Harrison letters likewise exemplify the importance of audience. Harrison and Hawkins may both have been engaged in Indian relations, but Jefferson considered Hawkins a kindred intellectual spirit and Harrison an effective military enforcer. To understand all three letters, however, one must be aware of the fact that they discussed two different Wests. In the months separating the Hawkins and Harrison letters from the Lewis letter, Jefferson was forced to redefine his understanding of the West as an area for territorial expansion that created a host of new challenges as well as new opportunities.[28]

All three documents are also products of Jefferson's presidency. That may seem an obvious matter, and yet it is critical to remember, in large part because Jefferson's presidency remains a strikingly understudied subject. The presidency is something of an afterthought to many historians in our time. For political junkies, Jefferson's arrival in the Executive Mansion in March 1801 is a conclusion rather than a beginning, marking the end to the political upheavals of the 1790s. With the Federalists in disarray and Jefferson's own ideas firmly in place, Jefferson's presidency often appears more like a pedestrian exercise of bureaucratic administration, including various achievements but always concluding with Jefferson's disastrous misadventure in the embargo of 1807–9.[29]

In his time, Jefferson came to the presidency convinced that Western policy was proceeding in the right direction. A series of military victories in the Northwest Territory after Jefferson's departure from the Washington administration resulted in substantial Indian land cessions and contributed to the collapse of pan-Indian unity. Meanwhile, diplomatic agreements with Spain and Great Britain during the 1790s clarified international boundaries, further stripping Indians of the ability to exploit ambiguous borders and international disputes. By the time Jefferson wrote to Harrison and Hawkins in 1803, he did so from a position of strength.[30]

A day after writing to Hawkins, Jefferson eagerly signed the act providing for Ohio statehood, a crucial step in the process of extending republican government for whites. Yet Jefferson continued to conceive of these matters within the confined geographical space of the Near West extending to the Mississippi River. There were no letters to his subordinates to match the expansionist zeal of his 1801 letter to Monroe. Instead, Jefferson and his cabinet focused on promoting trade down the Mississippi River and securing the federal government's authority over the Northwest and Mississippi Territories.[31]

All these plans were superseded by the Louisiana Purchase. Jefferson had long concluded that uninterrupted trade down the Mississippi River was vital to the security and unity of the Near West. By 1803 Jefferson joined in a broader national consensus that supported an aggressive diplomatic effort to secure those trading rights as well as the cession of the Gulf Coast territory that controlled the mouth of the Mississippi. After months of frustrated American efforts to secure these goals, France imposed an agreement that required the United States to take possession of a vast Western domain with the vaguest of boundaries.[32]

The Louisiana Purchase came as a surprise and not necessarily a welcome one. This hardly means that Jefferson could not accommodate himself to expansion into the Far West, but it was a difficult fit. In our time, the Purchase has become an example of Jefferson's continental expansionism, but in his time Jefferson himself had developed a Mississippi policy from 1801 to 1803 that expressly rejected the acquisition of territory in the Far West. Only complicating an understanding of these developments in our time are the numerous commentators who pointed out the benefits of the Louisiana Purchase; many of them served at the time and have since come to serve as stand-ins for Jefferson. In an effort to build public support, advocates of the Purchase unleashed a nationwide series of pamphlets and public speeches. Few of these commentators actually celebrated expansion per se, instead preferring to emphasize the way the Louisiana Purchase secured federal control of the Mississippi River through peaceful means. Tucked within this commentary were morsels of what has become the familiar narrative of the Jeffersonian Western outlook, aggressively expansionistic and acquisitive. David Ramsay's *Oration on the Cession of Louisiana to the United State* was among the few pamphlets to formulate a positive rationale for expansion into the Far West. "Here are plantations enough and enough for our children and our children's children, for centuries to come." When critics asked whether the United States actually needed so much land, Ramsay explained that "our increasing population, which doubles every 25 years, is a satisfactory answer."[33] Yet most pamphleteers discussed the Purchase as a means to safeguard the security and political economy of the Near West, not as a gateway to the Far West.[34]

Jefferson himself helped redefine the Louisiana Purchase for public consumption. In his first annual message after the Purchase, Jefferson still focused on the Mississippi. "[T]he property and sovereignty of the Mississippi and its waters secure an independent outlet for the produce of the western States," he explained in October 1803, "and an uncontrolled navigation through their whole course, free from collision with other powers and the dangers to our peace from that source." To this he added that "the fertility of the country, its climate and extent, promise in due season important aids to our treasury, an ample provision for our posterity, and a wide-spread field for the blessings of freedom and equal laws." Two years later he was laying a foundation for the positive benefits of expansion. "I know that the acquisition of Louisiana has been disapproved by some," he confided in his Second Inaugural Address, "from a candid apprehension that the enlargement of our territory would endanger its union." Borrowing the logic his own secretary of state, James Madison, had used in *The Federalist,* Jefferson asked, "[W]ho can limit the extent to which the federative principle may operate effectively? The larger our association, the less will it be shaken by local passions; and in any view, is it not better that the opposite bank of the Mississippi should be settled by our own brethren and children, than by strangers of another family? With which shall we be most likely to live in harmony and friendly intercourse?"[35]

Within the cabinet, however, a very different picture emerged. In his own correspondence, Jefferson made few comments like his remark to Monroe that "our rapid multiplication will expand itself beyond those limits, & cover the whole northern, if not the southern continent." Instead, he focused on security within existing boundaries, whether that meant establishing a federal presence in the towns that controlled the eastern banks of the Mississippi River, or engaging in a fruitless diplomatic effort to secure a Spanish cession of the Gulf Coast. Meanwhile, Jefferson's letters to Harrison, Hawkins, and Lewis formed part of a broader correspondence with his frontier officials that allowed far greater discretion. Harrison, Hawkins, and Lewis were among a generation of men whom President Jefferson selected with far greater confidence than the men who had served him when he was secretary of state. In the years after the Purchase, Jefferson's trusted subordinates on the territorial frontier flooded Washington with reports of foreign intrigue, the threat of Indian war or slave revolt, and the prospect of long-term resentment from the white Francophone and Hispanic residents of Louisiana. The only major dangers in the Far West that Jefferson put at the center of his public commentary were of a more homegrown variety. In 1806–7 Jefferson loudly denounced Aaron Burr for organizing what many Americans—including Jefferson—believed was a treasonous conspiracy to carve a separate republic in the Far West. In other words, Burr sought to steal the West that Jefferson so desperately wanted. Yet Jefferson himself occasionally considered trading major portions of the Louisiana Purchase for territory on the Gulf Coast he considered more valuable for the nation's security. To Jefferson, Burr's sin was less one of denying the Far West to the United States than acting against the federal government.[36]

Jefferson's complex, shifting attitudes toward the Far West became abundantly clear in his correspondence with Meriwether Lewis. In our time, the Lewis and Clark Expedition—famously coined the "Corps of Discovery" in the title of the book by Patrick Gass, a sergeant under Lewis and Clark[37]—has come to symbolize Jefferson's inquisitive Western gaze. In his time, Jefferson dramatically changed his notions of Western exploration. His personal interest in the natural history of the Far West, his public interest in promoting commerce, and his desire to prove his nation's (and his own) intellectual maturity to the Europeans had long inspired Jefferson to dream of a great scientific expedition that would survey the North American West. As president, Jefferson could pursue that venture with government support. When Jefferson selected Lewis, his personal secretary and protégé, to lead the expedition, this represented a venture on foreign soil. Jefferson also intended it to remain that way. In early 1803 he believed commercial linkages would enable the United States to trade in the West without shouldering the burdens of governing the West.[38]

Those goals go a long way toward explaining Jefferson's June 1803 instructions to Lewis and the way they differed from Jefferson's letters to Harrison and Hawkins. His mandate that Lewis treat Indians in a "friendly" manner clearly reflected Jefferson's efforts to build influence in a way that undermined the European hold on the Far West. Yet at no time did he instruct Lewis to constitute the advance guard of territorial expansion. Jefferson acknowledged that Lewis would depend on the Indians and that Indians dominated Western trade. In contrast, the rising power of the United States in the Near West, the growing number of white settlers, and the federal government's determination to assert sovereignty all combined in bellicose language to Harrison and Hawkins.

Jefferson wrote those instructions before news of the Louisiana Purchase reached the United States and transformed the Lewis and Clark Expedition. Jefferson sent subsequent instructions detailing how Lewis should establish federal sovereignty with the Indians and survey the land for federal control.[39] Equally important, Jefferson no longer planned a single expedition to explore commercial routes through the Northwest. Rather, the federal government dispatched a total of five expeditions during his presidency, of which the Lewis and Clark Expedition was only the most extensive and famous. These expeditions now had to provide information on territory the United States had to govern. The explorers in turn described the Far West as a place of commercial opportunity but also a place of powerful Indians. Significantly, they rarely celebrated the opportunities for white settlers that other Americans described in the Near West.[40]

Consider as well Lewis's experience after the expedition ended in 1806. In 1807 Jefferson appointed Lewis governor of the Louisiana Territory, a vast stretch of the West that encompassed everything acquired through the Louisiana Purchase with the exception of what is now the State of Louisiana. Lewis's manuscript journals of the expedition describe the landscape of the Far West with wonderment. Those journals also portray Lewis as the leader of a victorious Corps of Discovery that successfully secured Indian agreements to recognize federal sovereignty. Lewis's correspondence from the territorial capital of St. Louis tells a very different story: Lewis described political instability among whites and resistance from Indians. Likewise, Jefferson changed his tone. No longer dependent on distant Western Indians to provide supplies for American explorers, Jefferson instructed Lewis to take a harsh stance toward the Indians of the Eastern Plains.[41]

The public planning for the Lewis and Clark Expedition and the private correspondence between President Jefferson and Governor Lewis serve as a reminder not only of the different Wests that Jefferson saw but also of the ways that context and genre informed his explanation of the West. At the very moment that Jefferson the public administrator focused on securing federal sovereignty within confined geographic spaces, Jefferson the public communicator made expansion appear easy and inevitable.[42]

Lewis displayed those differences in tragic form. After the exploration of the Far West made Lewis into a national hero, the administration of the Far West left him a wreck. Lewis committed suicide in 1809, in his own time as much a cautionary tale as a subject for celebration.

> I considered as a great public acquisition the commencement of a settlement on that point of the Western coast of America, and looked forward with gratification to the time when its descendants should have spread themselves through the whole length of that coast, covering it with free and independent Americans, unconnected with us but by the ties of blood and interest, and employing like us the rights of self-government.
>
> Thomas Jefferson to John Jacob Astor, May 24, 1812

> These are occurrences which like waves in a storm will pass under the ship. But the Missouri question is a breaker on which we lose the Missouri country by revolt, and what more, God only knows.
>
> Thomas Jefferson to John Adams, December 10, 1819

> I still believe that the Western extension of our confederacy will ensure its duration, by overruling local factions, which might shake a smaller association.
>
> Thomas Jefferson to Henry Dearborn, August 17, 1821

There is something wonderfully appealing about Jefferson in retirement.[43] To his advocates, Jefferson's retreat to the comforts of Monticello marks a satisfying reward for a lifetime of public service.

To his critics, Jefferson's numerous personal tribulations were well deserved. And to everybody, the correspondence of Jefferson's retirement includes enough lyrical prose, cantankerous rages, and downright bizarre flights of fancy to satisfy any reader. Out of office, Jefferson no longer found himself forced to prescribe practical solutions to Western problems, nor did he need to do so through only semiprivate correspondence to often unfamiliar Western officials. Shifts on the global stage enabled Jefferson to unleash some of his most optimistic predictions about the West. Disputes in the domestic arena fueled some of Jefferson's worst fears. Race pushed him in both directions at once.[44]

During his first decade of retirement, Jefferson looked west with pleasure. He delighted in the creation of five new states that made a peaceful transition from territorial rule through the model Jefferson had first established in the "Report" of 1784. He observed this transition as the worst fears about the incorporation of the Louisiana Purchase—including his own—proved unfounded. White residents of the Purchase territories proved eager to become American citizens, in no small part because the Francophone residents of Louisiana found common cause with Anglophone newcomers in the creation of republican government and the subjugation of nonwhites. In what looked like the greatest test of loyalty—the British invasion of the Gulf Coast during the War of 1812—Westerners remained steadfast in their support of the union. The loyalty in both the Near West and the Far West appeared all the more striking in contrast to New England, which Jefferson identified as the home to everything from cultural corruption to antirepublican sentiment to treason.[45]

Jefferson addressed these matters in the most detailed and pragmatic terms in a February 1815 letter to William Crawford, the American minister to France who was about to assume office as secretary of war. "It may be thought that useless blood was spilt at New Orleans, after the treaty of peace had been actually signed and ratified. I think it had many valuable uses," Jefferson explained. "It proved the fidelity of the Orleanese to the United States. It proved that New

Orleans can be defended both by land and water; that the western country will fly to its relief (of which ourselves had doubted before); that our militia are heroes when they have heroes to lead them on." To Jefferson, the defense of New Orleans proved the theory he had espoused throughout his adult life, that unleashing white settlers onto the West would make the nation stronger, not weaker. Yet he also believed that it validated the particular institutional restraints he had imposed onto the West as secretary of state and as president.[46]

Jefferson reached those conclusions because the United States had also successfully crushed resurgent Indian militancy throughout the Mississippi Valley and the Deep South. In 1803 the information before Jefferson had described the Mississippi as the gateway not to white settlement but to a land of powerful, potentially violent Indian villages. By 1820 the reports Jefferson read described major land cessions in which Indians on both sides of the Mississippi surrendered territory in the face of an increasingly powerful federal government.[47] The federal leadership in Washington and public officials throughout the country increasingly saw the Far West as a place to deposit the Indians who had survived the war for racial supremacy in the Near West. In the process, they laid the foundation for the formal policy of removal announced by Andrew Jackson in 1830 and helped to transform the Far West itself. Rather than an Indian country that the United States was forced to govern at the expense of scarce resources, the Far West could solve the problem of intercultural contact by providing vast boundaries of racial separation.

Some of the first published responses to the Louisiana Purchase had suggested as much, and they have often been read in our time as early signs of the removal policy. In their time, however, those comments were desperate inventions of 1803, designed to secure passage for the Purchase in the face of considerable domestic concern. It was only in the 1810s that the federal leadership took seriously the prospect of using the Far West as a grand Indian reservation. The new Indian policy of the Far West succeeded in no small part because of transatlantic changes. In the wake of the Napoleonic Wars, the Madison and Monroe administrations secured treaties that clarified boundaries. Just as the treaties of the 1790s normalized relations with Europe and undermined Indian power in the Near West, the treaties of the 1810s helped secure federal sovereignty in the Far West.[48] In broad terms, Jefferson had moved from proclaiming the possibility of Indian incorporation to endorsing forced removal and predicting eventual extinction. Yet that transition in thought had hardly been smooth. Rather, it was his years as a policymaking official that accelerated this change, leaving him in retirement convinced of endless racial conflict between whites and blacks.

It was in these circumstances that Jefferson once again returned to his most boisterous predictions for a Western future. The United States was not yet at war when Jefferson wrote to John Jacob Astor describing a West dominated by "free and independent Americans." When Jefferson wrote those words to Astor in 1812, he did so as a private citizen increasingly detached from the policymaking realities he had known as president. Jefferson may have dispatched Lewis and Clark to the Pacific in an effort to infiltrate the European commercial grip, but as president he rarely discussed a federal claim to territory beyond the Rocky Mountains. In retirement, however, Jefferson endorsed Astor's scheme to build a trading outpost at the mouth of the Columbia River that would establish a foothold in the Pacific trade by constructing a claim to the Oregon Country. The letter to Astor marked a logical extension of Jefferson's commercial vision, but written with an expansionist outlook he had rarely expressed before.[49]

If Jefferson expressed considerable optimism about the West from 1809 to 1819, the years that followed brought a dramatic shift. In 1819 Jefferson concluded that arguments about the future of Missouri indicated how settlement and growth could endanger the very survival of the young republic. The Missouri Crisis appears in the grand narrative of Jefferson's Western concerns as the counterpart to his "Report." The story usually goes like this. In 1784 Jefferson established a model for excluding slavery from the Northwest that survived intact in the Northwest Ordinance of 1787. In 1819

Jefferson supported the proslavery constitution in Missouri, marking a sad move from opponent to advocate of slavery. Scholars have rightly shown that despite this apparent inconsistency, both cases reflected Jefferson's commitment to Western development and a broader notion of opportunity and self-determination for white settlers. Nonetheless, both documents also indicate a dramatic shift in Jefferson's defense of slavery.

Once again, however, these conclusions suggest the challenge of selecting texts from the Jefferson canon. The 1784 "Report" and Jefferson's letters addressing the Missouri Crisis remain among the most widely circulating documents in the various printed anthologies of Jefferson's writings, in no small part because they make such compelling reading. The 1784 "Report" remains a model of visionary planning. Meanwhile, Jefferson's comment to John Holmes at the height of the Missouri Crisis that "we have the wolf by the ears, and we can neither hold him, nor safely let him go" crystallized in vivid prose the national struggle over slavery and freedom.[50] Missing from those anthologies is the extensive correspondence chronicling Jefferson's efforts—in part owing to heavy pressure from whites in the region—to secure slavery in the West during the thirty-five years in between. As president, he struggled to build a system of governance in the Louisiana Purchase and in the Mississippi Territory that would successfully prevent the slave revolts that territorial officials feared could erupt at any moment on the vulnerable frontier. He never did so through a major public document like the 1784 "Report," and as a result, Jefferson's role as the expander of slavery in the Southwest often disappears in the shadow of Jefferson the emancipator of the Northwest. Rather, it was through the legal, bureaucratic, and institutional structures the administration established in the Southwest that Jefferson articulated his plan to preserve enslavement within the extended boundaries of the United States.[51]

In the years after Jefferson's death in 1826, Americans abandoned Jefferson's distinction between the Near West and the Far West. The teams like the Lewis and Clark Expedition that Jefferson had dispatched into the Far West did more than report to the president. They published a series of books and maps that contributed to a growing body of knowledge that Americans used to claim the West as their own.[52] Although Americans recognized various distinctions in demography, economy, and ecology, the West became a place of more uniform experiences and interpretations. A new generation of political leaders from the Western states Jefferson helped to create shared none of his fears about unchecked expansionism. They did so based on personal experience, but also at the behest of Western constituencies that since 1776 had only become louder in announcing the linkage Jefferson had seen between settlement, liberty, and opportunity. Westerners became among the leading architects of a more aggressive approach to Western expansion. Whites throughout the United States quickly signed on to an expansionist outlook that reached its most manifest expression in Manifest Destiny and the Mexican War. Although the federal government subdivided those new Western possessions along the territorial model first imagined by Jefferson, the old lines between the Near West and the Far West disappeared within a national domain that extended to the Pacific.[53]

When the union that Jefferson struggled so hard to preserve crumbled in 1861, the two governments that went to war were, appropriately enough, led by men who came of age in Western places designed by Thomas Jefferson. Abraham Lincoln's celebration of farmers, his attacks on slave power, and his racial prejudices emerged from a political culture of Illinois that had its foundations in the 1784 "Report." Likewise, Jefferson Davis's defense of slavery at all costs and his belief that a plantation economy could provide both economic prosperity and regional development were products of his life in a Mississippi that took shape during Jefferson's presidency. Meanwhile, both men came from states where Jefferson had helped crush Indian power and institute Indian removal. Lincoln and Davis considered themselves heirs to Jefferson's Western legacy, and rightly so. In the process, they only continued a process of interpreting Jefferson's Western vision that connects his time to our time.

Notes

1. For two particularly revealing studies of the way context and chronology informed different aspects of Jefferson's approach to the West, see James P. Ronda, "Jefferson and the Imperial West," *Journal of the West* 31 (July 1992): 13–19; and Anthony F. C. Wallace, *Jefferson and the Indians: The Tragic Fate of the First Americans* (Cambridge, Mass., 1999).

2. Every biographer of Jefferson eventually turns his or her attention to the West. When it comes to focused studies of Jefferson and the West, however, the following suggest the range of interpretive approaches for scholarly and popular audiences. See John Logan Allen, *Passage through the Garden: Lewis and Clark and the Image of the American Northwest* (Urbana, Ill., 1975); Laurie M. Carlson, *Seduced by the West: Jefferson's America and the Lure of the Land beyond the Mississippi* (Chicago, 2003); Donald Jackson, *Thomas Jefferson and the Stony Mountains: Exploring the West from Monticello* (Urbana, Ill., 1981); Lawrence S. Kaplan, *Thomas Jefferson: Westward the Course of Empire* (Wilmington, Del., 1999); Roger G. Kennedy, *Mr. Jefferson's Lost Cause: Land, Farmers, Slavery, and the Louisiana Purchase* (New York, 2003); Peter S. Onuf, *Statehood and Union: A History of the Northwest Ordinance* (Bloomington, Ind., 1987); Peter S. Onuf, "The Expanding Union," in *Devising Liberty: Preserving and Creating Freedom in the New American Republic,* ed. David Thomas Konig (Stanford, Calif., 1995), 50–80; James P. Ronda, ed., *Thomas Jefferson and the Changing West: From Conquest to Conservation* (Albuquerque, N.M., 1997; St Louis, 1997); and James P. Ronda, *Jefferson's West: A Journey with Lewis and Clark* ([Charlottesville, Va.], 2000).

3. Sources for the epigraphs are as follows: TJ to George Rogers Clark, January 1, 1780, in Jefferson, *Papers,* 3:259; Thomas Jefferson, *Notes on the State of Virginia,* in Jefferson, *Writings* [Peterson], 133–34, 136, 131; Jefferson, "Observations on Démeunier's Manuscript," June 22, 1786, in Jefferson, *Papers,* 10:53.

4. The surge in white migration to the West during the late-colonial period and the accompanying rise in elite speculation in Western lands remains one of the most consistent themes in the scholarship of late-colonial British North America. For examples from Virginia, see Thomas Perkins Abernethy, *Western Lands and the American Revolution* (New York, 1937); Robert D. Mitchell, *Commercialism and Frontier: Perspectives on the Early Shenandoah Valley* (Charlottesville, Va., 1977); Gregory H. Nobles, "Breaking into the Backcountry: New Approaches to the Early American Frontier, 1750–1800," *William and Mary Quarterly,* 3rd series, 46 (October 1989): 641–70 [hereafter, *WMQ*]; and Albert H. Tillson Jr., "The Southern Backcountry: A Survey of Current Research," *Virginia Magazine of History and Biography* 98, no. 3 (July 1990): 387–422

[hereafter, *VMHB*]. For other regions, see Rachel N. Klein, *Unification of a Slave State: The Rise of the Planter Class in the South Carolina Backcountry, 1760–1808* (Chapel Hill, N.C., 1990); and Alan Taylor, " 'A Kind of Warr': The Contest for Land on the Northeastern Frontier, 1750–1820," *WMQ*, 3rd ser., 46 (January 1989): 3–26.

5. Thomas Hallock, *From the Fallen Tree: Frontier Narratives, Environmental Politics, and the Roots of a National Pastoral, 1749–1826* (Chapel Hill, N.C., 2003), 96–117; Jackson, *Thomas Jefferson and the Stony Mountains*, 25–41; Bernard W. Sheehan, *Seeds of Extinction: Jeffersonian Philanthropy and the American Indian* (Chapel Hill, N.C., 1973), 75–77.

6. Jefferson, *Notes on the State of Virginia*, in Jefferson, *Writings* [Peterson], 290; Jefferson, "Observations on Démeunier's Manuscript," June 22, 1786, ibid., 588.

7. Cathy D. Matson and Peter S. Onuf, *A Union of Interests: Political and Economic Thought in Revolutionary America* (Lawrence, Kans., 1990), 68–70; Peter S. Onuf, *Jefferson's Empire: The Language of American Nationhood* (Charlottesville, Va., 2000), 68.

8. Jefferson, *Notes on the State of Virginia*, in Jefferson, *Writings* [Peterson], 148 (quotation). For Jefferson's notions of aesthetics and writing, see Albert Furtwangler, *Acts of Discovery: Visions of America in the Lewis and Clark Journals* (Urbana, Ill., 1993), 27–31; Hallock, *From the Fallen Tree*, 99–101; Robert Lawson-Peebles, *Landscape and Written Expression in Revolutionary America: The World Turned Upside Down* (Cambridge, 1988), 165–95; and Larzer Ziff, *Writing in the New Nation: Prose, Print, and Politics in the Early United States* (New Haven, Conn., 1991), 132–49.

9. Jefferson, *Notes on the State of Virginia*, in Jefferson, *Writings* [Peterson], 221.

10. "Report on Government for Western Territory," March 1, 1784, in Jefferson, *Writings* [Peterson], 376–77 (quotation). For the radical implications of the "Report on Government for Western Territory," see Jefferson, *Papers*, 6:581–600; Onuf, *Statehood and Union*, 51–56; and Peter S. Onuf, "New State Equality: The Ambiguous History of a Constitutional Principle," *Publius* 18 (Autumn 1988): 53–69.

11. For the past two decades, some of the most fascinating scholarship on the American Revolution has concerned the way Anglo-Americans joined the Revolutionary movement because they believed the call for independence was a direct response to their local needs. For examples from Virginia, Kentucky, and the trans-Appalachian backcountry, see Stephen Aron, *How the West Was Lost: The Transformation of Kentucky from Daniel Boone to Henry Clay* (Baltimore, 1996), 47–53; Michael A. Bellesiles, *Revolutionary Outlaws: Ethan Allen and the Struggle for Independence on the Early American Frontier* (Charlottesville, Va., 1993); Ronald Hoffman, Thad W. Tate, and Peter J. Albert, eds., *An Uncivil*

War: The Southern Backcountry during the American Revolution (Charlottesville, Va., 1985); Woody Holton, *Forced Founders: Indians, Debtors, Slaves, and the Making of the American Revolution in Virginia* (Chapel Hill, N.C., 1999); Klein, *Unification of a Slave State;* and Albert H. Tillson Jr., *Gentry and Common Folk: Political Culture on a Virginia Frontier, 1740–1789* (Lexington, Ky., 1991).

12. TJ to George Rogers Clark, January 1, 1780, in Jefferson, *Papers,* 3:259; see also TJ to George Washington, September 26, 1780, ibid., 664–66; Washington to Clark, June 8, 1781, *George Washington Papers* (Washington, D.C.: Library of Congress Microfilm Collection).

13. TJ to Clark, February 19, 1781, in Jefferson, *Papers,* 4:653. See also TJ to Clark, April 4, 1780, ibid., 3:356–57; TJ to Clark, September 29, 1780, ibid., 3:670–71; TJ to Clark, December 25, 1780, ibid., 4:233–38.

14. For Jefferson's feelings on his tenure as governor, see Malone, *Jefferson and His Time,* 1:352–69, and Merrill D. Peterson, *Thomas Jefferson and the New Nation: A Biography* (Oxford, 1970), 236–44.

15. For Jefferson's approach to correspondence, see Andrew Burstein, *The Inner Jefferson: Portrait of a Grieving Optimist* (Charlottesville, Va., 1995); Joanne B. Freeman, "Slander, Poison, Whispers, and Fame: Jefferson's 'Anas' and Political Gossip in the Early Republic," *Journal of the Early Republic* 15 (Spring 1995): 25–57; and Andy Trees, "Private Correspondence for the Public Good: Thomas Jefferson to Elbridge Gerry, 26 January 1799," *VMHB* 108, no. 3 (2000): 217–54.

16. Sources for the epigraphs are as follows: TJ to Charles Carroll, April 15, 1791, in Jefferson, *Papers,* 20:214; Thomas Jefferson, "A Memoir on the Discovery of Certain Bones of a Quadruped of the Clawed Kind in the Western Parts of Virginia," *Transactions of the American Philosophical Society* 4 (1799): 247; TJ to James Monroe, November 24, 1801, in Jefferson, *Works,* 9:317.

17. TJ to Carroll, April 15, 1791, in Jefferson, *Papers,* 20:214; TJ to George Washington, April 17, 1791, ibid., 144–46; TJ to James Monroe, April 17, 1791, ibid., 234–36.

18. Samuel Flagg Bemis, *Pinckney's Treaty: A Study of America's Advantage from Europe's Distress, 1783–1800* (Baltimore, 1926); Samuel Flagg Bemis, *Jay's Treaty: A Study in Commerce and Diplomacy* (New York, 1923); James E. Lewis Jr., *The American Union and the Problem of Neighborhood: The United States and the Collapse of the Spanish Empire, 1783–1829* (Chapel Hill, N.C., 1998), 21–23.

19. Stephen Aron, *American Confluence: The Missouri Frontier from Borderland to Border State* (Bloomington, Ind., 2006), 75–77; Gregory Dowd, *A Spirited Resistance: The North American Indian Struggle for Unity, 1745–1815* (Baltimore, 1992), 99–115; Richard H. Kohn, *Eagle and Sword: The Federalists and the Creation of the Military Establishment in America, 1783–1802* (New York, 1975), 91–127.

20. Wallace, *Jefferson and the Indians,* 165–74, 286–87.

21. TJ to Arthur St. Clair, August 6, 1791, in Clarence Edwin Carter, ed., *The Territorial Papers of the United States,* 28 vols. (Washington, D.C., 1934–75), 2:349.

22. Peter S. Onuf, "Liberty, Development, and Union: Visions of the West in the 1780s," *WMQ,* 3rd ser., 43 (April 1986): 179–213; Alan Taylor, "Land and Liberty on the Post-Revolutionary Frontier," in Konig, ed., *Devising Liberty,* 81–108.

23. For two revealing examples, see TJ to George Washington, November 8, 1791, in Jefferson, *Papers,* 22:274–88, and Jefferson, "Report on Negotiations with Spain," March 18, 1792, ibid., 23:296–317.

24. TJ to George Turner, November 9, 1792, ibid., 24:604.

25. Andrew R. L. Cayton, *The Frontier Republic: Ideology and Politics in the Ohio Country, 1780–1825* (Kent, Ohio, 1986), 51–67.

26. Cayton, *The Frontier Republic,* 71–74; John E. Ferling, *Adams vs. Jefferson: The Tumultuous Election of 1800* (New York, 2004), 170–74; Alan Taylor, *Liberty Men and Great Proprietors: The Revolutionary Settlement on the Maine Frontier, 1760–1820* (Chapel Hill, N.C., 1990), 212–32; David Waldstreicher, *In the Midst of Perpetual Fetes: The Making of American Nationalism, 1776–1820* (Chapel Hill, N.C., 1997), 264–65.

27. Sources for the epigraphs are as follows: TJ to Benjamin Hawkins, February 18, 1803, in Jefferson, *Writings* [Peterson], 1115; TJ to William H. Harrison, February 27, 1803, ibid., 118; and TJ to Meriwether Lewis, June 20, 1803, in Donald Jackson, ed., *Letters of the Lewis and Clark Expedition, With Related Documents, 1783–1854,* 2nd ed., 2 vols. (Urbana, Ill., 1978), 1:64.

28. Florette Henri, *The Southern Indians and Benjamin Hawkins, 1796–1816* (Norman, Okla., 1986); Robert M. Owens, "Jeffersonian Benevolence on the Ground: The Indian Land Cession Treaties of William Henry Harrison," *Journal of the Early Republic* 22 (Autumn 2002): 405–35.

29. Strikingly, many of the most revealing studies in political culture during the past decade—books that often make extensive reference to Jefferson and the Jeffersonian Republicans—are fundamentally books about the 1790s. In those books that do progress into the 1800s, Jefferson himself often disappears from the story. For examples of innovative work on the 1790s, see Joanne B. Freeman, *Affairs of Honor: National Politics in the New Republic* (New Haven, Conn., 2001); Jeffrey L. Pasley, *"The Tyranny of Printers": Newspaper Politics in the Early American Republic* (Charlottesville, Va., 2001); Andrew S. Trees, *The Founding Fathers and the Politics of Character* (Princeton, N.J., 2004); and Waldstreicher, *In the Midst of Perpetual Fetes.* Work on Jefferson's presidency will also require the publication of his entire corpus of correspondence. *The Papers of Thomas Jefferson* will soon release volumes concerning Jefferson's presidency.

30. Dowd, *Spirited Resistance,* 116–17.

31. For the connections between the 1790s and Jefferson's ongoing concerns about the West as president, see Lewis, *American Union and the Problem of Neighborhood,* 21–33, and Drew R. McCoy, *The Elusive Republic: Political Economy in Jeffersonian America* (Chapel Hill, N.C., 1980), 196–208.

32. For general surveys of the politics and diplomacy surrounding the Purchase, see Alexander DeConde, *This Affair of Louisiana* (New York, 1976), and Jon Kukla, *A Wilderness So Immense: The Louisiana Purchase and the Destiny of America* (New York, 2003).

33. Ramsay, *An Oration on the Cession of Louisiana to the United States: Delivered on the 12th of May, 1804, at Charleston* (Charleston, S.C., 1804), 8, 16.

34. Samuel Brazer, *Address, Pronounced at Worcester, on May 12th: 1804 in Commemoration of the Cession of Louisiana to the United States* (Worcester, Mass., 1804); David A. Leonard, *An Oration, Delivered at Raynham (Massachusetts), Friday, May 11th, 1804, on the Late Acquisition of Louisiana, at the Unanimous Request of the Republican Citizens of the County of Bristol* (Newport, R.I., 1804); Allan Bowie Magruder, *Political, Commercial, and Moral Reflections on the Late Cession of Louisiana to the United States* (Lexington, Ky., 1803); O[rasmus] C[ook] Merrill, *The Happiness of America: An Oration Delivered at Shaftsbury on the Fourth of July, 1804: Being the Twenty-Ninth Anniversary of American Independence* (Bennington, Vt., 1804); St. George Tucker, *Reflections on the Cession of Louisiana to the United States* (Washington City, 1803); [W.M.P.], *A Poem on the Acquisition of Louisiana: Respectfully Dedicated to the Committee Appointed for the Celebration of that Great Event in This City* (Charleston, S.C., 1804).

35. Jefferson, "Third Annual Message," October 17, 1803, in Jefferson, *Writings* [Peterson], 512; Second Inaugural Address, March 4, 1805, ibid., 519.

36. DeConde, *This Affair of Louisiana;* William E. Foley, *The Genesis of Missouri: From Wilderness Outpost to Statehood* (Columbia, Mo., 1989); Peter J. Kastor, *The Nation's Crucible: The Louisiana Purchase and the Creation of America* (New Haven, Conn., 2004); Onuf, *Jefferson's Empire,* 131–35.

37. Patrick Gass's book, titled *Journal of the Voyages and Travels of a Corps of Discovery: Under the Command of Capt. Lewis and Capt. Clarke of the Army of the United States: From the Mouth of the River Missouri through the Interior Parts of North America to the Pacific Ocean, during the Years 1804, 1805, & 1806,* originally published in 1807, is now conveniently reprinted as *The Journal of Patrick Gass, May 14, 1804–September 23, 1806,* vol. 10 of *The Journals of the Lewis and Clark Expedition,* 13 vols., ed. Gary E. Moulton (Lincoln, Neb., 1983–2001).

38. John Logan Allen, *Passage through the Garden: Lewis and Clark and the Image of the American Northwest* (Urbana, Ill., 1975), 59–63; Jackson, *Thomas*

Jefferson and the Stony Mountains; James P. Ronda, *Astoria and Empire* (Lincoln, Neb., 1990), 29–31, 42–44.

39. TJ to Lewis, November 16, 1803, in Jackson, ed., *Letters of the Lewis and Clark Expedition,* 1:137–38.

40. For Jefferson's concerted effort in the West, see Jackson, *Thomas Jefferson and the Stony Mountains,* 223–41. For the explorers' reports, see Lewis to TJ, April 7, 1805, and September 23, 1806, in Jackson, ed., *Letters of the Lewis and Clark Expedition,* 1:231–34, 319–24; *An Account of the Red River, in Louisiana, Drawn up from the Returns of Messrs. Freeman and Custis to the War Office of the United States, Who Explored the Same, in the Year of 1806* ([Washington?], [1806?]); John Sibley, *A Report from Natchitoches in 1807,* ed. Annie Heloise Abel (New York, 1922); and Zebulon Pike to James Wilkinson, July 5, 1807, in *The Journals of Zebulon Montgomery Pike, with Letters and Related Documents,* 2 vols., ed. Donald Jackson (Norman, Okla., 1966), 2:238–44.

41. TJ to Lewis, August 21, 1808, in Carter, ed., *Territorial Papers of the United States,* 14:219–21. Published in numerous forms over the past century, the definitive edition of Lewis's manuscript journals has recently been completed as Moulton, ed., *Journals of the Lewis and Clark Expedition.*

42. Onuf, *Jefferson's Empire,* 132–37.

43. Sources for the epigraphs are as follows: TJ to John Jacob Astor, May 24, 1812, in Jefferson, *Works,* 11:244; TJ to John Adams, December 10, 1819, in Lester J. Cappon, ed., *The Adams-Jefferson Letters: The Complete Correspondence between Thomas Jefferson and Abigail and John Adams* (Chapel Hill, N.C., 1959), 2:548–49; TJ to Henry Dearborn, August 17, 1821, in Jefferson, *Writings* [L&B], 15:330.

44. Jefferson's retirement correspondence is the subject of a major editorial project, *The Papers of Thomas Jefferson: Retirement Series.* Operating on an ambitious publishing schedule, the five published volumes are already providing new insights into Jefferson's life after public service. For revealing studies of Jefferson's retirement, see Andrew Burstein, *Jefferson's Secrets: Death and Desire at Monticello* (New York, 2005), and Malone, *Jefferson and His Time,* vol. 6.

45. Kastor, *Nation's Crucible;* Onuf, *Jefferson's Empire,* 127–29; Waldstreicher, *In the Midst of Perpetual Fetes,* 279–89.

46. TJ to William Crawford, February 11, 1815 [P.S. added February 26, 1815], in Jefferson, *Works,* 11:453–54.

47. For the collapse of Indian power, see Dowd, *Spirited Resistance,* 181–91; Richard White, *The Middle Ground: Indians, Empires, and Republics in the Great Lakes Region, 1650–1815* (Cambridge, 1991), 511–17; and Kathleen DuVal, *The Native Ground: Indians and Colonists in the Heart of the Continent* (Philadelphia, 2006), 226–40.

48. DuVal, *Native Ground,* 184–89; Kastor, *Nation's Crucible,* 205–8.

49. Ronda, *Astoria and Empire*, 40–45; William Earl Weeks, *John Quincy Adams and American Global Empire* (Lexington, Ky., 1992), 49–51.

50. TJ to John Holmes, April 22, 1820, in Jefferson, *Writings* [Peterson], 1434.

51. For Jefferson's commitment to preserving and extending slavery into the Southwest, see Adam Rothman, *Slave Country: American Expansion and the Origins of the Deep South* (Cambridge, Mass., 2005), and Kennedy, *Mr. Jefferson's Lost Cause*. This is as much a story of international affairs as it is one of domestic governance. Jefferson's condemnation of the racial revolt in Saint Domingue and his refusal to recognize an independent Haiti emerged in no small part from his fear of a similar revolt in the nearby southwestern United States. See Tim Matthewson, "Thomas Jefferson and Haiti," *Journal of Southern History* 61 (May 1995): 209–48.

52. *History of the Expedition under the Command of Captains Lewis and Clark, to the Sources of the Missouri, Thence across the Rocky Mountains and down the River Columbia to the Pacific Ocean: Performed during the Years 1804–5-6 by Order of the Government of the United States* (Philadelphia, 1814); Zebulon Montgomery Pike, *An Account of Expeditions to the Sources of the Mississippi: And through the Western Parts of Louisiana to the Sources of the Arkansaw, Kans, La Platte, and Pierre Jaun Rivers: Performed by Order of the Government of the United States during the Years 1805, 1806, and 1807, and a Tour through the Interior Parts of New Spain When Conducted through These Provinces by Order of the Captain-General in the Year 1807* (Philadelphia, 1810); *Atlas Accompanying an Account of Expeditions to the Sources of the Mississippi and through the Western Parts of Louisiana to the Sources of the Arkansaw, Kans, La Platte, and Pierre Jaun Rivers* (Philadelphia, 1810). For the link between landscape description and ownership, see James D. Drake, "Appropriating a Continent: Geographical Categories, Scientific Metaphors, and the Construction of Nationalism in British North America and Mexico," *Journal of World History* 15 (September 2004): 323–57; J. P. D. Dunbabin, "Red Lines on Maps: The Impact of Cartographical Errors on the Border between the United States and British North America, 1782–1842," *Imago Mundi* 50 (1998): 105–25; Gregory H. Nobles, "Straight Lines and Stability: Mapping the Political Order of the Anglo-American Frontier," *Journal of American History* 80 (June 1993): 9–35; and James P. Ronda, "'We Have a Country': Race, Geography, and the Invention of Indian Territory," *Journal of the Early Republic* 19 (Autumn 1999): 739–55.

53. For the role of Jefferson's memory and example in subsequent expansionism, see Thomas R. Hietala, *Manifest Design: Anxious Aggrandizement in Late Jacksonian America* (Ithaca, N.Y., 1985), 108–9; and Frank Lawrence Owsley Jr. and Gene A. Smith, *Filibusters and Expansionists: Jeffersonian Manifest Destiny, 1800–1821* (Tuscaloosa, Ala., 1997), 181–86. For the shifting role of

the West in American expansionism, see Stephanie LeMenager, *Manifest and Other Destinies: Territorial Fictions of the Nineteenth-Century United States* (Lincoln, Neb., 2004); Angela L. Miller, *The Empire of the Eye: Landscape Representation and American Cultural Politics, 1825–1875* (Ithaca, N.Y., 1993), 138–39, 178–84; Henry Nash Smith, *Virgin Land: The American West as Symbol and Myth* (Cambridge, Mass., 1950); and Shelley Streeby, *American Sensations: Class, Empire, and the Production of Popular Culture* (Berkeley, Calif., 2002).

Adam Rothman

Jefferson and Slavery

Once on a magnificent Sunday afternoon I sat with a group of Georgetown University undergraduates on the steps of the Jefferson Memorial, where we discussed the legacy and memory of the author of the Declaration of Independence. What better way to kick off a new semester of "Society and Politics in Jeffersonian America"? Jefferson loomed over us, larger than life. It dawned on me that I was about to spend the next few months attempting to topple that bronze statue from its granite pedestal, hammering away at the gleaming white edifice that shelters it. In 1943 Franklin Roosevelt dedicated the memorial as "a shrine to freedom," but today it is impossible to overlook the irony of that pronouncement.[1] The transformation in thought and perception provoked by the black freedom movement during the second half of the twentieth century has tarnished Jefferson's historical reputation while validating his loftiest ideals of universal liberty and equality. Jefferson is now indelibly linked to slavery as well as to freedom. He may seem less heroic than he used to, but history offers some compensation. Jefferson is now the gateway to a more enigmatic and fascinating world.

Jefferson's entanglement with slavery usually provokes two conflicting attitudes. On the one hand, Jefferson's defenders reject as "presentist" any criticism of Jefferson according to contemporary standards of morality. They assert that Jefferson should be judged by the standards of his own time rather than ours, and that by the standards of his time, Jefferson was a pioneering critic of slavery and a relatively benign slave owner. There are some problems with this position. One is that by Jefferson's own standard—the famous proposition from the Declaration of Independence that "all men are created equal, that they are endowed by their Creator with certain unalienable Rights, that among these are Life, Liberty and the pursuit of Happiness"—he fell far short of doing what was right by his slaves. It is true that Jefferson was a pioneering critic of slavery and deserves credit for his eloquent condemnations of the institution. He also had a hand in prohibiting slavery in the Northwest Territory and ending the slave trade to the United States. But he must also be held to account for adding insult to injury through his equally pioneering articulation of racist ideas and policies. Moreover, the claim that he was a benign slave owner is morally bankrupt. If we truly believe that slavery is wrong, then the only truly benign slave owners were the ones who freed their slaves, and not just the ones they had fathered. I do not mean to argue that some slave owners were not better than others. Slaves themselves knew too well the difference between masters who provided adequate food and shelter and rarely used the whip, and those who were cruel and neglectful. Rather, I am insisting that we never lose sight of the inevitable limits to slave owners' morality. As the fictional slave Gabriel puts it in Lafcadio Hearn's novel *Youma,* "there are masters who are better masters than others: there is no good master."[2] The whole concept of the benign slave owner originated in slave owners' own efforts to justify their behavior. To defend Jefferson as a good master, then, is to turn his own recognition of frustration and defeat into a moral victory. But more on these matters in due course.

On the other hand, Jefferson's critics often dismiss him as a mere hypocrite, a man who said one thing and did another. Jefferson's actions speak louder than his words; indeed, they drown out his words in a deafening crash of bad faith, broken promises, and racism. Although there is no disputing Jefferson's hypocrisy, this criticism does not take us very far toward understanding the man, nor the trap that he and his fellow slave owners had fallen into, nor the specific measures that he advocated to get out of it. Nor does Jefferson's own hypocrisy invalidate the ideals he so eloquently expressed. Even as they rejected colonization, abolitionists, including Frederick Douglass, would eventually wield Jefferson's principles and his iconic name in the struggle against a new generation of slave owners who explicitly repudiated them in favor of a counter-revolutionary defense of inequality and slavery. William Morris's *A Dream of John Ball* resonates in this instance: "I pondered all these things, and how men fight and lose the battle, and the thing that they fought for comes about in spite of their defeat, and when it comes turns out not to be what they meant, and other men have to fight for what they meant under another name."[3]

Thomas Jefferson was not just any old slave owner in any old place. He was a big planter in Virginia, the most populous of the North American states and the one with the most enslaved people. According to the first federal census in 1790, almost 40 percent of Virginia's 750,000 people were slaves, and 42 percent of all enslaved people in the United States lived in Virginia. Almost 45 percent of the people in Jefferson's Albemarle County were enslaved.[4] During the eighteenth century, the center of gravity of slavery in Virginia shifted from the Tidewater to the Piedmont on the strength of an expanding tobacco plantation economy.[5] Jefferson was one of the main beneficiaries of that surge. Using tax records from the 1780s, Jackson T. Main determined that Jefferson was one of the hundred wealthiest men in Virginia, with holdings of 12,050 acres of land and 149 slaves spread across two counties.[6] Jefferson was born into a slave society, and he viewed slavery as part of the United States' colonial legacy, since literally and figuratively he inherited it from his predecessors.

Jefferson's human property came into his possession through inheritance, marriage, purchase, and reproduction. He inherited 40 slaves from his father, received another 135 from his wife's father, purchased 18, and accrued another 400 over the course of his life by what historians generally refer to as the "natural reproduction" of his people. Yet the term "natural reproduction" is really a misnomer.

Enslaved people did have babies, of course, but as Jefferson knew, their reproduction *as slaves* was accomplished by the legislation that declared the offspring of enslaved women to be slaves, not by nature or biology. The law of descent was so deeply woven into the structure of Jefferson's society that it appeared to be one of the natural facts of life, even as it contradicted the usual pattern of inheritance in the English common law. Imagine how different the problem of slavery would have appeared if the status of the children of slave mothers had followed that of their fathers (as was briefly the case in Maryland in the seventeenth century) or, better yet, if all children had been born free. Of course, the growth of the enslaved population in Jefferson's Virginia, as in the other mainland colonies of North America, gave slavery there a unique aspect when compared to the rest of the Americas, where the slave population was sustained only by massive imports from Africa. Jefferson fully understood the profits to be gained through reproduction. Worried by high infant mortality among his enslaved people in 1819, he asked that the overseers allow slave women more time to care for their children. Regarding slave women, he wrote, "it is not their labor, but their increase which is the first consideration with us." Luckily for Jefferson, economic self-interest lined up with his sense of what was morally right, so he could encourage slave reproduction with a clear conscience: "in this, as in all other cases, providence has made our interests & our duties coincide perfectly." It should be noted that this Panglossian outlook was not limited to questions of slavery but was one of Jefferson's ingrained mental habits. His relentless optimism could take on a macabre form, as when he praised yellow fever for stunting the growth of America's cities.[7]

With important exceptions, Jefferson scholars have generally treated slavery as an intellectual and political problem rather than a lived experience or social reality—either for him or the enslaved people who labored for his happiness. Yet sources exist to bear witness to that reality. Jefferson's own correspondence, account books and memoranda; public tax, estate, and census records; the observations of visitors; the recollections and oral histories of slaves and free people; the shards, artifacts, and residue they left behind: all suggest a dense and complex community of human beings whom scholars have only begun to explore and whose full existence Jefferson himself only dimly comprehended. The Thomas Jefferson Memorial Foundation's Monticello Plantation Database has assembled names and other data on 609 enslaved people "who lived in slavery on Thomas Jefferson's Virginia plantations."[8] In alphabetical order, the database begins with Abbey, the daughter of Sally and Gawen, and ends with Zachary, the son of Lucy Gillette and a father whom we do not know. One good result of the controversy over the relationship between Thomas Jefferson and Sally Hemings is that it has energized historians to dig deeper into the social life of Jefferson's slaves.[9]

Theirs was a routine of work—the cultivation of tobacco, wheat, hemp, and foodstuffs; the artisanal craftsmanship of coopers, blacksmiths, and seamstresses; the domestic service of cooks, laundresses, and hostlers. Jefferson could invent devices to hide their labor from view inside the main house at Monticello, but he could not render their labor completely invisible—especially not to the slaves themselves, who were keenly aware of its value. Their families formed an intricate web, as the slave censuses in Jefferson's Farm Book graphically reveal. The Hemings clan stands out for its genetic and social proximity to Jefferson's innermost family circle, but other slave families inhabited Monticello and Poplar Forest, too, including the Colberts, Fossetts, Gillettes, Herns, Hubbards, and Hugheses (not to mention many others without recorded surnames). In the controversy about Sally Hemings and Jefferson's black descendants, the other slaves have largely been overlooked. The oral histories of former slaves from Monticello display an impressive genealogical knowledge, a sense of kinship that partially insulated them from one of the essential conditions of enslavement identified by sociologist Orlando Patterson: natal alienation, the symbolic obliteration of enslaved peoples' ancestry and heritage.[10]

The more scholars delve into the dynamics of community life on Jefferson's plantations, the less that life resembles the formerly conventional stereotypes of plantation history. The intricate kinship between white and black families, which Sally Hemings has come to symbolize, is only the tip of the iceberg.[11] For example, enslaved people had ample opportunities to truck, barter, and exchange (to use Adam Smith's famous phrase). Indeed, this phenomenon concerned Jefferson, who warned Thomas Mann Randolph in 1798 to prevent the slaves from growing their own tobacco. "I have ever found it necessary to confine them to such articles as are not raised for the farm. [T]here is no other way of drawing a line between what is theirs & mine."[12] Archaeologists at Poplar Forest have discovered locks and keys in the slave quarters, suggesting that enslaved people had possessions they wished to safeguard.[13] The idea of slaves owning, or at least possessing, their own property and having a customary right to "what is theirs" may seem counterintuitive, but as Patterson has argued, this *peculium* was a nearly universal privilege of slaves everywhere and at all times. It gave them a positive incentive to work and a stake in the system, but it also gave them a sense of the value of their own labor as well as their right to the fruits of it. Revelations like these pose a considerable intellectual challenge for scholars, who walk a tightrope in retaining a moral disgust for slavery while recognizing the range and complexity of social relations that it allowed.[14]

Even admitting this complexity, the plantation milieu was undeniably hierarchical and coercive, and so it remains puzzling that Jefferson came to champion a set of values so corrosive to the foundations of his own society. What was the relationship between slavery and Jefferson's ideals of liberty and equality? That this was a puzzle occurred to intellectuals in Jefferson's era. In 1775 the English biographer Samuel Johnson skewered the whiny Americans with his famous quip: "How is it that we hear the loudest *yelps* for liberty among the drivers of negroes?"[15] Johnson meant only to indict the colonists' hypocrisy and undermine their moral credentials, but he actually raised a difficult question. Orlando Patterson has offered one explanation of slaveholders' zeal for liberty. Slaveholders were acutely sensitive to threats to their liberty and slights to their honor precisely because they deprived others around them of freedom and honor. The slaveholders' esteem for freedom and honor was elevated by their immediate appreciation of the contrast between those who possessed these traits and those who lacked them. Hence, the fear of enslavement, so overwhelming in American Revolutionary rhetoric, drew its intensity and power from the colonists' horror at the condition in which they held their own slaves.[16] Edmund S. Morgan offers a different though not incompatible explanation for the apparent paradox of freedom-loving slave owners. He contends that the emergence of slavery in colonial Virginia obviated the need for an unruly class of free, poor people in Virginia, making it possible for Virginia's aristocrats to champion liberty and equality without reservation—or, rather, by reserving liberty and equality for the free, white population, which was the only population encompassed by that ambiguous term, "the people."[17] Yet both the Patterson and Morgan theses explain only why the Virginia gentry would have favored their own freedom. They cannot explain why Jefferson would have taken the crucial ideological leap of extending that ideal to all human beings—thus threatening the very social order that had nurtured him. To explain this startling development, we have to take into account two broader contexts: Jefferson's transatlantic world of letters and the revolt of the British mainland North American colonies.

Isaac Jefferson recalled that his old master "want rich himself—only his larnin."[18] Surrounded by books and in constant correspondence with a far-flung array of leading intellectuals, Thomas Jefferson joined the Enlightenment. His engagement with various strands of Western European thought—as represented by Locke, Montesquieu, and others—taught Jefferson that slavery was an obstacle to the fulfillment of the human mind rather than the necessary condition of his own mind's pursuits.[19] In the struggle for national independence, Jefferson universalized this antislavery position and deployed it to advance the American colonies' claims to self-government, refute charges of hypocrisy like the one leveled by Samuel Johnson, and attack the moral legitimacy of the king and the colonial system. Jefferson's notorious, excised assault on the transatlantic slave trade in his original draft of the Declaration of Independence accomplished all of these goals at once. Jefferson criticized King George III for engaging in this "cruel war against human nature itself," preventing the colonial legislatures from prohibiting it, and then inciting rebellions among the slaves, "thus paying off former crimes committed against the LIBERTIES of one people, with crimes which he urges them to commit against the LIVES of another."[20] Jefferson boldly identified Africans as a people deserving of life and liberty. He decried the slave trade as "piratical warfare" and repudiated the buying and selling of human beings. All of these were precocious criticisms of the Atlantic slave trade, which was in fact dominated by British carriers in the eighteenth century. But what also lurked insidiously in this passage, as Peter Onuf has argued, is Jefferson's sense of Africans and Americans as separate and distinct, "one people" and "another." He implied not just that Africans stood outside the Revolution, but also that they were the pawns of its enemies.[21]

In the early 1780s Jefferson had another opportunity to take stock of the meaning and significance of slavery for the future of his country. *Notes on the State of Virginia,* Jefferson's response to queries posed by a French diplomat, was both his most fully developed contribution to the transatlantic world of letters and a piece of nationalist propaganda. The *Notes* ranged widely across the geography, demography, economy, politics, culture, history, and future of Virginia. It joined empirical detail with sublime rhetoric. Students' eyes glaze over as they slog through the tedious lists and tables of plants and animals in Query IV, but then they open up again and focus intently when Jefferson veers unexpectedly into an extended defense of the Amcrican Indian character and once again when he confronts the problem of slavery. It is in *Notes on the State of Virginia* that Jefferson discloses his full horror of slavery and reveals his preferred solution, which he regretfully concludes cannot be accomplished. How does Jefferson arrive at this dead end?

We must logically begin with Query XVIII, entitled, "*The* particular *customs and manners that may happen to be received in that state?*"[22] Suppose someone were to ask you to describe the customs and manners of the people in your neighborhood. What would you focus on? Most of us would dwell on patterns of etiquette. Are the people rude or friendly? What are their favorite foods? Do they appreciate the arts or enjoy sports? We might not think to describe whether they are just, whether they house the homeless and feed the hungry, or whether they conserve energy or protect the environment. Yet it is worth remembering that there has been a long tradition of thinking about manners in a different light. In *Leviathan,* for instance, the grim Thomas Hobbes had written, "By manners, I mean not here decency of behaviour, as how one man should salute another, or how a man should wash his mouth, or pick his teeth before company, and such other points of the *small morals,* but those qualities of mankind that concern their living together in peace and unity."[23] This latter concept of manners resembles what Jefferson had in mind when he wrote *Notes on the State of Virginia*. Manners involve the unwritten norms of conduct and behavior, the habits and rituals that regulate social relations between people. When a society's manners are healthy, it will enjoy peace, but when they are foul, conflict will rage.

That concept of manners explains why, seemingly out of nowhere, Jefferson launched into an eloquent, anguished exposé of the destructive impact of slavery on his nation. "The whole commerce between master and slave is a perpetual exercise of the most boisterous passions," he writes, "the most unremitting despotism on the one part, and degrading submissions on the other. . . . The parent storms, the child looks on, catches the lineaments of wrath, puts on the same airs in the circle of smaller slaves, gives a loose to his worst of passions, and thus nursed, educated, and daily exercised in tyranny, cannot but be stamped by it with odious particularities."[24] Modern readers instinctively read this in the light of Jefferson's relationship with Sally Hemings, but sexual abuse is only a symptom of the general and basic evil of slavery that Jefferson alluded to here. Unfettered power corrupts, opening the way for passion to triumph over reason. Jefferson predicted that slavery would have fatal consequences for republican society. Slavery deformed the morals of the citizenry, created a dangerous domestic enemy, sapped the desire to work, and unmoored the American belief in liberty. At last Jefferson comes to his wit's end: "Indeed I tremble for my country when I reflect that God is just: that his justice cannot sleep for ever: that considering numbers, nature and natural means only, a revolution of the wheel of fortune, an exchange of situation, is among possible events: that it may become probable by supernatural interference!"[25] Now keep in mind that Jefferson did not believe in miracles; nor was he prone to invoking the prospect of divine intervention. That he invoked it here signals Jefferson's intellectual crisis. He appears temporarily unhinged by slavery. His "smile of reason" has turned into a frown.[26] But then Jefferson regained his composure and inched back from the precipice. He optimistically concluded that the times were changing and everything would be just fine. "The spirit of the master is abating, that of the slave rising from the dust, his condition mollifying, the way I hope preparing, under the auspices of heaven, for a total emancipation, and that this is disposed, in the order of events, to be with the consent of the masters, rather than by their extirpation."[27] No more trembling.

What, then, was to be done to prevent this looming national catastrophe and hasten the day of total emancipation? Jefferson provided his answer in Query XIV, entitled "*The administration of justice and description of the laws?*"[28] In describing plans for republicanizing the laws of Virginia, Jefferson elaborated on a proposed law for the eradication of slavery in the state. The law would have emancipated all slaves born after its passage, allowed them to remain with their parents until a certain age, and educated them at public expense "to tillage, arts or sciences" until the age of eighteen for females and twenty-one for males, when they would be "colonized" outside the state, established elsewhere as a "free and independent people," and replaced by white immigrants.[29] This perverse scheme of affirmative action for the children of slaves exemplifies the central features of the republican antislavery program. It provided for a very gradual transition to a free, white society that would have taken generations to accomplish. It respected slave owners' property interests insofar as it did not propose to emancipate slaves born before the passage of the act, although slave owners would have viewed the denial of their claim to the offspring of female slaves as a major infringement on their property rights. It established an intermediate stage between slavery and freedom for the freed children of slaves, who as minors were not entitled to full citizenship rights in any case. It required the state to educate and prepare them to become free men and women, and finally, it envisioned their deportation once they reached the age of maturity. What a bittersweet moment that would have been for those young Afro-Virginians who finally attained their freedom at the cost of their family and country!

Anticipating one obvious objection, Jefferson asked, "Why not retain and incorporate the blacks into the state?" His famous answer was that emancipation without deportation would lead to a genocidal race war. "Deep rooted prejudices entertained by the whites; ten thousand recollections, by the blacks, of the injuries they have sustained; new provocations; the real distinctions which nature has made; and many other circumstances, will divide us into parties, and produce convulsions which will probably never end but in the extermination of the one or the other race."[30] Jefferson could have stopped there, but instead he wasted no time in providing an example of the deep-rooted prejudices entertained by the whites. He launched into a long and notorious rumination on the ugliness, physical differences, and moral and intellectual inferiority of black people as compared with whites, concluding, "This unfortunate difference of color, and perhaps of faculty, is a powerful obstacle to the emancipation of these people."[31] As Barbara Fields has argued, Jefferson ended up blaming race—not racism, the true culprit—for the impasse at emancipation.[32] Other Virginia slave owners were more forthright than Jefferson in identifying the real sticking point, which was not the slaves' incapacity for freedom but slave owners' reluctance to give up their property and make do without slave labor.

As Patrick Henry acknowledged in a letter to Anthony Benezet in January 1773, "I am drawn along by the general inconvenience of living here without them."[33] Jefferson's account of the difficulties facing his proposal for the gradual eradication of slavery never fully confronted the political and economic interests arrayed against it. These he concealed behind the smokescreen of race.

Thomas Jefferson's retreat into race-thinking was not a personal quirk or character flaw. Other liberal intellectuals who faced analogous tasks of justifying inequality in different places and at different times took a similar tack. The political theorist Uday Mehta contends that liberalism, while ostensibly universalistic, has been historically exclusionary in practice, and that liberalism's exclusionary practices have a theoretical foundation. That foundation is the implicit demand for what he calls "a thicker set of social credentials that constitute the real bases of political inclusion." It turns out that just being human is not enough to claim the enjoyment of one's natural rights. For John Locke, reason was a necessary credential for political inclusion, so children and the insane could not be included in the circle of people entitled to exercise and enjoy their rights. In the nineteenth century, John Stuart Mill required a sufficiently advanced stage of civilizational development, which in his mind excluded the people of India from self-government and justified British colonialism. A similar logic applies to Jefferson's attempt to reconcile democratic republicanism with slavery. For Jefferson, race became the vocabulary of legitimate exclusion, the rational explanation for why people of African descent lacked the necessary credentials for political inclusion in the United States.[34]

Readers often puzzle over the relationship between Jefferson's attack on slavery in Query XVIII and his racist defense of colonization in Query XIV. The two passages seem opposed to each other in body and spirit. Yet the two passages can be reconciled by paying close attention to the criticisms that Jefferson levels against slavery. The key to understanding Jefferson's racist exclusionism is Jefferson's inability to imagine enslaved people as having any patriotism toward the country that enslaved them. In Query XVIII he wrote:

> And with what execration should the statesman be loaded, who permitting one half the citizens thus to trample on the rights of the other, transforms those into despots, and these into enemies, destroys the morals of the one part, and the amor patriae of the other. For if a slave can have a country in this world, it must be any other in preference to that in which he is born to live and labour for another: in which he must lock up the faculties of his nature, contribute as far as depends on his individual endeavours to the evanishment of the human race, or entail his own miserable condition on the endless generations proceeding from him.[35]

In this passage, Jefferson transformed slaves from the "one people" of the Declaration of Independence's excised slave trade clause into "one half the citizens" of Virginia. Yet he transforms them into citizens only to deny that they have any patriotism. The robbery of their labor alienates them from their country. Whether patriotism could be demanded or expected from slaves was an issue in the intriguing case of Billy, a "Mulatto slave" belonging to the estate of John Taylor. Billy was convicted of treason in 1781 after having been captured from an enemy vessel. Two members of the Prince William County jury protested Billy's conviction on the grounds that the court lacked proof that he had voluntarily taken up arms and, moreover, that the treason charge was improper, since "a slave in our opinion Cannot Commit Treason against the State not being Admited to the Priviledges of a Citizen owes the State No Allegiance and that the Act declaring what shall be treason cannot be intended by the Legislature to include slaves who have neither lands or other property to forfiet." Their argument against the treason charge was consistent with the view that Jefferson later expressed in Query XVIII that slaves could have no allegiance to the country they lived in. As governor of Virginia in 1781, Jefferson did indeed grant Billy a reprieve (although he did not explain why), and a month later the Virginia House of Delegates and Senate quashed the "illegal" indictment, saving Billy's neck and the property interest of John Taylor's estate.[36]

Twenty-one of Jefferson's own slaves defected to the British in 1781.[37] Perhaps he understood their flight as the understandable response of an oppressed and alienated people. It is more likely that he thought they had been enticed away, deceived, or stolen by the British. But what about those who remained behind, or the enslaved people who actively supported the Revolution—how did Jefferson understand their motives and actions? A small number of enslaved Virginians joined the Revolutionary cause as soldiers, sailors, and spies, and the state of Virginia eventually manumitted a few of them in recognition of their service.[38] Jefferson may have dismissed these enslaved "patriots" as exceptional, narrowly self-interested, or motivated by personal ties to their masters. He could not allow that they might have been fighting for their country or its avowed principles, as one enslaved Virginian named Saul insisted in a 1792 petition asking that the Virginia legislature emancipate him in recognition of his military service during the war. "He was taught to know that War was levied upon America, not for the Emancipation of Blacks, but for the Subjugation of Whites," read the petition, "and he thought the number of Bond-men ought not to be augmented."[39]

In Query XVIII, Jefferson condemned slavery for depriving enslaved people of their God-given natural right to freedom, but the consequences of the crime prevented a simple restoration of their rights. To borrow a term from twentieth-century debates over racial integration, Jefferson suggested that slavery had "damaged" enslaved people and rendered them unfit for freedom. They had been kept ignorant and stripped of the moral sense, thus unmanning them for citizenship. To set them free under these conditions would be cruel to them and dangerous to society.[40] Jefferson struck precisely this note in his famous letter to Edward Coles thirty years later, observing that "men probably of any color, but of this color we know, brought from their infancy without necessity for thought or forecast, are by their habits rendered as incapable as children of taking care of themselves."[41] That slaves required some tutelage to prepare them for freedom was a common argument among slavery's American and European critics throughout the late eighteenth and nineteenth centuries. It legitimized schemes to create way stations between slavery and freedom that would teach former slaves to exercise their newfound liberty in the right way, which usually meant working for their former masters as if nothing had changed. The argument undergirded Victor Hugues's repressive labor policy in Guadeloupe in the late 1790s as well as the apprenticeship system in the British West Indies in the 1830s and the *patronato* in Cuba in the 1880s.[42]

Jefferson's inability to imagine a basis for African American citizenship in the United States emerged from his concept of slavery as an abstract philosophical horror, which obscured the actual lived experience of the enslaved people all around him. Contrary to his allegation, enslaved Afro-Virginians and African Americans in general were not alienated from the country where they lived and worked for their masters' benefit. At a place like Monticello they had sunk deep roots into the ground, nurtured kin and community, taken pride in their work, and realized its value. Jefferson understood this enough to recognize that selling one of his slaves to a Georgia trader was the equivalent of sentencing him to exile.[43] That he could propose to sweep all those accomplishments away by his callous scheme of deportation shows just how shallow his legendary affection for the African American men and women under his control really was. Time and again throughout the nineteenth century, most African Americans would repudiate such ideas of so-called colonization to distant lands. One who did so in fiery terms was the radical abolitionist David Walker, who challenged Jefferson head-on in his 1829 *Appeal to the Colored Citizens of the World*. Walker declared, "America is more our country, than it is the whites—we have enriched it with our *blood and tears*."[44] He rooted black patriotism in the blood sacrifice of his people. The country belonged to them because they had built it and died for it, albeit involuntarily. The experience had not alienated them from the land but rather deepened their claim to it in ways that Jefferson could not permit himself to fully comprehend.

Despite the best efforts of the American Colonization Society, which did manage to ship around thirty thousand people to Liberia in the nineteenth century, Jefferson's vision of post-nati emancipation and deportation did not come to fruition. While free black resistance thwarted colonization, a proslavery retrenchment in Virginia blocked emancipation in any legislative form and constricted manumission.[45] Virginia slave owners were attached to the wealth and labor embodied by their slaves, and they gilded that attachment with arguments drawn from their Christian heritage and Revolutionary experience.[46] Faced with this intransigent public opinion, Jefferson devised another strategy aimed at displacing the problem of slavery altogether through a dual strategy of ending slave importation and encouraging slave exportation. "Diffusion," as it is known, restricted slave population growth to biolegal reproduction while granting slave owners the freedom to transport their human property to the newly organized territories and states of the Southwest. Virginians explicitly articulated this agenda in debates over the status of slavery in the Mississippi and Orleans Territories in 1798 and 1804, and Jefferson endorsed it. He seemed to believe that these policies would slowly reduce the density of slaves in the eastern states, diminish the danger they posed, and eventually result in the softening of slave owners' attitudes toward emancipation. Diffusion attached both slavery and the hope of emancipation to Western expansion. It imagined a voluntary, market-driven transition to freedom that also undermined the possibility of slave rebellion. It would have taken a very long time to accomplish, which was a hallmark of all Jefferson's schemes for abolition, even had it not already been fatally compromised by the persistent growth of Virginia's slave population. Daniel Raymond laid diffusion to rest in 1819, writing that it was "about as effectual a remedy for slavery as it would be for the smallpox."[47]

Jefferson's approach to the problem of slavery was remarkably consistent from the publication of *Notes on the State of Virginia* until his death. He favored prohibiting slave imports; emancipating, educating, and deporting the children of slaves; permitting slave owners to carry their human property into the West; and ultimately replacing slaves with free white immigrants. In short, he wanted to kill slavery and hide the body. The free white republic would not appear overnight, but Jefferson was confident it would eventually be achieved. "The revolution in public opinion which this cause requires," he wrote shortly before his death, "is not to be expected in a day, or perhaps in an age; but time, which outlives all things, will outlive this evil also."[48] He hoped subsequent generations would continue the work of moral progress, although during the Missouri Crisis he feared they would throw it all away. In the meantime, as Jefferson advised Edward Coles, the best that could be done under the circumstances was "to feed and clothe them well, protect them from ill usage, require such reasonable labor only as is performed voluntarily by freemen, & be led by no repugnancies to abdicate them, and our duties to them."[49] Thus, the very idea of the benign slave owner originated as a sigh of resignation, an admission of momentary moral retreat. As slavery bloomed in the southern United States in the first half of the nineteenth century, reestablishing itself on the basis of cotton and sugar, southwestern expansion, and the domestic slave trade, that sigh of resignation condensed into proslavery dogma.

Ultimately, Jefferson's antislavery commitments were distorted by a black hole at the center of his political universe. Although largely invisible to Jefferson himself and to subsequent generations of historians, it exerted a powerful gravitational pull on everything around it. That black hole is another name for what the historical anthropologist Michel-Rolph Trouillot has called "unthinkable history." In an essay on the Haitian Revolution, Trouillot explains that "the unthinkable is that which one cannot conceive within the range of possible alternatives, that which perverts all answers because it defies the terms under which the questions were phrased." For Trouillot, the slave rebellion at the core of the Haitian Revolution was "unthinkable" in the terms of Enlightenment discourse, "unthinkable" to slave owners and their allies all around the Atlantic world. It is not that they did not know about it or talk about it. In fact, they were obsessed with it and wrote about it incessantly. The point is that they lacked the intellectual tools to really understand it properly, and so they tried to suppress and trivialize it. Trouillot points out that these tendencies were largely reproduced in subsequent historical scholarship. Where is Haiti, for instance, in R. R. Palmer's magisterial history, *The Age of the Democratic Revolution*?[50]

For a long time, Jefferson scholars ignored the presence and perspective of African Americans. Theirs was an unthinkable history, as the controversy over Jefferson's alleged relationship with Sally Hemings revealed. Dumas Malone, Jefferson's great biographer, insisted that a sexual relationship between Jefferson and Hemings would have been "distinctly out of character, being virtually unthinkable in a man of Jefferson's moral standards and habitual conduct."[51] Malone's choice of words tells the tale. He reduced a complex interaction to the single question of Jefferson's character, and he dismissed countervailing testimony offered by Jefferson's black descendants. Thus, he rendered the Jefferson-Hemings affair "unthinkable." Similarly, Jefferson's defenders often suggest that it is inconceivable that Jefferson could have advocated immediate abolition and black citizenship. These cards were simply not on the table. But why not? That these options were unthinkable to Jefferson should not make them unthinkable to Jefferson's historians. There is a current vogue among historians for taking historical subjects on their own terms. If this were truly achieved, we would be nothing more than stenographers. Instead, historians have an obligation to look at history in ways that our historical subjects did not, with the benefit of hindsight, using all the analytical tools at our disposal, including many that were not available to the people we study. This means that we must explain why Jefferson could not imagine immediate abolition and black citizenship. The answer lies in the black hole generated by slavery, which never permitted the real desires of enslaved African Americans to see the light of day.

Jefferson's inability to imagine immediate abolition and black citizenship rested on the suppression of the hopes and dreams of the enslaved people all around him. Jefferson left behind mountains of words. They have been celebrated, inscribed in the walls of monuments, transformed into national scripture. His slaves left behind mere shards and fragments of thought, like the extraordinary memoir of Madison Hemings, which Jefferson's historians have too often neglected, ridiculed, or trivialized. This asymmetry reflects the imbalance of power between Jefferson and his slaves and the imbalance of honor paid to them. Had Jefferson and other slave owners granted enslaved people an opportunity to express themselves freely, the slave owners might have learned that the people under their dominion preferred to be free; wanted to stay where they were; and for once, wanted to labor for their own happiness. But of course, there was no such opportunity. For one thing, law and custom barred enslaved people from learning to read and write, and those who did learn had to be very cautious in exercising their talents.[52] Moreover, the threat of reprisal deterred enslaved people from saying anything within earshot of their owners except what they thought their masters were willing to hear—the famous tactic of "puttin' Ole Massa on."[53] Late in his life, Jefferson appears to have had a fleeting moment of awareness that his scheme for colonization depended on this suppression of African Americans' own true preferences. In his 1824 letter to Jared Sparks, in which (not coincidentally) he acknowledges Haitian independence, Jefferson admonished the younger generation not to delay in getting rid of the blacks before it was too late. "A million and a half are within their control; but six millions, (which a majority of those now living will see them attain,) and one million of these fighting men, will say 'we will not go.' "[54] And that is indeed what happened once slavery's gravitational field collapsed and the genuine voices of newly freed people were finally heard through the din and ruin of war.

Notes

1. Edward T. Folliard, "Shrine to Freedom," *Washington Post,* April 14, 1943, 1.

2. Lafcadio Hearn, *Youma: The Story of a West-Indian Slave* (New York, 1890), 119.

3. William Morris, *A Dream of John Ball and a King's Lesson* (London, 1913), 39–40.

4. These figures are from the Historical Census Browser, University of Virginia, Geospatial and Statistical Data Center, http://fisher.lib.virginia.edu/collections/stats/histcensus/index.html (accessed September 28, 2007).

5. Philip D. Morgan and Michael L. Nicholls, "Slaves in Piedmont Virginia, 1720–1790," *William and Mary Quarterly*, 3rd. ser., 46 (April 1989): 211–51 [hereafter, *WMQ*].

6. Jackson Turner Main, "The One Hundred," *WMQ*, 3rd ser., 11 (July 1954): 377.

7. TJ to Joel Yancey, January 17, [18]19, in Edwin Morris Betts, ed., *Thomas Jefferson's Farm Book, with Commentary and Relevant Extracts from Other Writings* (Princeton, N.J., 1953), 43. On the social, as opposed to natural, reproduction of the enslaved population in the United States, see Marie Jenkins Schwartz, *Born in Bondage: Growing Up Enslaved in the Antebellum South* (Cambridge, Mass., 2000). For Jefferson's remarks on yellow fever, see TJ to Benjamin Rush, September 23, 1800, in Jefferson, *Writings* [Peterson], 1080–81.

8. "Introduction," Monticello Plantation Database, http://plantationdb.monticello.org/ (accessed September 27, 2007).

9. Two important contributions to the social history of enslaved people living at Monticello and Jefferson's other plantations are Barbara J. Heath, *Hidden Lives: The Archaeology of Slave Life at Thomas Jefferson's Poplar Forest* (Charlottesville, Va., 1999), and Lucia C. Stanton, " 'Those Who Labor For My Happiness': Thomas Jefferson and His Slaves," in *Jeffersonian Legacies*, ed. Peter Onuf (Charlottesville, Va., 1993), 147–80. To these must be added Annette Gordon-Reed, *The Hemingses of Monticello: An American Family* (New York, 2008).

10. Orlando Patterson, *Slavery and Social Death: A Comparative Study* (Cambridge, Mass., 1982), 5–10. Annette Gordon-Reed provides an important vindication of Madison Hemings's memoir in *Thomas Jefferson and Sally Hemings: An American Controversy* (Charlottesville, Va., 1997). Gordon-Reed's book also reprints the memoirs of Madison Hemings and Israel Jefferson.

11. I use the racial designation *black* with the caveat that it utterly fails to comprehend the range and diversity of complexion and skin color among people of African descent.

12. TJ to Thomas Mann Randolph, June 14, [17]98, in Betts, ed., *Thomas Jefferson's Farm Book*, 269.

13. Heath, *Hidden Lives*, 62–64.

14. Patterson, *Slavery and Social Death*, 182–86. Dylan C. Penningroth offers an incisive analysis of property ownership among enslaved people in the United States in *The Claims of Kinfolk: African American Property and Community in the Nineteenth-Century South* (Chapel Hill, N.C., 2003), chap. 2.

15. Quoted in David Brion Davis, *The Problem of Slavery in the Age of Revolution, 1770–1823* (Ithaca, N.Y., 1975), 275.

16. Patterson, *Slavery and Social Death,* 94–97. See also F. Nwabueze Okoye, "Chattel Slavery as the Nightmare of the American Revolutionaries," *WMQ,* 3rd ser., 37 (January 1980): 3–28.

17. Edmund S. Morgan, *American Slavery, American Freedom: The Ordeal of Colonial Virginia* (New York, 1975).

18. Rayford W. Logan, "Memoirs of a Monticello Slave," *WMQ,* 3rd ser., 8 (October 1951): 568.

19. Lewis P. Simpson, *Mind and the American Civil War: A Meditation on Lost Causes* (Baton Rouge, La., 1989), chap. 1.

20. "Declaration of Independence," in Jefferson, *Writings* [Peterson], 22.

21. Peter S. Onuf, " 'To Declare Them a Free and Independant People': Race, Slavery, and National Identity in Jefferson's Thought," *Journal of the Early Republic* 18 (Spring 1998): 1–46. For the strategic deployment of antislavery rhetoric in the American Revolution, see Peter A. Dorsey, " 'To Corroborate Our Own Claims': Public Positioning and the Slavery Metaphor in Revolutionary America," *American Quarterly* 55 (September 2003): 353–86.

22. *Notes on the State of Virginia,* in Jefferson, *Writings* [Peterson], 288–89.

23. Thomas Hobbes, *Leviathan,* ed. A. P. Martinich (Petersborough, Canada, 2002), 75.

24. *Notes on the State of Virginia,* in Jefferson, *Writings* [Peterson], 288.

25. Ibid., 289.

26. Simpson refers to Jefferson's "smile of reason" in *Mind and the American Civil War,* 14. On Jefferson's momentary lapse of reason, see Barbara J. Fields, "Of Rogues and Geldings," *American Historical Review* 108 (December 2003): 1399. For Jefferson's view of divine intervention in history, see Eugene R. Sheridan, "Liberty and Virtue: Religion and Republicanism in Jeffersonian Thought," in *Thomas Jefferson and the Education of a Citizen,* ed. James Gilreath (Washington, D.C., 1999), 244–45.

27. *Notes on the State of Virginia,* in Jefferson, *Writings* [Peterson], 289.

28. Ibid., 264–70.

29. Ibid., 264.

30. Ibid.

31. Ibid., 270.

32. Fields, "Of Rogues and Geldings," 1398–99.

33. Quoted in "Letters of Anthony Benezet," *Journal of Negro History* 2 (January 1917): 88. I am grateful to Maurice Jackson for bringing Patrick Henry's letter to my attention.

34. Uday S. Mehta, "Liberal Strategies of Exclusion," *Politics and Society* 18 (December 1990): 427–54 (quotation at 429).

35. *Notes on the State of Virginia,* in Jefferson, *Writings* [Peterson], 288.

36. Jefferson, *Papers,* 5:640–43. Billy's case is discussed in Malick W. Gha-

chem, "The Slave's Two Bodies: The Life of an American Legal Fiction," *WMQ*, 3rd ser., 60 (October 2003): 834–36.

37. Cassandra Pybus, "Jefferson's Faulty Math: The Question of Slave Defections in the American Revolution," *WMQ*, 3rd ser., 62 (April 2005): 243–64.

38. On the perhaps five hundred Afro-Virginians who fought on the Revolutionary side, see L. P. Jackson, "Virginia Negro Soldiers and Seamen in the American Revolution," *Journal of Negro History* 27 (July 1942): 247–87. Twenty-five of the 150 Afro-Virginian soldiers and sailors Jackson identified by name were slaves.

39. Quoted in Willie Lee Rose, *A Documentary History of Slavery in North America* (New York, 1976), 62.

40. On slavery's damage to the moral sense, and hence to one's capacity for citizenship, see Ari Helo and Peter Onuf, "Jefferson, Morality, and the Problem of Slavery," *WMQ*, 3rd ser., 60 (July 2003): 583–614.

41. TJ to Edward Coles, August 25, 1814, in Jefferson, *Writings* [Peterson], 1345.

42. On French antislavery and the Caribbean, see Laurent Dubois, *A Colony of Citizens: Revolution and Slave Emancipation in the French Caribbean, 1787–1804* (Chapel Hill, N.C., 2004), especially chap. 6. On the transition from slavery to freedom in comparative perspective, see Frederick Cooper, Thomas C. Holt, and Rebecca J. Scott, *Beyond Slavery: Explorations of Race, Labor, and Citizenship in Postemancipation Societies* (Chapel Hill, N.C., 2000).

43. TJ to Thomas Mann Randolph, June 8, 1803, in Betts, ed., *Thomas Jefferson's Farm Book*, 19.

44. David Walker, *David Walker's Appeal, to the Coloured Citizens of the World*, ed. Peter P. Hinks (University Park, Pa., 2000), 67.

45. Eva Sheppard Wolf, *Race and Liberty in the New Nation: Emancipation in Virginia from the Revolution to Nat Turner's Rebellion* (Baton Rouge, La., 2006).

46. For a sampling of these arguments, see Fredrika Teute Schmidt and Barbara Ripel Wilhelm, "Early Proslavery Petitions in Virginia," *WMQ*, 3rd ser., 30 (January 1973): 133–46.

47. I discuss diffusionism at greater length in Adam Rothman, *Slave Country: American Expansion and the Origins of the Deep South* (Cambridge, Mass., 2005), 24–31 (quotation at 210).

48. TJ to James Heaton, May 20, 1826, in Jefferson, *Writings* [Peterson], 1516.

49. TJ to Edward Coles, August 25, 1814, ibid., 1346.

50. Michel-Rolph Trouillot, "From Planters' Journals to Academia: The Haitian Revolution as Unthinkable History," *Journal of Caribbean History* 25, nos. 1–2 (1991): 81–99 (quotation at 85).

51. Malone quoted in Clarence Walker, "Denial Is Not a River in Egypt," in

Sally Hemings and Thomas Jefferson: History, Memory, and Civic Culture, ed. Jan Ellen Lewis and Peter S. Onuf (Charlottesville, Va., 1999), 194. See also Gordon-Reed, *Thomas Jefferson and Sally Hemings.*

52. James Oakes, "Why Slaves Can't Read: The Political Significance of Jefferson's Racism," in Gilreath, ed., *Thomas Jefferson and the Education of a Citizen,* 177–92.

53. See Eugene Genovese, *Roll, Jordan, Roll: The World the Slaves Made* (New York, 1974), 609–12 (quotation at 610). Genovese traces the practice to West African etiquette, and he argues that however necessary it may have been as a strategy for survival, the habit of lying had deep moral costs for enslaved people in the long run.

54. TJ to Jared Sparks, February 4, 1824, in Jefferson, *Writings* [Peterson], 1487.

Thomas E. Buckley, S.J.

Placing Thomas Jefferson and Religion in Context, Then and Now

The letter Thomas Jefferson penned to the Baptist Association of Danbury, Connecticut, in January 1802 ranks among the most important ever composed by any president. The previous October the Baptists had written him a congratulatory letter on his inauguration. In it they expressed their desire that complete religious freedom might one day be achieved in Connecticut. There the Congregational clergy enjoyed a church establishment linked to the Federalist Party. So effectively did the Congregationalists dominate the state that the Reverend Timothy Dwight of Yale College was referred to as the pope of Connecticut.[1] The Baptist clergy knew that the First Amendment did not pertain to the states but only to the federal government. However, they expressed their hope that Jefferson's well-known views in support of religious liberty would so influence the United States and even the world that one day "Hierarchy and tyranny" would be destroyed.[2] Three months later Jefferson replied in memorable language:

> Believing with you that religion is a matter which lies solely between Man & his God, that he owes account to none other for his faith or his worship, that the legitimate powers of government reach actions only, &

> not opinions, I contemplate with sovereign reverence that act of the whole American people which declared that their legislature should "make no law respecting an establishment of religion or prohibiting the free exercise thereof," thus building a wall of separation between Church & State.

The spread of this perspective, he asserted, would "restore" to human beings their "natural rights."[3]

What has made the letter so significant is, of course, the way in which the concept of "separation of Church and State" has passed into American jurisprudence. The Supreme Court, in its earliest precedent-setting decisions on the First Amendment, turned to Jefferson's letter to the Danbury Baptists and the history of the long argument over religious freedom in Virginia during the Revolutionary era. Jefferson was at the center of that fight; and the Virginia Act for Establishing Religious Freedom, which the state approved in 1786, set the stage for the First Amendment's religion clause a few years later.

In *Reynolds v. United States* in 1878, which upheld a federal ban on Mormon polygamy in Utah territory, Chief Justice Morrison Waite, at the urging of a distinguished historian, George Bancroft, turned to the Virginia story to understand the First Amendment. In the preamble of Jefferson's statute, Waite found a definition of "religion" as "opinion" that the government could not touch, though actions were a different matter. The Chief Justice also quoted Jefferson's Danbury letter and the "wall of separation" metaphor.[4] Seventy years later, in the *Everson* and *McCollum* decisions of 1947 and 1948, the Court applied the Establishment Clause to the states and endorsed a strict separationist interpretation of the First Amendment. Again, as in the *Reynolds* case, the justices made Jefferson's perspective normative.[5] Therefore, what Jefferson thought and wrote about religion, particularly in its relationship to civil society, holds enormous importance for church-state jurisprudence and consequently for our lives today. No aspect of his thought so roused his political opponents during his lifetime or has proved more contentious after his death as his views on religion and its association with government. Both friends and foes, then and afterward, too often misunderstand his positions, chiefly because they ignore the complex circumstances within which he formulated his developing perspectives on God, religious freedom, and the place of religion in a republic. No one, however, underestimates the significance of his thought. Just as his Declaration of Independence unleashed the political revolution that established this nation, so his Virginia Statute for Religious Freedom—as it is commonly known—inaugurated a social revolution that transformed the relationship between church and state first in Virginia and then by example and by law throughout the United States.

To understand that transformation and Jefferson's role in it, we need some sense of the varied contexts that framed his developing thought on religion and its place in society. The religious world into which Jefferson was born in 1743 provided the first setting. Shortly after that event, Peter and Jane Randolph Jefferson brought their firstborn son to be baptized according to the ritual in the Book of Common Prayer of the Church of England. That was the established church of the colony of Virginia. In its first session in 1619, the General Assembly had passed a series of laws to set up the church "according to the Ecclesiastical Lawes and orders of the church of Englande." The instructions to Governor Sir Francis Wyatt in 1621 mandated that the colonists follow the "religion of the church of England as near as may be."[6] Virginia was to be an extension of the nation as a whole, "a Christian body politique," as William Crashaw put it. Its magistrates and ministers—state and church—formed its "very life and being."[7]

The way in which parishes were established makes this evident. In England the parish was a subdivision of both the county and the diocese. In Virginia, as the settlers moved inland, they established counties and parishes as they had known them in England. The parish was a well-defined geographical area for purposes of local government, both civil and ecclesiastical. Everyone who lived within its boundaries was a parishioner. Baptism made one a member of the church, and everyone—at least all of the white population—was baptized. Virginians conceived of their society in organic terms. Just as all belonged to a single political entity—the English colony of Virginia governed from Jamestown and later from Williamsburg—so all should be members of the Church of England, each in his or her proper place in the parish church on Sunday. Relationships were neatly ordered and hierarchical.[8]

By the time of the American Revolution, Virginia held ninety-five parishes with clergymen in all of them. Fredericksville Parish, where the Jefferson family lived in Albemarle County, held three churches and a chapel. The minister rotated among them on Sundays. In his absence a clerk or lay reader read the service. Parish affairs were managed by a vestry of twelve men, two of whom served as churchwardens. Originally elected by parishioners, the vestry eventually became self-perpetuating; vestry service was part of the *cursus honorem,* as younger members of the gentry class were first seated in vestries and on the bench of the county courts and then stood for election to the House of Burgesses. Jefferson began that path to preferment by taking a seat on the Fredericksville Parish vestry at the age of twenty-four.[9]

Virginians considered this church-state relationship to be mutually beneficial. The "*national church,*" as Jefferson's teacher, James Maury, styled it, was "incorporated and blended with the state." As such, it formed "a necessary and essential part of the political system of the nation."[10] The church supported the state by its public worship and by teaching the Christian gospel, the moral law, and the obligations of good subjects of the crown. The colonial government supported the church by favorable laws, public taxes, and benevolent oversight. Church and state worked together in friendly alliance for the well-being of the whole society; and whether in church or state, the laity, and particularly the gentry class, maintained control. Nominally episcopal in polity, the church's government in Virginia was in reality more congregational, with a lay vestry wielding important powers in each parish. No bishop was on hand to supervise the clergy or to administer confirmation or ordination. Virginians who wished to be ordained sailed to England for that rite. Ministers seeking a parish would apply to a vestry to be hired at a salary and with such benefits as Virginia law stipulated.

The typical Sunday worship in which Jefferson might have participated included Morning Prayer and the litany from the Book of Common Prayer, followed by a sermon. This service was designed to join the congregation in a common relationship to God—one based more on prayer and action than on a shared faith or doctrine. Three or four times a year the clergyman would administer Holy Communion, but communicants were generally few in number, held back perhaps by a sense of unworthiness. Preaching, rather than liturgy and sacraments, was the key for Low Church Anglicanism, and only an ordained minister could preach. While Virginia's established clergy included a few evangelicals in the eighteenth century, most sermons in Jefferson's day were aimed at the head rather than the heart and focused on behavior, not doctrine. As in England at that time, the emphasis was on moral rationalism. A good moral life rather than adherence to traditional Christian creeds was the test of a Christian.[11]

Ministers occasionally stated that the Sermon on the Mount with its teachings on behavior contained everything necessary for salvation. Jefferson would agree, and he would fit quite comfortably in the Episcopal Church community even as his personal religious beliefs developed, changed, and occasionally reversed. In the 1790s Joseph Priestley's work made a profound impression on him, and Jefferson no longer accepted the Trinity or the divinity of Christ; later, he seemed to move decisively toward Unitarianism.[12] But however privately skeptical he became of traditional Christian doctrines, his public religious practice remained thoroughly conventional. Throughout his life he often enough attended whatever religious services were convenient, contributed generously to the maintenance of his local clergyman, and publicly identified himself as a member of the Episcopal Church.[13] As he informed a Presbyterian clergyman who had solicited him for a contribution in 1823 to build his church: "I have been from my infancy a member of the Episcopalian church, and to that I owe and make my contributions." The records demonstrate that he consistently made such donations, even when it was not financially convenient.[14]

But while the ministers and services might suit him, the church establishment did not. The roots of this dissatisfaction may be found in his earliest real education as a teenage boy in the home of the Reverend James Maury. Anglican clergymen commonly supplemented their salaries by running small schools for the sons of local gentry. Jefferson's formal training began under the tutelage of the Reverend William Douglas. According to Jefferson's own account, he learned little from Douglas; and it was a relief when in early 1758 at the age of fourteen, thanks to arrangements made by his father, he switched to the log-cabin academy operated by Maury, the well-liked rector of Fredericksville Parish. Perhaps because so few of the papers from Jefferson's early life survive, his biographers usually pass over this period quickly. Dumas Malone, for example, follows Jefferson's own autobiography in praising Maury as a "correct classical scholar"; but Malone further surmises that from Maury "Jefferson gained none of his characteristic political principles or religious ideas."[15]

Can we be so sure? What else might Jefferson have learned besides Latin and Greek in those impressionable years between the ages of fourteen and seventeen? His father, Peter Jefferson, had just died. He had no older brothers or sisters. He lived in the Maury home where the forty-year-old minister welcomed him into his ever-growing family circle. When Mary Walker Maury gave birth to her ninth child Abraham in 1758, the clergyman and his wife honored the teenaged Jefferson by inviting him to serve as their new son's godfather. The older Maury sons were among his schoolmates, and for the rest of his life Jefferson numbered them among his close friends.[16] James Maury is best known in history for his role as the unsuccessful litigant in the Parson's Cause, a lawsuit to recover damages suffered when the Virginia Assembly, at a time when the value of tobacco had dramatically increased, temporarily allowed Virginians to pay their tithes in money rather than tobacco. Many years later, when William Wirt was collecting materials for a biography of Patrick Henry, he asked Jefferson for his recollections of the Parson's Cause. The sage of Monticello remembered little, except that he had "often" heard Maury attack the "iniquity of the . . . two-penny act."[17] The minister was not silent about his opinions. What else was Jefferson likely to have overheard or discussed with his teacher?

Let me suggest three lessons. First, there is the fundamental equality before God of all people. Jefferson was still living in Maury's home and may well have been present at a Sunday baptism the minister performed in October 1759. As the service began, Maury invited those who wished to present their children for baptism to come forward. As some slaves advanced with the white people up the aisle of the church, Thomas Johnson, a churchwarden, suddenly intervened and ordered them back to their benches. As Maury reported the event afterward, he thought that Johnson only meant that the slaves were not to mingle with the whites. So the minister told them to stop. But Johnson announced that, for the sake of "order," blacks and whites could not be baptized "together." When the slaves left the church that morning without having their children baptized, Maury was outraged. Johnson thought the clergyman could baptize the slave children at another time and place. Maury would have none of it. From his perspective, "making such a Distinction between free and bond, white and black, in this and similar cases . . . appears an Innovation upon the Gospel, which nowhere . . . warrants such Distinctions." Instead, he felt, it violated explicitly the scriptural command "to . . . baptize all Nations . . . without any partial Regards to their several Colors, Conditions or Countries." For himself, Maury had no intention of remaining "tame and passive" before this attempt to prevent "the Admission of new Members into the Church of Christ." This was a matter of conscience for which he would one day have "to render an Account."[18] One can only wonder what turn the dinner conversation took in the Maury household over an event such as this.

A second lesson: the importance of enlisting reason in the service of religion. This must have been a favorite theme for Maury, even before he composed his essay attacking the "pretensions" of Baptist preachers, published posthumously in 1771. In this pamphlet Maury laid out his case for the reasonableness of Christianity as embodied in the established church. The Separate Baptists had moved into Virginia in significant numbers in the 1760s. Unlike earlier congregations of Quakers and Presbyterians, the Baptists had refused to accept the colony's restrictions on religious dissenters. Their charismatic preaching and enthusiastic services drew crowds and won converts, particularly among the lower classes. Maury protested on both rational and scriptural grounds. The Christian, Maury argued, "is not required to believe an article, or perform a precept," until he had "received rational satisfaction of the credibility of the one and obligatory force of the other. His religion then may justly be termed an address to his reason." Is this what he taught Jefferson? Years later, Jefferson would advise his young nephew, Peter Carr, "Fix reason firmly in her seat, and call to her tribunal every fact, every opinion. Question with boldness even the existence of a god; because, if there be one, he must more approve the homage of reason, than that of blindfolded fear. . . . Your own reason is the only oracle given you by heaven, and you are answerable not for the rightness but uprightness of the decision."[19]

Maury might well have agreed. In a third lesson, the minister laid out a basis for religious dissent and a rationale for separating from the established church. In 1755 he had described "Liberty of Conscience" as a "natural Right of Mankind."[20] Then the issue had been Presbyterians without preaching licenses; now it concerned Baptists. But the Anglican minister's supreme principle remained the same: the rights of conscience. One could—in fact, one should—leave the Church of England if he or she was sincerely convinced "that conformity is sinful and contrary to the laws of God." Years later Jefferson in his *Notes on the State of Virginia* would write: "The rights of conscience we never submitted, we could not submit. We are answerable for them to our God."[21] Did Maury plant that seed?

The clergyman was certainly unhappy with the growth of the Presbyterians and Baptists in Virginia at the expense of the Church of England, but he supported toleration and rejected coercion. Reason was crucial. He called upon those who had separated from the church to revisit that decision and make it not "as the result of giddiness, humour or caprice," but rather by "deliberation, principle and judgment." They should accept no one's assertion of "an immediate mission from God" unless he could prove it; instead, Maury urged them to "consult your own reason" and the scriptures.[22] Jefferson would follow that advice, and he would boldly use his reason to address the Bible, even to the extent of constructing his own version of the New Testament. His later confidence that "truth is great and will prevail" if reason is just left free was instilled first by a pious Anglican minister. All three lessons profoundly shaped Jefferson's public and private religion.

From Maury's tutelage Jefferson passed to the study of philosophy at the College of William and Mary under the guidance of William Small and then to read law in the office of George Wythe. His circle of friends in Williamsburg included two future clergymen, and Jefferson took an interest in their careers. One of them was James Maury Fontaine, a nephew of Maury, who was studying theology in preparation for the ministry. A few years later Jefferson would strongly recommend Fontaine for the position of chaplain to the House of Burgesses, singling out Fontaine's "acuteness of penetration, accuracy of judgment, elegance of composition, propriety of performing the divine service." In Jefferson's view, these were the qualities he would need to write good sermons and lead Morning Prayer.[23] By the time he penned that letter, Jefferson was already a vestryman of his former teacher's Fredericksville Parish, having sworn the oath the previous year "to conform to the Doctrine and Discipline of the Church of England as by law established." He remained active on the vestry until moving out of the parish to Monticello.[24] Another clerical friend was James Ogilvie, a Scottish immigrant, who served as a tutor in Fredericksville Parish in the early 1760s. Later, when Ogilvie ran into difficulties obtaining ordination in England, Jefferson wrote strong letters in his behalf in the summer of 1770.[25]

As Jefferson was recommending Ogilvie for the ministry, he was also ordering books to replace his library, which had been destroyed when a fire burned Shadwell, his family's home. We know what he wanted—in his late twenties—to have available on his bookshelves. In the category of "religion" he included such titles as Cicero's *Tusculan Disputations,* which fostered stoicism; Locke's "Conduct of the mind in search of truth," seven volumes of Laurence Sterne's sermons—not a household word today, Sterne was an Anglican clergyman best known for *Tristram Shandy;* David Hume's essays in four volumes; along with Henry Home, Lord Kames's *Essays on the Principles of Morality and Natural Religion,* which attacked Hume's moral skepticism. From the writings of William Sherlock, Dean of St. Paul's Cathedral in London, Jefferson selected his *Practical Discourse Concerning Death* and *Practical Discourse Concerning a Future Judgment.*[26] He was then, as he would be for the rest of his life, vitally interested in what are essentially religious questions.

When Jefferson ordered those books, he was already a member of the House of Burgesses from Albemarle County and a vestryman of Saint Anne's Parish. His life in politics had begun. As a burgess and then as a delegate from Virginia's assembly to the Continental Congress, he assumed a leadership position in the movement toward independence. In that capacity, his religious perspective became more public and broadly reflective of the consensus of Americans. According to Edmund Randolph, Jefferson and Charles Lee were the two burgesses who in May 1774 drew up the resolution passed by the House for a public day of prayer and fasting. In "an allowable trick of political warfare," Randolph wrote, they wanted "to electrify the people from the pulpit." Later in the summer, Jefferson and John Walker, his fellow representative from Albemarle, issued a call for a day of "fasting, humiliation and prayer" in the parish of St. Anne. Charles Clay, the rector of St. Anne's and another of Jefferson's clerical friends, agreed to lead special prayers and preach a sermon appropriate to the occasion.[27] That same summer Jefferson spelled out basic principles in a set of instructions he drafted for the Virginia delegates to the Continental Congress. The source of their rights, the "rights of human nature," was not the British constitution, much less George III; rather, it was "the god who gave us life, gave us liberty at the same time."[28] The following year, Jefferson—now a Virginia delegate in Philadelphia—helped draft the Declaration of the Causes and Necessity for Taking Up Arms. After a lengthy recital of the abuse that Americans had suffered under British rule, he concluded, "We do then most solemnly, before god and the world declare . . . we will . . . use . . . all those powers which our creator hath given us, to . . . preserve that liberty which he committed to us in sacred deposit." The statement ended by appealing for the "assistance of Almighty god."[29] He returned to these basic themes when he penned his first draft of the Declaration of Independence. He appealed to the "laws of nature and of nature's god." They demonstrated "that all men are created equal and independent, that from that equal creation they derive rights inherent and inalienable, among which are the preservation of life, and liberty, and the pursuit of happiness."[30]

In these documents, Jefferson set forth the foundational principles of what would become the American civil religion: a belief in natural rights that are the gift of a creator God, the fundamental equality of all men and women, and a reliance upon divine Providence. No sooner was the Declaration signed than Congress constituted Jefferson, Benjamin Franklin, and John Adams as a committee to devise a great seal for the United States. Jefferson's proposal, as Adams reported to his wife the next month, included the Exodus event: "The Children of Israel in the Wilderness, led by a Cloud by day, and a Pillar of Fire by night."[31] The United States becomes, in Jefferson's view, the New Israel guided by divine providence. Jefferson's proposal for the seal was not adopted, but as president a quarter of a century later, he would incorporate this image from the Hebrew Bible into a further elaboration of American civil religion. Though religious references laced his addresses and messages to Congress, his Second Inaugural Address contained perhaps the most elaborate: "I shall need," he said, as he invited his fellow citizens to prayer, "the favor of that Being in whose hands we are, who led our fathers, as Israel of old, from their native land and planted them in a country flowing with all the necessaries and comforts of life; who has covered our infancy with His providence and our riper years with His wisdom and power, and to whose goodness I ask you to join in supplications with me."[32]

Jefferson could easily incorporate religious references into his public statements because in his political context, he spoke not just for himself but for all Americans. His language was inclusive. Later Americans would call it nondenominational. What he said, his countrymen believed. Religion became then a unifying element that brought people together—rather than a divisive one. Thus, Jefferson became an architect of American civil religion as Robert Bellah would much later define it, a bonding force for our national life in a society made up of people of many diverse faiths. Civil religion exists alongside of and set apart from our personal religious beliefs and commitments, but, hopefully, not in opposition to them. As Bellah differentiated it from a Christian perspective, this is not a saving, redemptive faith but an ordering faith. It helps to organize our national life as a people. It grows out of a set of religious beliefs, symbols, and rituals that are part of the American historical experience interpreted in terms of transcendence.[33]

While Jefferson developed the foundations for an American civil religion, he also insisted that one's personal beliefs demanded respect: that each person should be free to believe or not, and to act on that belief as each saw fit. This aspect of religion was foremost in his mind as he left Philadelphia and returned to Williamsburg for the next session of the General Assembly in the fall of 1776. During the previous June a revolutionary convention in Virginia had drafted a republican form of government and a Declaration of Rights for the newly independent state. The sixteenth article dealt with "religion, or the duty which we owe to our Creator" and stated that "all men are equally entitled to the free exercise of religion, according to the dictates of conscience; and that it is the mutual duty of all to practise Christian forbearance, love, and charity, towards each other."[34] What did that mean for the established church? Nobody was quite sure, but the convention rejected a proposal made by James Madison to disestablish it.[35]

That autumn, Baptists and Presbyterians petitioned for relief and religious equality. Jefferson attempted to end the establishment and all the colonial laws in any way specifying religious belief or practice. Much later, he wrote that this effort had "brought on the severest contests" he ever experienced.[36] He respected his opponents, who included most of the Assembly's leadership, even as he disagreed with them. As 1776 ended, the legislators eliminated religious taxation for dissenters and suspended it for Anglicans (who were now calling themselves Episcopalians), but they refused to go further. The Church remained "established" and tied to the state by a network of laws, some of which had become anachronistic in the new situation of independence. The clergy lived off their farms, their schools, and whatever people voluntarily contributed. Jefferson, for example, gave generously to the subscription for his friend Charles Clay at St. Anne's.[37]

But he would not let the issue of religious freedom rest. Two years later, as a member of a small committee assigned to revise all the former colony's laws to accord with the new situation of independence, Jefferson drew up his statute for establishing religious liberty. The word "establishing" is significant. This law was designed to institutionalize religious freedom, just as laws had once instituted and supported a state church. The new establishment he envisioned was one of complete liberty of conscience. The preface he composed is the clearest statement of his thoughts on religion and the freedom it must possess; in it, he established that:

> (1) Religion is a matter of opinion determined by the use of human reason.
>
> (2) Because "Almighty God hath created the mind free," belief must be based on the evidence submitted to the mind. Therefore, Jefferson concluded, belief was not an act of the will but rather must "follow involuntarily the evidence proposed" to people's minds. God, he said, had chosen "to extend [religion] by its influence on reason alone."

(3) Consequently, civil government has no authority in the realm of religious thought and its expression—either in terms of coercion or support (which is often a form of coercion). Religious freedom is part of our natural rights that are antecedent to any rights of government.

(4) Church and State must remain separate, though Jefferson does not use that term; what he wrote was that "to suffer the civil magistrate to intrude his powers into the field of opinion and to restrain the profession or propagation of principles on supposition of their ill tendency is a dangerous fal[l]acy, which at once destroys all religious liberty."[38]

It was a bold statement of principles followed by a brief enabling clause that provided for complete freedom of belief and worship. In that same session of 1779 the legislature also debated an opposing measure: a bill concerning religion, closely modeled on a measure already approved in South Carolina, that would establish the Christian religion with a general assessment (tax) on everyone. Ultimately, the legislature tabled both religious bills and voted Jefferson into the governorship, a largely powerless position, which he found frustrating and humiliating when the British raiders invaded the state and he could do little or nothing.[39]

But the defeat of his religious liberty statute hurt more. A few years later, while serving in Paris as American minister to France, he poured out his frustration in his *Notes on the State of Virginia*. Discussing the state of religion in the Old Dominion, he distinguished between activities appropriate to civil government and to the individual: "The legitimate powers of government extend to such acts only as are injurious to others." Then came the zinger: "But it does me no injury for my neighbour to say there are twenty gods, or no god. It neither picks my pocket nor breaks my leg." That separation of belief from action would later cause him major political problems. But Jefferson was supremely confident that left to itself, reason would discover the truth. Only "error," he wrote, "needs the support of government."[40]

The climactic struggle over church and state in Virginia came in the middle of the 1780s after the Revolution and before the Constitutional Convention of 1787. By the time the first postwar assembly met in Richmond in 1784, many people realized that the Church "established by law" was in critical condition. No replacements had been coming from England for those clergymen who died during the war years or who had resigned their positions. Church buildings and property had suffered extensive damage. Many thoughtful people were also concerned that a republic depended ultimately upon the virtue of its citizens and officeholders alike. Religion supported such virtue, and Patrick Henry, George Washington, John Marshall, and others thought that religion needed and deserved state support.

Two important measures responded directly to the crisis. First, a meeting of the established church's clergy requested the Assembly to organize them as something other than the Church of England in Virginia. The law still tied them to the state. In response, the Assembly passed a bill "incorporating the Protestant Episcopal Church" in Virginia. This elaborate law reconfirmed the church in its church buildings and other property, but more important, it also established the church's polity. Henceforth, a convention composed of a clergyman and vestryman from each parish would form its governing body. In effect, the General Assembly decided how the Episcopal Church would operate in Virginia.[41] The second measure that fall of 1784 was a general assessment proposal, a bill introduced by Patrick Henry to establish a provision for "teachers of the Christian religion," with each person to designate the clergyman or religious group who was to receive his taxes. After extensive debate and Henry's election as governor, which removed him from the legislature, the bill was postponed for statewide discussion.

The next spring a petition war broke out on a scale never seen before or afterward in the Old Dominion. Nobody welcomed the idea of paying more taxes—the state was in the economic doldrums—but the incorporation of the Episcopal Church enraged the growing ranks of former dissenters, especially the Presbyterians and the Baptists. They saw this measure "as a snake in the grass"—a covert way of reviving the old, hated establishment. The legislature had exalted the Episcopalians to a "Superior pitch of Grandeur," the

Presbyterians complained, and made them again "the Church of the State."[42] Now the assessment proposal looked like the frosting on the icing. All Virginians who were not dissenters would wind up paying for the local Episcopal vicar, and the old establishment with its new name and new legal standing would revive and again dominate the religious landscape. James Madison drafted his famous Memorial and Remonstrance, an exhaustive list of objections to the assessment, but it was not nearly as popular or well subscribed as those that were composed and circulated at Baptist and Presbyterian meetinghouses.

When the legislature met in the autumn, the assessment was not even considered. Instead, Madison pulled Jefferson's bill out of limbo and guided it through the Assembly. The key element in its successful passage was the evangelical bloc. In the Incorporation Act and assessment proposal, the former dissenters had seen one potential future and rejected it. Jefferson's bill offered an alternative vision of complete freedom to believe, to worship, and to evangelize without government restraint, not just in Virginia but for the whole nation. Moreover, the contests of 1784–85 over religion revealed their political leverage, which they would now use on the state legislature, first to repeal the incorporation of the Episcopal Church; and then to repeal all Virginia laws concerning religion except Jefferson's statute; and finally to seize the property that the Assembly had repeatedly guaranteed to the Episcopal Church.[43] That move completed the most notable social revolution of the Revolutionary era.

Jefferson stood aside from that last battle. He had other, more pressing and more personal concerns. In recent years it has become common to decry the political partisanship prevalent in Washington and the nation generally and to hanker after a more harmonious time. For TV viewers on election night, the media produces a color-coordinated electoral shorthand that pits red states against the blue and revels in arguments about religion and politics. In 2004 we experienced a closely fought election that, for many Americans, was determined on the basis of moral and/or religious concerns such as abortion, the faith-based initiative, and gay marriage.[44]

Thomas Jefferson would have found himself on similar, if unwelcome, terrain. The election of 1800 that he eventually won produced the nastiest campaign in the early republic. The chief issue was Jefferson's religion or lack thereof. Four years earlier, the choice of a successor to George Washington pointed the way for this line of attack on Jefferson. The contest in 1796 was between Vice President John Adams and Jefferson, the former secretary of state. William Loughton Smith, a high-toned Federalist congressman from Charleston, South Carolina, published a series of articles in the *Gazette of the United States* that were then collected into a tidy pamphlet entitled *The Pretensions of Thomas Jefferson to the Presidency Examined; and the Charges Against John Adams Refuted.* Smith attacked Jefferson by equating Jefferson's support for "*religious freedom*" with "*freedom from religion.*" Smith zeroed in on Jefferson's writings that we have already considered, particularly his *Notes on the State of Virginia* and his Virginia statute.

Recall what Jefferson wrote in his *Notes:* "it does me no injury for my neighbour to say there are twenty gods, or no god. It neither picks my pocket nor breaks my leg." Smith pounced. "[D]o I receive no injury, as a member of society," he asked, "if I am surrounded with atheists"? Smith argued that by his "*levity* or . . . *impiety,*" Jefferson degraded Christianity. He quoted Jefferson: "There are religions [in Virginia] of *various* kinds indeed . . . BUT ALL GOOD ENOUGH." The South Carolinian found that same studied indifference toward religion throughout the lengthy preamble to Jefferson's statute. The effect of that law in Virginia was at best highly questionable, but Jefferson could hardly be concerned. "Who ever saw him in a place of worship," Smith asked.[45]

Four years later, when Vice President Jefferson challenged Federalist president John Adams, conservative Federalist clergy like Timothy Dwight and his Congregational brethren in Connecticut dragged out all of Smith's religious arguments and invented a few more of their own. From the pulpit of Christ Church in Philadelphia, the Episcopal clergyman James Abercrombie attacked Jefferson's irreligion and urged other ministers "to aid me in support of our great and common cause." It would be a disaster, he warned, for "a Christian community, *voluntarily*, to place at their head, as their *ruler* and *guide*, an acknowledged *unbeliever*, . . . an *enemy* to their faith."[46] What did Jefferson really want, asked a writer in the Maryland press. Turning to the Virginia statute and the efforts then being made in its name to seize the Episcopal Church's property there, "Caius" wondered whether the call for religious freedom had merely been a prelude to wiping out "the Christian religion" entirely.[47]

The most searing invective came from the pen of William Linn, the Presbyterian pastor of New York's collegiate Dutch Reformed Church. With the help of another New York clergyman, John Mitchell Mason, Linn produced *Serious Considerations on the Election of a President*, which appeared first as a newspaper series in various cities and then in pamphlet form.[48] Linn based his opposition to Jefferson entirely on religious grounds. If the United States elected this Deist who rejected Christianity, he would "destroy religion, introduce immorality, and loosen all the bonds of society." Linn claimed that the Virginian wanted "a government where the people have *no religious opinions and forms of worship*." As evidence of what to expect if Jefferson were elected, Linn cited a widely reported "Sunday-feast" that the vice president had enjoyed in Fredericksburg in violation of the Sabbath on his way home to Monticello.[49]

The attack of the Federalist clergy and Linn's invective in particular infuriated Jefferson. In a private letter to Benjamin Rush that year, he wrote, "I have sworn upon the altar of god eternal hostility against every form of tyranny over the mind of man."[50] He bided his time, however, and his First Inaugural Address was a model of conciliation: "We are all Republicans, we are all Federalists." He made the peaceable religious pluralism in America the model for political pluralism.[51] But the Danbury letter eight months later provided the opening he wanted. If the context prompting the Baptist preachers' letter was Connecticut's oppressive church-state policy, Jefferson's context was the religious politics of the 1800 campaign. As James Hutson, the chief of the Manuscript Division of the Library of Congress, demonstrated by calling in the FBI to examine

Jefferson's rough draft of his Danbury letter, the president fully intended to use this occasion to strike back. The Federalists had used presidential proclamations of days of prayer and fasting to push their policies and attack their Republican opponents. Jefferson initially intended to use his response to the Danbury letter to explain why he refused to "proclaim fastings & thankgivings" as Washington and Adams had done. His draft identified this practice with "the Executive of another nation as the legal head of its church"—a clear reference to the British monarch. The First Amendment forbade such "religious devotions" and left them to the decision of each state.

Before composing his final draft, however, the president consulted the two New England politicians in his cabinet: Postmaster General Gideon Granger of Connecticut and Attorney General Levi Lincoln of Massachusetts. Granger thought the president's words were fine—he had suffered unrelenting political attacks at home and was ready for combat. But Lincoln cautioned Jefferson that the letter might offend Republicans in New England who were used to such proclamations from their governors and would not want the practice disparaged by linking it to the British crown. Jefferson accepted Lincoln's advice and left his explanation for another day. But, as Hutson demonstrates, the Danbury letter was not a detached statement of political principles but a political statement designed to skewer Jefferson's enemies. Two days later, to underscore the point that he was not irreligious, Jefferson attended services conducted by a visiting Baptist preacher, John Leland, in the hall of the House of Representatives. Thereafter, whenever he was resident in Washington, the president publicly participated in religious worship on Sundays. He also authorized such services in the public buildings of the executive branch. Such "neutral aids" did not violate his understanding of the First Amendment.[52] Nor did it prevent him from assisting with federal dollars the ministry of both Protestant and Catholic missionaries to the Native Americans.[53] A century before Theodore Roosevelt, Jefferson made the presidency a "bully pulpit" for developing the American civil religion.

Perhaps Jefferson's clearest statement on the boundaries of the church-state relationship is contained in a letter he wrote to a clergyman friend, the Presbyterian Samuel Miller of Princeton, in 1808. In it, he stated:

> I consider the government of the US. as interdicted by the Constitution from intermeddling with religious institutions, their doctrines, discipline, or exercises. This results not only from the provision that no law shall be made respecting the establishment, or free exercise, of religion, but from that also which reserves to the states the powers not delegated to the U.S. Certainly no power to prescribe any religious exercise, or to assume authority in religious discipline, has been delegated to the general government. It must then rest with the states, as far as it can be in any human authority.[54]

Jefferson never completely recovered from the campaign of 1800. Nor has his reputation today. How ironic that some individuals and organizations appeal to Jefferson as the progenitor of a modern secularism that would separate religion from government. That's what his archenemy William Linn said in 1800. Years later, in a letter to De Witt Clinton, a Republican ally in New York, the president strongly denied that he had ever made such a statement or desired a "government without religion." That was a "lie" that he attributed to Linn.[55] The separation he envisioned was between church and state, not religion and government; and he was nothing if not precise about his use of language. And that separation, he argued, was beneficial to religion and the churches. "I do not believe it is for the interest of religion," he wrote Miller, "to invite the civil magistrate to direct it's exercises, it's discipline, or it's doctrines; nor of the religious societies that the general government should be invested with the power of effecting any uniformity of time or matter among them."[56] But that separation did not banish God from the public square.

Jefferson's religion was both private and public. In both contexts, expressions of belief and prayer came easily to him. Shortly before his old friend John Page died in 1808, Jefferson wrote privately to him: "God bless you, and give you health of days, until he shall do better for you."[57] As president, his public messages to Congress were matter-of-fact statements that dealt with foreign trade, diplomatic relations, the federal debt, Indian affairs, and the like, but invariably, they included a reference to God's providential care of the United States. Referring to his own retirement in his last such message, Jefferson concluded, "I carry with me the consolation of a firm persuasion that Heaven has in store for our beloved country long ages to come of prosperity and happiness."[58]

NOTES

1. Robert J. Imholt, "Timothy Dwight, Federalist Pope of Connecticut," *New England Quarterly* 73 (September 2000): 386–411. See also Colin Wells, *The Devil and Doctor Dwight: Satire and Theology in the Early American Republic* (Chapel Hill, N.C., 2002).

2. The text of the letter to Jefferson is in Daniel L. Dreisbach, *Thomas Jefferson and the Wall of Separation between Church and State* (New York, 2002), 142–44. Dreisbach offers the most complete treatment of this event.

3. TJ to Messrs. Nehemiah Dodge, Ephraim Robbins, and Stephen S. Nelson, a Committee of the Danbury Baptist Association in the State of Connecticut, January 1, 1802, Presidential Papers Microfilm, Thomas Jefferson Papers, Manuscript Division, Library of Congress, Washington D.C. [hereafter, DLC], ser. 1, reel 25, November 15, 1801–March 31, 1802. Also http://memory.loc.gov/ammem/collections/jefferson_papers/.

4. *Reynolds v. United States*, 98 U.S. 145 (1878). For the background to this decision, see Donald L. Drakeman, "The Church Historians Who Made the First Amendment What It Is Today," *Religion and American Culture: A Journal of Interpretation* 17 (2007): 27–56.

5. *Everson v. Board of Education*, 330 U.S. 1, 39 (1947); *McCollum v. Board of Education*, 333 U.S. 203 (1948). For the significance of these decisions, see Philip Hamburger, *Separation of Church and State* (Cambridge, Mass., 2002), 454–78.

6. H. R. McIlwaine, ed., *Journals of the House of Burgesses of Virginia, 1618–58/59* (Richmond, Va., 1915), 13; William Waller Hening, ed., *The Statutes at Large: Being a Collection of All the Laws of Virginia, from the First Session of the Legislature in the Year 1619*, 13 vols. (Richmond, Va., 1809–23), 1:114.

7. Alexander Whitaker, *Good News from Virginia* (London, 1613), A5. Crashaw furnished the dedication to this work. For Crashaw's perspective and the importance of religion to the early settlement of Virginia, see Perry Miller, *Errand into the Wilderness* (Cambridge, Mass., 1956), 99–140.

8. For a superb study of Virginia's colonial church, see John K. Nelson, *A Blessed Company: Parishes, Parsons, and Parishioners in Anglican Virginia, 1690–1776* (Chapel Hill, N.C., 2001).

9. Rosalie Edith Davis, ed., *Fredericksville Parish Vestry Book, 1742–1787* (Manchester, Mo., 1978), November 25, 1767, 86.

10. James Maury, *To Christians of Every Denomination among Us, Especially Those of the Established Church, an Address . . .* (Annapolis, Md., 1771), 31. Evans Imprint, 1st ser., no. 42253.

11. See Nelson, *Blessed Company*, 187–210; Edward L. Bond, *Damned Souls in a Tobacco Colony: Religion in Seventeenth-Century Virginia* (Macon, Ga., 2000); and Bond, "Anglican Theology and Devotion in James Blair's Virginia, 1685–1743: Private Piety in the Public Church," *Virginia Magazine of History and Biography* [hereafter, *VMHB*] 104, no. 3 (1996): 313–40.

12. The best brief exposition of Jefferson's personal religion and its development is Eugene R. Sheridan's "Introduction," in *Jefferson's Extracts from the Gospels: "The Philosophy of Jesus" and "The Life and Morals of Jesus"* (in *Papers of Thomas Jefferson*, 2nd ser., ed. Dickinson W. Adams, which has been slightly revised and published as Sheridan, *Jefferson and Religion* [Charlottesville, Va., 1998]). Also helpful are Edwin S. Gaustad, *Sworn on the Altar of God: A Religious Biography of Thomas Jefferson* (Grand Rapids, Mich., 1996), and Charles B. Sanford, *The Religious Life of Thomas Jefferson* (Charlottesville, Va., 1984).

13. Henry S. Randall, *The Life of Thomas Jefferson*, 3 vols. (New York, 1858), 3:555. Two clergymen were present at his marriage to Martha Wayles Skelton in 1772 (Malone, *Jefferson and His Time*, 1:159–60). Jefferson carefully recorded the births, marriages, and deaths of his children in his personal copy of the Episcopal Book of Common Prayer (ibid., 430, 434). For examples of Jefferson's attendance at religious services and contributions to the Episcopal Church, see *Jefferson's Memorandum Books: Accounts, with Legal Records and Miscellany, 1767–1826*, 2 vols. (in *Papers of Thomas Jefferson*, 2nd ser., ed. James A. Bear Jr. and Lucia C. Stanton [Princeton, N.J., 1997], 1:529, 613; 2:821, 1051, 1138). When church tithes ended, he led the subscription drives for his local clergyman, Charles Clay, and the parish clerk in 1777. Two years later, he wrote a glowing testimonial for Clay as his rector (Jefferson, *Papers*, 2:6–9, 3:67). As Virginia's wartime governor in 1779, he issued a "Proclamation Appointing a Day of Thanksgiving and Prayer" (ibid., 3:177–79). He was an early and generous benefactor of the Bible Society of Virginia (Bear and Stanton, eds.,

Jefferson's Memorandum Books, 2:1297); in the 1820s he contributed to the support of the new Episcopal minister in Charlottesville and paid the tuition for his three grandsons to study with him (ibid., 2:1362–1412, passim); and he provided religious funeral services for members of his family and others buried at Monticello (ibid., 1:370–71, 415; 2:1029, 1268, 1279, 1399).

14. Thomas Jefferson to [Benjamin Holt Rice], August 10, 1823, Virginia Historical Society, Richmond (photocopy of original in the Pierpont Morgan Library, New York, N.Y). While president, he contributed $100 in 1805 to build "an Episcopal church" in Washington, D.C. (Bear and Stanton, eds., *Jefferson's Memorandum Books,* 2:1154), and Jefferson subscribed $200 in 1824 for "an Episcopalian church" in Charlottesville (ibid., 2:1403).

15. Thomas Jefferson, "The Autobiography of Thomas Jefferson," in *The Life and Selected Writings of Thomas Jefferson,* ed. Adrienne Koch and William Peden (New York, 1944), 4; Malone, *Jefferson and His Time,* 1:40–45 (quotation at 44). Maury's cousin described him as "much beloved by his parishioners." See Peter Fontaine Jr. to Moses Fontaine, June 7, 1754, in Ann Maury, *Memoirs of a Huguenot Family* (New York, 1853; rpt., Baltimore, 1973), 363. For Maury's biography and approach to education, see Helen Duprey Bullock, ed., "A Dissertation on Education in the Form of a Letter from James Maury to Robert Jackson, July 17, 1762," *Papers of the Albemarle County Historical Society* 2 (1941–42): 36–60.

16. Malone, *Jefferson and His Time,* 1:40; TJ to James Maury, July 20, 1804, DLC.

17. TJ to William Wirt, August 14, 1814, Jefferson Papers of the University of Virginia, 1732–1828, Main Series 3 (microfilm), roll 7: July 1813–17. A full account of the Parson's Cause may be found in Robert Douthat Meade, *Patrick Henry: Patriot in the Making* (Philadelphia, 1957), 114–38.

18. James Maury to Commissary Dawson, October 10, 1759, in Papers of Patrick Henry, DLC.

19. Maury, *To Christians of Every Denomination,* 3; TJ to Peter Carr, August 10, 1787, in Jefferson, *Papers,* 12:15, 17.

20. James Maury to [Thomas Dawson], October 6, 1755, in "Letters of Patrick Henry, Sr., Samuel Davies, James Maury, Edwin Conway and George Trask," *William and Mary Quarterly,* 2nd ser., 1 (October 1921): 278 [hereafter, *WMQ*].

21. Maury, *To Christians of Every Denomination,* 33; Thomas Jefferson, *Notes on the State of Virginia,* ed. William Peden (Chapel Hill, N.C., 1955), 159.

22. Maury, *To Christians of Every Denomination,* 37, 42.

23. TJ to William Preston, August 18, 1768, in Jefferson, *Papers,* 1:23. Fontaine did not receive the position but remained as rector of Ware Parish in Gloucester until his death in 1795. See Joan R. Gundersen, *The Anglican Ministry in Virginia, 1723–1766: A Study of a Social Class* (New York, 1989), 252. For

an example of Fontaine's sermon style, see the except from the funeral service he performed for Frances Burwell Page, John Page's first wife, in William Meade, *Old Churches, Ministers and Families of Virginia,* 2 vols. (Philadelphia, 1910), 1:334–35.

24. Davis, ed., *Fredericksville Parish Vestry Book,* November 25, 1767, November 30, 1770, pp. 86, 88, 96.

25. James Ogilvie to TJ, March 28, 1770; TJ to Thomas Adams, July 11, 1770; TJ to Peyton Randolph, July 23, 1770; TJ to James Ogilvie, February 20, 1771; Ogilvie to TJ, April 26, 1771, all in Jefferson, *Papers,* 1:38–40, 48–51, 62–64, 67–68; Gundersen, *Anglican Ministry in Virginia,* 272. Ogilvie was eventually ordained and returned to Virginia to serve first in Henrico Parish and then as rector of Westover Church, though in 1778 he would be banished as a loyalist.

26. TJ to Robert Skipwith, August 3, 1771, in Jefferson, *Papers,* 1:76–81.

27. Edmund Randolph, *History of Virginia,* ed. Arthur H. Shaffer (Charlottesville, Va., 1970), 203. For Jefferson's account of these events, see Jefferson, "Autobiography," 8–10; "Resolution of the House of Burgesses Designating a Day of Fasting and Prayer," and TJ and John Walker to the Inhabitants of the Parish of St. Anne, in Jefferson, *Papers,* 1:105–7, 116–17.

28. "Draft of Instructions to the Virginia Delegates in the Continental Congress," in Jefferson, *Papers,* 1:121–37 (quotations at 134, 135).

29. Declaration of the Causes and Necessity for Taking Up Arms, ibid., 1:187–219 (quotations at 202, 203).

30. Jefferson's "original Rough draught" of the Declaration of Independence, ibid., 423–28 (quotations at 423).

31. John Adams to Abigail Adams, August 14, 1776, in *Adams Family Correspondence,* ed. L. H. Butterfield et al. (Cambridge, Mass., 1963–), 2:96.

32. Thomas Jefferson, Second Inaugural Address, March 4, 1805, in *A Compilation of the Messages and Papers of the Presidents, 1789–1897,* 10 vols., comp. James D. Richardson (Washington, D.C., 1896–99), 1:382.

33. Robert N. Bellah, "Civil Religion in America," in *American Civil Religion,* ed. Russell E. Richey and Donald G. Jones (New York, 1974), 21–44.

34. Hening, ed., *Statutes at Large,* 9:111–12.

35. William T. Hutchinson et al., eds., *The Papers of James Madison,* 17 vols. (Chicago, 1962–91), 1:174; for the Declaration of Rights, see Daniel L. Dreisbach, "George Mason's Pursuit of Religious Liberty in Revolutionary Virginia," *VMHB* 108, no. 1 (2000): 5–44.

36. Jefferson, "Autobiography," 41.

37. "Subscription to Support a Clergyman in Charlottesville," in Jefferson, *Papers,* 2:6–8.

38. "A Bill for Establishing Religious Freedom," ibid., 545–53 (quotations at 545, 546).

39. For the legislative action on the religion bills in 1779, see Thomas E. Buckley, S.J., *Church and State in Revolutionary Virginia, 1776–1787* (Charlottesville, Va., 1977), 46–62.

40. Jefferson, *Notes on the State of Virginia,* 159, 160.

41. Hening, ed., *Statutes at Large,* 11:532–37.

42. Accomack County, October 28, 1785; Miscellaneous Petition, November 2, 1785, in Religious Petitions, 1774–1802, presented to the General Assembly of Virginia (microfilm), Library of Virginia, Richmond, Va. For the legislative history of these sessions and the passage of Jefferson's Statute, see Buckley, *Church and State,* 89–165.

43. Thomas E. Buckley, S.J., "Evangelicals Triumphant: The Baptists' Assault on the Virginia Glebes, 1786–1801," *WMQ,* 3rd ser., 45 (January 1988): 33–69.

44. See, for example, Stephen J. Farnsworth and S. Robert Lichter, *The Nightly News Nightmare: Television's Coverage of U.S. Presidential Elections, 1988–2004,* 2nd ed. (Lanham, Md., 2007).

45. [William Loughton Smith], *The Pretensions of Thomas Jefferson to the Presidency Examined; and the Charges Against John Adams Refuted. Addressed to the Citizens of America in General; and Particularly to the Electors of the President* (United States [Philadelphia?], 1796), 36–40; Jefferson, *Notes on the State of Virginia,* 157, 159; Malone, *Jefferson and His Time,* 3:282. For Smith's politics, see George C. Rogers, *Evolution of a Federalist: William Loughton Smith of Charleston (1758–1812)* (Columbia, S.C., 1962).

46. *Gazette of the United States and Daily Advertiser* [Philadelphia], August 30, 1800. See also Constance B. Schulz, " 'Of Bigotry in Politics and Religion': Jefferson's Religion, the Federalist Press, and the Syllabus," *VMHB* 91 (January 1983): 73–91.

47. *Federal Gazette and Baltimore Daily Advertiser,* August 4, 12, 1800.

48. [William Linn], *Serious Considerations on the Election of a President: Addressed to the Citizens of the United States* (Trenton, N.J., 1800).

49. *Connecticut Courant* [Hartford], September 8, 1800. For a contemporary comment on the Sunday event, see R. Troup to Rufus King, October 2, 1798, in *The Life and Correspondence of Rufus King . . . ,* 6 vols., ed. Charles R. King (New York, 1894–1900), 2:432.

50. TJ to Benjamin Rush, September 23, 1800, in Adams, ed., *Jefferson's Extracts from the Gospels,* 320.

51. Thomas Jefferson, First Inaugural Address, March 4, 1801, in Richardson, comp., *Compilation of the Messages and Papers of the Presidents,* 1:322. For favorable Federalist reaction, see George Cabot to Rufus King, March 20, 1801; and R. Troup to Rufus King, March 23, 1801, both in King, ed., *Life and Correspondence of Rufus King,* 3:407–9. See also Robert M. Johnstone Jr., *Jefferson and the Presidency: Leadership in the Young Republic* (Ithaca, N.Y., 1978).

52. James H. Hutson, "Thomas Jefferson's Letter to the Danbury Baptists: A Controversy Rejoined," *WMQ*, 3rd ser., 56 (October 1999): 775–90 (quotations at 783); and Hutson, *Religion and the Founding of the American Republic* (Washington, D.C., 1998), 84–97.

53. Thomas E. Buckley, S.J., "Reflections on a Wall," *WMQ*, 3rd. ser., 56 (October 1999): 799.

54. TJ to Samuel Miller, January 23, 1808, in Jefferson, *Works*, 11:7.

55. TJ to De Witt Clinton, May 24, 1807, ibid., 10:404–5.

56. TJ to Samuel Miller, January 23, 1808, ibid., 11:8.

57. TJ to Page, September 6, 1808, Jefferson Papers, UVa, Series 3, roll 6.

58. Thomas Jefferson, Eighth Annual Message, November 8, 1808, in Richardson, comp., *Compilation of the Messages and Papers of the Presidents*, 1:456.

Jan Ellen Lewis

Jefferson and Women

Thomas Jefferson's attitudes about women were remarkably conventional, so conventional, for the most part, that to describe them is essentially to provide an account of the standard views about sexual difference and women's roles held by men of his time, place, and social standing. To be sure, different men (and women, for that matter) had somewhat different ideas: the views and practices of a Jefferson, a Hamilton, an Adams, or a Franklin are so different, and so well known, that it may be sufficient merely to mention them and a few details of their lives to make the point that not all men of the same class and status share identical views and experiences.

Think only of Hamilton's acknowledgment, in embarrassing detail, of his affair with Maria Reynolds. Or John Adams's remarkable partnership with his remarkable wife, Abigail. Or Benjamin Franklin's common-law marriage to a woman who raised as her own the baby that Franklin had fathered out of wedlock only a short time earlier. Or, finally, Thomas Jefferson, who married rather late—at age twenty-nine—but, by all accounts, remarkably happily. After his wife died, from the complications of childbirth, after just ten years of marriage, Jefferson entered into a thirty-eight-year liaison with his slave Sally Hemings, herself the half-sister of his deceased wife.

Yet to say that within a culture, people can behave quite differently does not add a whit to the knowledge that all historians already possess. The varieties of human behavior are infinite. The challenge for anyone who would like to say something significant about Jefferson is that, although the particulars of his personal life are fascinating, his attitudes were almost wholly conventional. It is tempting, then, to provide a biography, to explore in detail Jefferson's experiences with women—not only his marriage and his liaison, but his embarrassing assault on Betsy Walker (the wife of his neighbor and friend from childhood, John Walker), his puzzling affair, or nonaffair, with Maria Cosway, his complex attachments to his white daughters and granddaughters. I am going to resist that temptation, however, for several reasons. First, this Jefferson was already rather well known to us, from the work of Andrew Burstein and others, and he has become even better known in Annette Gordon-Reed's recent biography of the Hemings family, which tells us a great deal about Jefferson's personal life.[1]

More important, I am reluctant to talk wholly about the private, personal Jefferson. To do so risks accepting without question Jefferson's own belief, forcefully stated, that private life is private and has no bearing upon public matters. On his deathbed, Jefferson told his namesake and favorite grandson that the insults of his political enemies had never really hurt him: "[H]e had not considered them as abusing him; they had never known *him*. They had created an imaginary being clothed with odious attributes, to whom they had given his name."[2] In a volume such as this, which considers Jefferson and religion, politics, Indians, slaves, ideas, and history, it is not helpful to say that either the private Jefferson or the public one was the real *him*, and the other Jeffersons were, by implication, imaginary or false ones.

I am interested in intersections, the places where the various Jeffersons met, whether imaginary or real Jeffersons—to accept, for a moment, Jefferson's own construction—and especially the places where Jefferson's ideas about women and gender intersected his ideas about politics and race. But here we come back to the dilemma with which I started: Jefferson's views were so conventional that to describe them is, to a significant extent, to describe the evolution of conventional notions of woman's sphere in the Revolutionary era.

So I must beg your indulgence while I retrace a history that has, by now, become quite familiar to all who know the outlines of the Jefferson biography. It becomes interesting, however, when it intersects with Jefferson's thought more generally—but it will take us a few moments to get there.

Let me start, then, with the young Jefferson, the one we meet in the first pages of the first volume of the Boyd edition of *The Papers of Thomas Jefferson*. Of course, to meet Jefferson in this way is to confront a puzzle: how does this apparently conventional young member of the Virginia gentry so quickly become the patriot leader? One day, Jefferson is commiserating with his friends about his troubles with the ladies, and the next, he is writing *A Summary View of the Rights of British America*. I exaggerate only slightly. The text of *A Summary View* begins on page 121 of the first volume of the *Papers*, and although there are a few documents that touch on politics in the preceding pages, and a few pieces of correspondence from Jefferson's legal practice, most of the documents in the first hundred pages or so of the volume are letters between Jefferson and his male friends. Of these, a significant number concern the women that Jefferson and his friends were courting.

So, how did this conventional young man virtually overnight become—to use one of the clichés that are applied to Jefferson—the apostle of liberty? Phrasing it that way, however, suggests that the mature, political Jefferson bore little or no relationship to the younger, more conventional one, that Jefferson had to emerge from his love-struck youth before he could become a political leader, like a larva becoming a butterfly. In their youthful letters, however, Jefferson and his friends were defining themselves as men, as the kind of men they would be: this was the work that the correspondence performed. These young members of the gentry were situating themselves in their society and in relationship to one another and defining their society and their place in it. The women, who themselves were never correspondents, were merely incidental, markers of the positions occupied by the men.[3]

Let me try to clarify what I mean by focusing, for a moment, on several of the early letters. The tone of Jefferson's second surviving letter, to his good friend John Page, is jocular. In it, Jefferson compares himself to Job. He is "in a house surrounded with enemies"—the mice who have chewed up his papers and his silk garters, and the rain, leaking through the roof, which had soaked and ruined the silhouette of Rebecca Burwell that he had placed in his pocket watch. The silhouette was a gift from Rebecca, and its destruction has left Jefferson disconsolate, in three languages. He assures Page, however, that "although the picture be defaced there is so lively an image of her imprinted in my mind that I shall think of her too often I fear for my peace of mind." Note that Jefferson is performing a role—the romantic lover—for his friend Page, not for the female object, or supposed object, of his affection.

Jefferson moved quickly from despair to animation, however, begging Page for gossip and imploring him to "remember" him "affectionately to all the young ladies of my acquaintance." Now Page must perform Jefferson's heterosexuality for the young women in their acquaintance. Jefferson gave his friend instructions on just which pleasantry to convey to each young woman, a long paragraph of instructions that Jefferson concluded with one further injunction: "Tell—tell—In short tell them all ten thousand things more than either you or I can now or ever shall think of as long as we live."[4] Making an impression on young women, courting them, was entirely performance—telling them whatever they wanted to hear. The content of the words, which would be of critical importance once Jefferson was drafting Revolutionary pamphlets and petitions, was irrelevant.

In the letters Jefferson exchanged with his friends, filled with chatter about young women, he was trying out and trying to make sense of the world of heterosexual relations. Young Jefferson seemed obsessed by women, but, at the same time, almost indifferent to them. Rebecca Burwell appears in his letters as Miss Burwell, Miss Becca Burwell, R.B., Miss R.B., Belinda, ἁδνίλέβ (that is, Belinda spelled backwards, and the Roman letters turned into Greek), and, most simply, SHE. In Jefferson's letters, she is everywhere but nowhere—a plenitude of pet names, her chief quality her ability to call forth Jefferson's ability to multiply her names. These secret names and endearments, however, were not for her, a code shared between lovers, but for Jefferson's male friends. The only meaningful discourse was that between men. Women were the language that men shared. They bonded as men engaged in the daunting rituals of courtship, in the process making themselves legible to each other by puzzling over the illegibility of women.

Jefferson's friends seemed possessed by a mania to marry. "You say you are determined to be married as soon as possible: and advise me to do the same," Jefferson wrote one friend. And after telling Page that some of their friends were engaged, he asked Page, "Why cannot you and I be married too . . . when and to whom we would chuse? Do you think it would cause any such mighty disorders among the planets? . . . I verily beleive [*sic*] Page that I shall die soon, and yet I can give no other reason for it but that I am tired with living."[5] Here was the problem: Jefferson and his friends were in training to be masters of their universe, not only their plantations but also their local governments, and, in Jefferson's case, also a leader in the Revolutionary movement. And yet they could not, as much as they wanted, marry when and whom they chose. They were at the mercy of the young women they courted. "What do you think of my affair," Jefferson asked Page, "or what would you advise me to do?" Rebecca Burwell had turned Jefferson into Hamlet: "Had I better stay here and do nothing, or go down and do less"—that is, "receive my sentence, and be no longer in suspence: but, reason says if you go and your attempt proves unsuccessful you will be ten times more wretched than ever."[6] And so Jefferson did nothing, and Rebecca Burwell married Jacquelin Ambler instead. No wonder Jefferson seemed depressed: his future, he thought, was out of his hands.

Jefferson, of course, eventually married. He later described the ten years he and his wife had together before her death as a period of "unchecquered happiness."[7] He had found a woman, a young widow, Martha Wayles Skelton, whom he could love deeply and who also brought him a handsome fortune. There is a hint in his letters that the wedding almost did not come off. Nine years after his first letter to Page, Jefferson was still worrying about marrying. He mentioned a friend who was "wishing to take to himself a wife; and nothing obstructs it but the unfeeling temper of a parent who delays, perhaps refuses to approve her daughter's choice." Jefferson found himself in a similar situation, "not from the frowardness of parents, nor perhaps want of feeling in the fair one, but from other causes as unpliable to my wishes as these."[8] The precise impediment is not clear; it is evident, though, that once again, Jefferson found that something stood in the way of his getting what he wanted.[9]

It is in this context—a young man's quest to establish himself—that Jefferson's early, gossipy letters should be understood. Courtship was a competitive enterprise, not entirely unlike the political one in which Jefferson would later make such a mark. As Joanne B. Freeman has noted, Jefferson was an avid gossip, and if the chit-chat about who was courting whom did not serve as "conduits for other people's aggression" in the way that political gossip did, it certainly revealed an underlying anxiety about who was getting ahead and who was being left behind.[10] And, as he would later, when insisting that he was sick and tired of politics and wanted nothing more than to retire to his mountaintop, from time to time Jefferson proclaimed himself weary of the whole enterprise of courting the ladies. In one of his more gossipy letters ("You have heard I suppose that J. Page is courting Fanny Burwell. W. Bland, and Betsy Yates are to be married thursday se'nnight") Jefferson denied not only that he was a gossip ("Who told you that I reported you was courting Miss Dandridge and Miss Dangerfeild?") but that he even planned to marry. "Many and great are the comforts of a single state." True, "St. Paul . . . says that it is better to be married than to burn. Now I presume," Jefferson joked, "that if that apostle had known that providence would at an after day be so kind to any particular set of people as to furnish them with other means of extinguishing their fire than those of matrimony, he would have earnestly recommended them to their practice."[11] Who needed to court young heiresses when more willing women could be had for a considerably lower price? In this gossipy letter, Jefferson's anxieties about the mercenary nature of the relationship between the sexes came through.

Once he married, Jefferson's anxieties about sex and gender abated, and he soon made his stunning entrance on the political scene. By marrying a beautiful and affluent young woman, Jefferson was able to settle down, in several senses of the term. Whatever his earlier anxieties about marrying, he found great joy in domesticity, and it became for him, even after his wife's death, the measure of human happiness. Jefferson moved, then, from a kind of conventional misogyny to a kind of conventional valorization of domesticity. We see this appreciation for the domestic life not only in Jefferson's reminiscences about his married life but also in his subsequent contrast of the satisfactions of private life and the pure and unabated miseries of the public sphere. Not only was his marriage one of "unchequered happiness," but his wife's death in "a single event wiped away all my plans and left me a blank which I had not the spirits to fill up."[12] Twenty years earlier, the anxieties of courtship had left Jefferson depressed and listless; now it was the death of his beloved wife. Jefferson had grown up.

Jefferson carried this image of happy domestic life with him for the rest of his days; it became a touchstone for him. Jefferson's comparisons of the miseries of public service with the rewards of family life are too well known to require more than a brief mention. "It is in the love of one's family only," he once told his younger daughter, "that heartfelt happiness is known." In government, he found "every thing which can be disgusting," at home with his family, "every thing which is pleasurable to me." His protestations notwithstanding, Jefferson spent most of his adult life in public service; his family—and his idea of family, as those who knew his real self and as his only source of "heartfelt happiness"—anchored him, making his public service possible. I have written about this aspect of Jefferson's life and thought elsewhere.[13] For our purposes we should note only that Jefferson's views about family life were wholly conventional, and also that a happy marriage enabled Jefferson to shed his early misogyny, or at least rub off its sharp edges.

There is, I believe, only one other period in Jefferson's life when his misogyny percolated to the surface. That was when he was in France, between 1784 and 1789, serving as the new nation's minister. Once again, Jefferson was single, engaged in an intense flirtation with the unhappily married artist Maria Cosway and perhaps beginning what would turn out to be a long liaison with his slave Sally Hemings. Whether owing to his own unsettled domestic life, or because he was living in a foreign culture, or some combination of the two, Jefferson had a lot to say about women, in particular about their appropriate roles in society. Some of these comments reveal if not a streak of misogyny, at least an anxiety about female sexuality and the risks that it posed for both the male body and the body politic.

Jefferson made it quite clear to anyone who asked that Europe was no place for a young man. The only question was how old he had to be before he could travel safely. John and Abigail Adams's daughter Nabby remembered Jefferson's saying that "no man was fit to come abroad until 35," while he told Walker Maury that "no American should come to Europe under 30 years of age."[14] He told Charles Thomson that he did not know "one good purpose on earth which can be effected by a young gentleman's coming here." He worried in particular about one of their young friends. "I am in hopes he is discreet and that you need not fear the corruption of his morals." Jefferson worried that such young men might form "a connection, as is the fashion here, which he might be unwilling to shake off when it shall be proper for him to return to his own country [is that what Jefferson did with Maria Cosway, shake her off?] and which might detain him disadvantageously here." The temptations of Paris, "where beauty is a begging in every street," were often too great.[15] The problem, quite obviously, was women, beautiful women. One sees here a glimmer of the young Jefferson, concerned that men make appropriate marriages in America. A European dalliance—a European woman—might get in the way.

Jefferson warned young men directly and even more explicitly. When John Banister Jr. asked Jefferson's advice about where to study in Europe, Jefferson told him to go to William and Mary. England, with its "drinking, horse-racing and boxing," was bad enough, but the rest of Europe was even worse. There a young man "is led by the strongest of all the human passions into a spirit for female intrigue destructive of his own and others happiness, or a passion for whores destructive of his health." Moreover, "in both cases," he "learns to consider fidelity to the marriage bed as an ungentlemanly practice and inconsistent with happiness." And once again, the fundamental threat comes from women, as the young man "recollects the voluptuary dress and arts of the European women and pities and despises the chaste affections and simplicity of those of his own country."[16] Jefferson told Walker Maury that a young man could not come to Europe without threat to his "virtue . . . health and . . . happiness."[17] One cannot help thinking that Jefferson himself must have been sorely tempted. For our purposes here, what is more important is the intensity of Jefferson's feeling that beautiful European temptresses threatened the happiness and health of young American men. The fault was entirely with the women.

To be sure, this sort of misogyny was not unusual. It was, as Hanna Fenichel Pitkin has pointed out, a staple of republican thought.[18] And although Jefferson's political thought was in many ways fundamentally liberal—his belief in the superiority of private life, for example—it also incorporated a misogynist streak, one that he expressed in republican terms. This misogyny, I have tried to suggest, became most pronounced in those periods in his life when he was unattached and either beset by or perhaps was himself besetting women. And when he was in France, it became embedded in a republican critique of monarchy. If we return to Jefferson's letter to John Banister Jr., we can see how the pieces fit together. When a young American man such as Banister goes to Europe, Jefferson warned, "he is fascinated with the privileges of the European aristocrats, and sees with abhorrence the lovely equality which the poor enjoys with the rich in his own country: he contracts a partiality for aristocracy or monarchy." While acquiring manners that were superficially pleasing, the young man "acquires a fondness for European luxury and dissipation and a contempt for the simplicity of his own country." And, of course, "he is led by the strongest of all the human passions into a spirit for female intrigue . . . or a passion for whores."[19] Hence, aristocracy was seductive and whorish, and seductive women were aristocratic: aristocracy, luxury, dissipation, and women who will destroy a man's health and happiness are all of a piece.

Jefferson's critique of the Old World was deeply gendered, which meant that he could not help depicting America as a gender utopia. In a well-known letter to Anne Willing Bingham, a beautiful young woman who was married to one of the wealthiest men in Philadelphia, he compared the "empty bustle of Paris" with the "tranquil pleasures of America," each of which he embodied as a woman. In Paris, "*madame*" was lucky to make it out of bed before noon, perhaps squeezing in a little visiting before having her hair done. Then came more visiting, supper, and after that, "cards; and after cards, bed; to rise at noon the next day, and to tread, like a mill horse, the same trodden circle over again. Thus the days of life are consumed, one by one, without an object beyond the present moment." Jefferson drew a contrast with America, where—and remember that he was writing to one of his country's wealthiest women—"the society of your husband, the fond cares of the children, the arrangements of the house, the improvements of the grounds, fill every moment with a healthy and an useful activity." Utility was the measure of a healthy society, and utility consisted in serving the needs of a woman's family and her social circle more generally. Proper gender relations made American society properly bourgeois. "The intervals of leisure are filled by the society of real friends, whose affections are not thinned to cob-web, by being spread over a thousand objects." Here Jefferson set out a vision of the properly functioning society and made women its anchor.[20] "Be you my dear," Jefferson once instructed his elder daughter, not yet twenty years old and just married into a family beset by turmoil, "the link of love, union, and peace for the whole family."[21]

Jefferson, of course, was working toward a conventional understanding of sex roles, one that assigned politics to men and domestic life to women. As I have argued elsewhere, this gendered order was deeply important to Jefferson psychologically: he needed his family to sustain him and to provide him with a refuge from the conflicts of politics.[22]

This gendered order was also a cornerstone of Jefferson's politics and his political economy as well. Let us begin with his politics. Jefferson took it as a given that women did not belong in politics. In France, he complained to Anne Willing Bingham in the spring of 1788, "All the world is now politically mad. Men, women, children talk nothing else. . . . the women of this capital, some on foot, some on horses, & some in carriages hunting pleasure in the streets, in routs & assemblies, and forgetting that they have left it behind them in their nurseries." This was pandemonium. The contrast between the Parisian women and American ones, who "have the good sense to value domestic happiness above all other," was "a comparison of Amazons and Angels."[23]

Jefferson's tone with his female friend was lighthearted; he no doubt thought he was being pleasant, perhaps even flirtatious. When he brought up the same subject with George Washington half a year later, however, the tone was serious. Jefferson was troubled by "the influence of women in the government." As France moved toward revolution, he worried—and remember that he is writing to the man who will shortly become the first president of the United States—that French attempts at reform would come to naught because of it. "The manners of the nation allow them to visit, alone, all persons in office, to sollicit the affairs of the husband, family, or friends." He had no such worries for his own country, in which, "fortunately for the happiness of the sex itself," female influence "does not endeavor to extend itself in our country beyond the domestic line."[24] In political life as in social, the United States was a gender utopia, a new and improved world, for men, and, Jefferson thought, for women too.

Let us turn, now, to Jefferson's political economy. His European travels gave him an opportunity to observe society in the countryside as well as the city, and there, too, he saw the baneful effects of Old World despotism. As Jefferson crossed the Rhine from Holland to

Germany, he found that the "transition from ease and opulence to extreme poverty is remarkable. . . . The soil and climate are the same; the governments alone differ." Moreover, "With the poverty, the fear also of slaves is visible in the faces of the Prussian subjects." In the villages he visited, "The women do everything. . . . They dig the earth, plough, saw, cut and split wood, row, tow the batteaux, &c." It disturbed Jefferson to see white women engaging in such heavy labor. He saw the same thing in eastern France, and it led him to meditate on the proper roles for men and women. "While one considers" women "as useful and rational companions, one cannot forget that they are also objects of our pleasures; nor can they ever forget it. While employed in dirt and drudgery, some tag of a ribbon, some ring, or bit of bracelet, earbob or necklace, or something of that kind, will show that the desire of pleasing is never suspended in them. It is an honorable circumstance for man, that the first moment he is at his ease, he allots the internal employments to his female partner, and takes the external on himself. And this circumstance, or its reverse, is a pretty good indication that a people are, or are not at their ease." By "ease" Jefferson meant free from the necessity of toil: no proper society would make its women work outdoors, doing backbreaking labor, if it had any real choice in the matter.

Jefferson's ruminations took him back to America and one of his favorite topics, the Native Americans. "Among the Indians . . . every Indian man is a soldier or warrior, and the whole body of warriors constitute a standing army, always employed in war or hunting. To support that army, there remain no laborers but the women." But "here"—in Europe—"is so heavy a military establishment, that the civil part of the nation is reduced to women only. But this is a barbarous perversion of the natural destination of the two sexes. Women are formed by nature for attentions, not for hard labor."[25]

When he returned to America, Jefferson tried to get Indians to adopt "natural" gender roles. He hoped that once game became scarce through overhunting, Indian men would willingly take up farming and free their women for work indoors. Once Indians became farmers, everyone would benefit. "When they withdraw themselves to the culture of a small piece of land, they will perceive how useless to them are their extensive forests, and will be willing to pare them off from time to time in exchange for necessaries for their farms and families."[26]

We may be stunned by how self-serving Jefferson's vision was: as Indian men became farmers, they would happily sell parcels of their land in order to purchase American manufactured goods, at the same time tying themselves into global commercial networks and satisfying the land-lust of the growing hordes of white settlers. How convenient. Self-serving as this scheme might have been, at least Jefferson understood its inner logic, and, if pressed, he could have justified its underlying premises. After all, he believed that this sort of commerce, based on the family farm, created the conditions for peace and prosperity.

But, where, one wonders, did Jefferson imagine that slavery fit into this scheme? His ideal—and this is commonplace—was the freehold family farm.[27] In his travels through Europe, in his observations about Native Americans, and in his paeans to American self-sufficiency, he seemed to assume that men should work outdoors and women indoors, caring for the home and manufacturing cloth. In this context, the War of 1812 was actually a good thing. "Household manufacture is taking deep root with us," Jefferson told James Ronaldson in 1813. "I have a carding machine, two spinning machines, and looms with the flying shuttle." "Scarcely a family fails to clothe itself," he reported happily to Du Pont de Nemours, and to Philip Mazzei, he wrote, "We are getting the spinning machines into all our farm houses. I have nearly 100. spindles in operation for clothing our own family."[28] In only the last of these boasts about increased American self-sufficiency is there even a hint that anyone other than the farmwife and her daughters was doing the spinning, and even there the slippage is evident: we are getting spinning machines into all of our farmhouses; I have nearly a hundred spindles in operation to clothe my own family. Which farmhouse can contain a hundred spindles?

Jefferson, however, never directly confronted this contradiction.

Instead, he left the impression that industrious farm women were making cloth at home, liberating the United States from foreign dependency. Moreover, as David Waldstreicher has recently argued, Jefferson made home manufacture of cloth the measure of (white) female virtue, praising, for example, a Mrs. Mason, whose production of homespun during the War of 1812 made her "a more dangerous adversary to our British foes, than all our Generals." "Silence about slavery and its politics undergirds the celebration of a white woman's virtue," Waldstreicher argues.[29]

In this context, Jefferson's 1810 letter to Madison, in which he set out a scheme for providing every farm in Virginia with merino sheep, is quite extraordinary. Once again, I am touching on a subject—here, Jefferson's merino mania—that is well known. In this particular letter, we see several of Jefferson's characteristic obsessions come together: merino sheep, American economic self-sufficiency, and the breeding of animals (with talk of half-bloods, three-quarters bloods, and so on). In this particular scheme, Jefferson set out a plan that would put a merino ram in every county in the state in only seven years, and then, in only a year or two more, a ewe as well.[30] Unless one knew that the state Jefferson was discussing was Virginia, one would think that he was describing a plan to encourage the production of fine wool on family farms. The slippage is stunning.

Or is it? In another of his letters from Paris, this a long one to the South Carolinian William Drayton, Jefferson described his travels through the south of France, which, because its climate was, he thought, similar to that of South Carolina and Georgia, seemed to offer useful lessons. Jefferson closely examined the cultivation of rice, comparing the varieties native to different regions and trying to obtain samples. He was intrigued by accounts of a "dry rice" from Cochin-China, which not only was supposed to have a superior taste and appearance but also could grow on dry land. If it could "supplant" the varieties raised in the Deep South, "it would be a great happiness, as it would enable us to get rid of those ponds of stagnant water, so fatal to human health and life." We know, and Jefferson knew, that in America, rice was a slave crop. How do we know that Jefferson knew? Bear with me for a moment more.

Jefferson continued his descriptions of French agriculture. He recommended against viniculture: "It is a species of gambling." The caper, however, was worth considering. Most of the labor consisted of picking the capers, which had to be done every day from mid-summer to mid fall, "[b]ut this is the work of women and children." Jefferson considered this fact, the employment of women and children in relatively easy labor, to be an advantage. Thus, he recommended figs and mulberries. "Their culture, too, is by women and children, and, therefore, earnestly to be desired in countries where there are slaves. In these, the women and children are often employed in labors disproportioned to their sex and age. By presenting to the master objects of culture, easier and equally beneficial, all temptation to misemploy them would be removed, and the lot of this tender part of our species be much softened." Here, then, finally, was Jefferson's recognition that in America, slave women—this was the nature of slavery—worked outdoors. And here also is the assertion that slave women, and children, are, like white women, the "tender part of our species" and should be spared backbreaking labor. One of the objects of Jefferson's plans for agricultural reform was to lighten the labor of slave women, to make their condition closer to that of their white sisters.

Of all the plants that Jefferson observed, he was most enthusiastic about the olive tree, with which he hoped to "cover the southern States." If South Carolinians revered those who had introduced rice, "a plant which sows life and death with almost equal hand, what obligations would be due to him who should introduce the olive tree. . . . Were the owner of slaves to view it only as the means of bettering their condition, how much would he better that, by planting one of those trees for every slave he possessed!." In earnestly recommending the olive tree to his countrymen in South Carolina and Georgia, Jefferson noted that he himself had been "an eye witness to the blessings which this tree sheds on the poor."[31]

Jefferson's views on slavery are too well known to require analysis here. Suffice it to say that we most often think of him as a man caught on the horns of a dilemma of his own making. On the one hand, he understood—after all, he was one of the authors of the proposition—that human slavery was a violation of the principle of human equality. On the other hand, his racism and his political paralysis made it impossible for him to do anything more than free a handful of his own slaves. As Adam Rothman, Peter Onuf, and others have brilliantly shown, rather than confront this dilemma, Jefferson retreated into fanciful schemes for diffusion and colonization.[32]

It is certainly possible to consider Jefferson's ideas about mulberries and olive trees as equally fanciful. The South Carolina Lowcountry is not Provence. But in his agricultural schemes, we see the desire to improve slaves' working conditions and the recognition that labor in the rice swamps was "fatal to human health and life." We also see Jefferson's unhappy recognition that slavery typically required women to do what he considered men's work. Perhaps, he mused, the mulberry offered a way out.

Jefferson returned from France, then, with several things: a well-developed sense of the superiority of America, with its equality, simplicity, and proper gender relations; a plan for the amelioration of slavery; and one thing more—a slave mistress. It is impossible to know exactly when Jefferson entered into his liaison with Sally Hemings, but if the memoir of their son Madison, which has proved accurate in so many particulars, is to be credited, it was while the two of them were in Paris.[33] There is every indication that this was a long-term relationship, lasting perhaps until Jefferson's death in 1826.

And Jefferson left something in France, as well: the extremes of his misogyny. For the most part, his subsequent writings are free from the invective against political women and prostitutes and the hostility to women more generally that had risen to the surface twice earlier in his life, once when he was courting and then, later, when he was in France and unattached. Perhaps American women really were more chaste, as Jefferson suggested, and once he was home, he no longer had to deal with women who were more aggressive than he liked.

Or perhaps, once he returned to America with the woman who would turn out to be his lifelong companion, he settled down, and the anxieties that gave rise to his misogyny abated. The evidence for this hypothesis is at best tenuous. It consists almost entirely of a simple correlation: Jefferson's anxieties about women manifested themselves at those times when he was unattached. We do not see the same sort of intense misogyny again after Jefferson's return from France, which is also the time when he entered into his long relationship with Sally Hemings.

It is very difficult, of course, to know what their relationship was like. We have very little to go on: their son Madison's brief memoirs, a few comments by others, the details that can be reconstructed about their lives together, the utter absence of any discussion of Sally Hemings in Jefferson's letters. But I cannot help wondering if the relationship functioned in some ways for Jefferson as a marriage.[34] To be sure, the relationship was not a marriage. There was no religious or legal ceremony. Sally Hemings had none of the legal rights of a spouse. The children she bore Jefferson were not legitimate; they were not even acknowledged. There were certainly no public declarations of love or belonging. An outsider, reading only Jefferson's letters, could not have missed Jefferson's devotion to his wife. An outsider, reading Jefferson's letters, could have missed Sally Hemings altogether. This was not a marriage.

But the liaison seems to have provided Jefferson with some measure of psychological peace. Remember that many of Jefferson's paeans to domesticity date from the period after the commencement of his liaison with Sally Hemings. I do not want to go so far as to claim that Jefferson thought of Sally Hemings as "family"; I want to suggest only that the connection to her afforded him sufficient contentment that he could rhapsodize about domestic happiness rather than rail about the female sex.

In this context, we might revisit Madison Hemings's memoirs. Of his mother, he said, "It was her duty, all her life which I can remember, up to the time of father's death, to take care of his chamber and wardrobe, look after us children and do such light work as sewing, &c." His sister Harriet "learned to spin and to weave in a little factory on the home plantation."[35] Here was the gendered division of labor that Jefferson associated with an ideal American farm society. Of course there is slippage, as there always seems to be when we are talking about Jefferson and either gender or slavery. This was the sort of work that might be expected of a farmwife; it was certainly not appropriate for the wife of a wealthy planter. But perhaps by giving his Hemings children and Sally Hemings herself the kind of useful but unpunishing work that women and children performed on the freehold farm of his imagination, Jefferson was able to reconcile himself not only to his unorthodox domestic arrangements but also to slavery itself.

Notes

1. Andrew Burstein, *Jefferson's Secrets: Death and Desire at Monticello* (New York, 2005); Fawn M. Brodie, *Thomas Jefferson: An Intimate History* (New York, 1974); Annette Gordon-Reed, *The Hemingses of Monticello: An American Family* (New York, 2008). See also Jon Kukla, *Mr. Jefferson's Women* (New York, 2007), although Kukla's interpretation, which emphasizes Jefferson's misogyny and "predatory sexuality" (55), differs from the interpretation I offer here. I would like to thank Annette Gordon-Reed for many valuable discussions and several specific suggestions and John Boles and Randal Hall for asking me to write this article.

2. Sarah N. Randolph, *The Domestic Life of Thomas Jefferson . . .* (New York, 1871), 428. I have examined Jefferson's views on the family and the importance of privacy for it in " 'The Blessings of Domestic Society': Thomas Jefferson's Family and the Transformation of American Politics," in *Jeffersonian Legacies,* ed. Peter S. Onuf (Charlottesville, Va., 1993), 109–46; and "The White Jeffersons," in *Sally Hemings and Thomas Jefferson: History, Memory, and Civic Culture,* ed. Jan Ellen Lewis and Peter S. Onuf (Charlottesville, Va., 1999), 127–60.

3. Eve Kosofsky Sedgwick, *Between Men: English Literature and Male Homosocial Desire* (New York, 1985). Jefferson's first surviving letter from a woman, a Mrs. Drummond, dates from 1771. Mrs. Drummond to TJ, March 12, 1771, in Jefferson, *Papers,* 1:65–66. In fact, this is the only letter either to or from a woman in the entire first volume of the Boyd edition of Jefferson's papers. Needless to say, some correspondence may have been lost, and after his wife's death, Jefferson himself destroyed his correspondence with her. Brodie, *Thomas Jefferson,* 22.

4. TJ to John Page, December 25, 1762, in Jefferson, *Papers,* 1:4–6.

5. TJ to William Fleming, March 20, 1764, ibid., 16; TJ to John Page, January 20, 1763, ibid., 8.

6. TJ to John Page, January 20, 1763, ibid., 7.

7. TJ, "Autobiography," in Jefferson, *Writings* [Peterson], 46.

8. TJ to James Ogilvie, February 20, 1771, in Jefferson, *Papers,* 1:63.

9. Kenneth A. Lockridge, *On the Sources of Patriarchal Rage: The Commonplace Books of William Byrd and Thomas Jefferson and the Gendering of Power in the Eighteenth Century* (New York, 1992).

10. On political gossip as "conduits for other people's aggression," see Joanne B. Freeman, *Affairs of Honor: National Politics in the New Republic* (New Haven, Conn., 2001), 74.

11. TJ to William Fleming, March 20, 1764, in Jefferson, *Papers,* 1:16.

12. TJ to Chastellux, November 26, 1782, in Jefferson, *Writings* [Peterson], 780.

13. TJ to Mary Jefferson Eppes, October 26, 1801; TJ to Martha Jefferson Randolph, May 31, 1798, in *The Family Letters of Thomas Jefferson,* ed. Edwin Morris Betts and James Adam Bear Jr. (Columbia, Mo., 1966), 210, 164; Lewis, " 'The Blessings of Domestic Society,' " 109–46.

14. Abigail Adams Smith quoted in Brian Steele, "Thomas Jefferson's Gender Frontier," *Journal of American History* 95 (June 2008): 25; TJ to Walker Maury, August 19, 1785, in Jefferson, *Papers,* 8:409.

15. TJ to Charles Thomson, November 11, 1784, in Jefferson, *Papers,* 7:518–19.

16. TJ to John Banister Jr., October 15, 1785, ibid., 8:635–37.

17. TJ to Walker Maury, August 19, 1785, ibid., 409.

18. Hanna Fenichel Pitkin, *Fortune Is a Woman: Gender and Politics in the Thought of Niccolò Machiavelli* (Berkeley, Calif., 1984).

19. TJ to John Banister Jr., October 15, 1785, in Jefferson, *Papers,* 8:636.

20. TJ to Anne Willing Bingham, February 7, 1787, in Jefferson, *Writings* [Peterson], 887–88.

21. TJ to Martha Jefferson Randolph, July 17, 1790, in Betts and Bear, eds., *Family Letters,* 60–61.

22. Lewis, " 'The Blessings of Domestic Society,' " 109–46.

23. TJ to Anne Willing Bingham, May 11, 1788, in Jefferson, *Writings* [Peterson], 922–23.

24. TJ to George Washington, December 4, 1788, ibid., 932–33.

25. TJ, "Memorandums on a Tour from Paris to Amsterdam, Strasburg, and back to Paris," March 3, 1788, ibid., 629–58 (quotations at 634, 640, 651–52).

26. TJ to Governor William H. Harrison, February 27, 1803, ibid., 1118.

27. See, for example, Henry Nash Smith, *Virgin Land: The American West as Symbol and Myth* (Cambridge, Mass., 1950).

28. TJ to James Ronaldson, January 12, 1813, in Jefferson, *Writings* [L&B],

13:205; TJ to E. I. Du Pont de Nemours, November 8, 1812, ibid., 18:276; TJ to Philip Mazzei, December 29, 1813, in Jefferson, *Works,* 9:442.

29. See David Waldstreicher, "Why Thomas Jefferson and African Americans Wore Their Politics on Their Sleeves: Dress and Mobilization between American Revolutions," in *Beyond the Founders: New Approaches to the Political History of the Early American Republic,* ed. Jeffrey L. Pasley, Andrew W. Robertson, and Waldstreicher (Chapel Hill, N.C., 2004), 79–103. Jefferson's comment about Mrs. Mason is on p. 95; Waldstreicher's is on p. 97.

30. TJ to James Madison, May 13, 1810, in Jefferson, *Writings* [Peterson], 1223–25.

31. TJ to William Drayton, July 30, 1787, in Jefferson, *Writings* [L&B], 6:193–204. I thank Professor Annette Gordon-Reed for pointing me toward this important document.

32. Adam Rothman, *Slave Country: American Expansion and the Origins of the Deep South* (Cambridge, Mass., 2005); Peter S. Onuf, *Jefferson's Empire: The Language of American Nationhood* (Charlottesville, Va., 2000).

33. On the reliability of Madison Hemings's memoirs, see Annette Gordon-Reed, *Thomas Jefferson and Sally Hemings: An American Controversy* (Charlottesville, Va., 1997).

34. For contrasting views, see the recent works of Rhys Isaac and Andrew Burstein. Isaac calls the relationship between Thomas Jefferson and Sally Hemings "a custom-of-the-place marriage" ("Monticello Stories Old and New," in Lewis and Onuf, eds., *Sally Hemings and Thomas Jefferson,* 119). Andrew Burstein, however, is skeptical that Hemings functioned as a "substitute wife." "Jefferson's feelings toward Sally Hemings," Burstein has recently written, "no matter the duration of their physical intimacy, cannot be analogous to marital affection, first because of the work she did, and second, because Jefferson was not open about the relationship" (*Jefferson's Secrets,* 154).

35. Gordon-Reed, *Thomas Jefferson and Sally Hemings,* 248.

ANDREW BURSTEIN

Jefferson in the Flesh

Thomas Jefferson devoted his energies to scientific study at least as much as he speculated on the art of government. Nothing was too big or too small for his mind: he was interested in the operations of all-encompassing natural forces and the interior nature of the human organism. As a materialist and an empiricist, he subscribed to the Newtonian universe and to a neurophysiological basis for mental activity. This pairing of interests—the material outer world and the material inner world—in many ways defines Jefferson's lifelong intellectual perspective. When we read Jefferson's correspondence with like-minded thinkers, we cannot but appreciate his efforts to devise a syntax that combined practical science with progressive self-fashioning—a way of tempering human imperfection through improved knowledge.

With an almost fawning fascination, Jefferson expressed awe in imagining the mind of the astronomer and mathematician David Rittenhouse of Philadelphia, who had made the jump from theory to practice as no American besides Benjamin Franklin had, building a mechanical orrery that accurately traced the movements of the planets. The master of Monticello had, from early in his public life, scanned the skies with his telescope. He kept careful temperature readings and tested a great variety of seeds to determine what kinds of plants would thrive in his central Virginia surroundings. He almost never wrote about agricultural science without appending the word "practical" or "practicable." He set the descriptive standards by which Meriwether Lewis and William Clark collected samples and recorded observations of the living things they encountered on their journey west. The objects Jefferson surrounded himself with at Monticello included his drafting board, maps, medicines, mechanical inventions, fossils, plants, and garden tools. As president of the American Philosophical Society, he regularly stood in the middle of a national conversation concerning investigative theories of physical nature.

Nature was perfect, but imperfectly understood. As Jefferson aimed to reduce human vulnerability by promoting remedies for ignorance that were upheld by Enlightenment science, he engaged with health issues in a very public and proactive way. He teamed with Dr. Benjamin Waterhouse of Harvard to disseminate knowledge of immunization and to open clinics devoted to vaccination throughout the United States. In devising a structure for the University of Virginia, he laid out the campus pavilions in such a way as to prevent disease from spreading easily; and he insisted on the construction of a medical amphitheater. For this purpose, too, he collected medical texts and a wide range of preserved organs and medical supplies, and he developed a detailed program of medical education. He sent his eldest grandson, Thomas Jefferson Randolph, to study anatomy with Dr. Caspar Wistar, in Philadelphia, hoping that "Jeff" would become a surgeon.

The entrepreneurial portrait painter Charles Willson Peale attended a dinner at the President's House in 1801, when the guest of honor was the Prussian botanist-zoologist-geologist-geographer Alexander Von Humboldt. Peale reported that the conversation never strayed into politics but focused intently on "natural history, and improvements of the conveniences of life." In considering "conveniences," we should not be thinking merely of labor-saving devices, because the term also connoted physical ease and comfort. Jefferson relied heavily on science to solve the problems of his generation in becoming "fit" for the future.

Science gave Jefferson laws to abide by, a language by which to order human experience, and means greater than religion offered to appreciate how the Earth sustained life. If science was, to his mind, the guide to progress, then medicine was the science of greatest urgency, because it offered a realistic hope of defeating that which stood in the way of human happiness. In other words, even before embracing the cause of liberty in combating tyranny, Jefferson had to contend with, and assume responsibility for, the nature and needs of his own body; he had to associate with the cause of life in combating pain and death. His private library (which contained over one hundred medical texts that we know of) and his correspondence with physicians, educators, naturalists, and others demonstrate over time how much he thought about personal health issues and how he applied his reading and thinking about health to his general system of belief.

We have often contended with the cerebral Jefferson—Jefferson as a thinking man and political practitioner—but rarely have we read what he read and what he wrote in such a way as to understand him viscerally. We know he was a man of the flesh—DNA evidence has opened a debate on this subject—but we do not really know him *as* a man of the flesh. This essay examines a man of the flesh as a man of science. Rational living, to Jefferson's way of thinking, required not just intellect but also blood flow, nervous energy, and the arousal and application of feelings.[1]

Jefferson lived in what can justly be styled the age of "trembling nerves." Gender difference and human sexuality were seen in terms of the impact that neurological functions had on the human organism. Jefferson subscribed to a science that asserted the following: women were naturally weak and susceptible, owing to the organization of their nerves, and men were stronger and generally willful and deliberative, but subject to the same pathological forces. The central nervous system, located in the sensorium of the brain, naturally excited nerve fibers that coursed through the body's sympathetic reactive system and caused people to experience either pleasure or pain. Without this operation there would be no memory, no language, and no perception. To understand human behavior, then, one had to make sense of nervous sensation.

Jefferson not only embraced this thinking but also took it well beyond science and incorporated neurophysiological vocabulary as metaphors in what he wrote for both private and public consumption. He enlarged on such words as "vibrations," "spasms," "tremors," "irritations," and "agitations"—and in the worst case, "convulsions" of the body politic. Spasms could be positive, as in "generous spasm of the heart"; but the other words in this list were employed to warn of dangers to the health of an organism. Physical sensation was a vital force behind the human personality: bigotry was a "disease," he declared; newspapers were "vulgar vehicles of passion"; selfish indulgence was a form of sensual excess; human history marked the "agonizing spasms of infuriated man." And as Eva Sheppard Wolf notes in her essay for this volume, Jefferson, when doubting the reasoning ability of the least educated voters, in essence compared such people to undeveloped species that "secrete" (a mere biological function) rather than think through their choices. Looking back on his career, he wrote paradigmatically in 1818: "It was my lot to be cast into being at the period of the commencement of a political convulsion, which has since continued to agitate the whole civilized world." We can infer from his word choice Jefferson's concern with corporeal balance and imbalance.[2]

Jefferson's correspondents understood this vocabulary and recognized that it added power to an established political ideology. Jefferson distinguished his Federalist political opposition from his Democratic-Republicans on the basis of their ostensibly different nervous constitutions. In 1795, as party conflict was starting to peak, he connected the Federalists with a kind of nervous disease: as men who were all too willing to trade moral principles for political favors, they were "[n]ervous persons, whose languid fibres have more analogy with a passive than active state of things." In 1802 he elaborated on this theme: Federalists were the "weakly and nerveless, the rich and corrupt seeking more safety and accessibility in a strong executive." Republicans were, in contrast, naturally "firm" and "healthy," of "sound minds and bodies"; they were "the healthy, firm and virtuous, feeling confidence in their physical and moral resources."[3]

Among the medical guides Jefferson owned were studies of general works of home use, physiology, pharmacology, and surgery. In addition, he owned specific works about air quality, human differentiation, childhood diseases, dentistry, poisons, water cures, cowpox inoculation, yellow fever, gout, bile, female concerns, masturbation, hysterics, and venereal diseases. Most were in English, but a good number were in French.

As a widely traveled intellectual, Jefferson was able to compare cultures on various levels. In the matter of sexual mores, the one-time minister to France alluded often to differences in outlook between the open-minded French and virtue-proclaiming Americans. He allowed the French their indulgences but sought to steer young American men away from early exposure to sex—particularly with prostitutes. We understand sex to be culturally constructed, but in Jefferson's day medical thinkers had much to say, in universal terms, on the subject. Well-read men of science such as Jefferson accepted at face value certain propositions about men's and women's sexual natures that medical professionals constantly evoked, beginning with the understanding that sex was part of the study of nervous sensations. The neurological language Jefferson applied to political partisanship—convulsions, spasms, irritations, and agitations—applied equally to human sexuality. In social terms, emphasis was put on women to resist temptation (their sexual nature), while men continued to act almost with impunity, restrained by a limited sense of shame. That self-restraint meant little when a man crossed class lines and engaged in sex with a woman who was not of the gentry.

We can only understand Jefferson's sexual impulses by identifying the assumptions he held. One was that women needed to be controlled. Jefferson was keenly aware of so-called diseases of the female imagination, for these were widely written about throughout the medical enlightenment. Most notable was the *furor uterinus,* or nymphomania, thought to be a disorder of the mind more than of the female sex organ. Eighteenth-century physicians were relying, in this instance, on their Greek ancestors, who were the first to name the condition. Lewdness coming from women was noted frequently, perhaps most famously in *Lysistrata,* the heroine of which play berated her entire gender as degenerate; the medical texts Jefferson read clinically denoted "a preternatural Irritation in the Parts of Generation; whence violent Impressions are made on the Brain." Hysteric passions or fits, "paroxysms" and "convulsive Constriction or Contraction," were indications of bodily and/or spiritual disharmony, for which the treatment was a tepid bath, bleeding (in serious cases, bleeding the jugular), and opiates.[4]

A woman's "generative fire" had to be controlled at all costs. The seriousness with which the female sexual imagination was treated by men who superintended women's well-being should not be underestimated: immodesty was considered a threat to society at large, yet at the same time, women were obliged to satisfy the male gaze. A woman should be desirable but also composed and controlled. Men should smile at her, but not hungrily. In short, people were meant to hide who they were and what they were thinking about the opposite sex. Jefferson's quiet self-possession, his soft-spoken demeanor, was legendary; but his attraction to married women at different times in his life was known by select friends and even became a partisan issue during his presidency, coincident with the newspaper charges that he was intimate with his slave Sally Hemings.

His ostensible transgression was not simply in having had sex but in being a different sort of man than his public image suggested. In the case of his attraction to his slave, the issue was her low social station along with her imagined color—the former element tends to get lost in most discussions of the subject: he "stooped" to conquer. Women's availability, regardless of class distinctions, was rooted in their passionate nature. Every female needed to work at her modesty, though little was expected of the lower classes, and slaves (especially female) were routinely sexualized.

Jefferson admired wit and intelligence in women, and he urged his daughters and granddaughters to submit to a rigorous education, stressing literature, the French language, and a basic appreciation for mathematics and the sciences; especially important were the fine arts, music, and household skills such as sewing. These occupations effectively were thought to protect young elite women from sexual knowledge. At the same time, Jefferson insisted that female delicacy was natural and not to be questioned; he saw women in terms of what they lacked, or as a complement to men, but not as men's equals—they were defined *in relation to* men. He disputed the opinion of those, such as Mary Wollstonecraft, who held that gender distinctions based on nervous sensations were false. Jefferson knew his son-in-law Thomas Mann Randolph Jr. to be ill-tempered, but he instructed his elder daughter Martha to yield to Randolph as a wife should yield to her husband. She bore him twelve children before effectively banishing him from the household. Shortly after her wedding, Jefferson exhorted Martha: "Your new condition will call for abundance of little sacrifices. . . . The happiness of your life depends now on the continuing to please a single person. To this all other objects must be secondary; even your love to me." He reckoned motherhood to be "undoubtedly the keystone of the arch of matrimonial happiness."[5]

Whether for purposes of procreation or his own inner fulfillment, a man was led to concern himself with the medical requirement that he engage in sexual intercourse on a fairly regular but not too frequent (or infrequent) basis. Balance was essential, because overindulgence could excite the passions and do long-term damage—sex was "a convulsion"—"it disposes the nerves to convulsive motions." The weakness a man felt after intercourse was proof of the engagement of easily exhausted nerves in this activity: "When a convulsion comes on, the nervous parts become more extended, or rather are put into extraordinary action, the consequence whereof is an excessive relaxation." No nerve was not disordered by this action, and the entire nervous system became weakened to the point where digestion and perspiration ceased to occur normally. The final result was a kind of dementia, "a sensible diminution of the powers, of the memory, and even of the understanding."

Similar reasoning applied to masturbation: "Nothing so much weakens as that continual bent of the mind, ever occupied with the same object. The masturbator, entirely devoted to his filthy meditations, is subject to the same disorders as the man of letters, who fixes his attention upon a single question." Whether it was diet or intensive study or sex, one should not adopt any practice that threatened to deplete his vital forces; the model of the healthy body, as Roy Porter has recently explained, was "a vital economy, demanding energetic and regular replenishment of stimulus."[6]

The author of the above warning about masturbation was the renowned Swiss physician Samuel A. D. Tissot (1728–97), whose entire works (sixteen volumes) Jefferson owned in the original French; in addition, he owned the English-language *Tissot's Advice*. If we combine the general understanding of female sexuality with Tissot's strictures, it makes perfect sense that Jefferson remained a sexual being in the years after his wife died—when he was thirty-nine. To suggest moral irregularity in Jefferson's behavior is to apply later standards to a privileged man of the eighteenth century.

No one in Jefferson's century had greater reach than Dr. Tissot when it came to commenting on neurosexual aspects of the human condition. Tissot was best known for his work on onanism, for condemning masturbation. His widely reprinted *De la santé des gens de lettres* (*An Essay on Diseases Incidental to Literary and Sedentary Persons*) most directly pertained to Jefferson. Tissot gave much of his attention to men of letters who strained their bodily systems through overwork, intense thought, and too much time spent at a desk. He recommended a regimen of physical exercise, a semi-vegetarian diet, and regular sexual activity with a healthy, attractive, and fruitful female. A widower, as Jefferson was, thus had the doctor's approval to take care of his physical needs in the manner that men of Jefferson's class ordinarily availed themselves of, so that they did not waste their seed through the unprofitable exertion of masturbation.

Jefferson, we know, followed Tissot's advice with respect to diet and exercise. It seems likely, then, that a long-term sexual relationship with Sally Hemings would also have fulfilled the purposes of a health-seeking man of letters. In all that he wrote, Tissot joined physical and moral health, without subscribing to puritanical policies. In short, according to the best minds of the eighteenth century, sex was as healthy for the female who received the attentions (and semen) of a man as it was for the man who achieved release (and whose health was of preeminent concern to him).

As to the moral component in Tissot's writing, the Swiss medical theorist tells of a celebrated physician of the fifteenth century who lived into his nineties and was asked how he retained his sharp memory and vigorous health. He answered that it was the effect of "innocence of morals, a tranquility of the spirit, and frugality." The cultural environment Jefferson thrived in strongly suggests that he did not regard a sexual relationship with his house servant as immoral; his reserve, his unruffled manner, his famed lack of an irritable temper, and his careful accounting of everyday life through lists, catalogs, and record-keeping, show that, in spite of his accrued debts, he could rationalize that he was a man of good order and good sense, seeking to extend his life. Tissot's answer to everything was to act moderately—some sex, but not an excessive amount.

The medical enlightenment typified by Tissot's prescriptions for men of letters linked the state of the nerves to the state of the mind. This was why the physician was so concerned with men's speaking and reading habits. Great orators who strained their voices were subject to problems with the lungs as well as "the organs of digestion," which could prove "disastrous" if left unchecked; but Jefferson, of course, shied from public speaking and spoke normally in a calm cadence, thus preserving the health of these key organs. The eyes of constant readers, Tissot wrote, were easily irritated, causing "continual fatigue," even for men "in the flower of their age." Though famous for his rotating bookstand, which held numerous books at once while he conducted research into whatever subject he was writing about, Jefferson boasted in his later years that he only occasionally needed reading glasses, even in the evening hours. His gradual loss of hearing, not covered in Tissot's treatise, was simply a natural phenomenon as the body aged.[7]

Thus, the picture we get of Jefferson, when we regard him not simply as a man of the liberal enlightenment but also as a man of the medical enlightenment, is a picture of a patient. He is acting often as his own physician, experimenting until he finds a regimen that satisfies him, as he did in bathing his feet in cold water every morning when he awoke, so as to ward off colds. He insisted that this worked. When he dined, he ate moderately, and he stayed thin; he diluted his wine and measured it, so as not to overindulge. He was a man for whom control and self-control were critical.

But he did not get his ideas about human sexuality only from the eighteenth-century medical enlightenment. There is reason to consider that his society's concern with sex—and legal definitions of race—in terms of bloodlines goes much further back in time. To say that ancient Greek ideas about sex still had a hold on the men of the early American republic sounds at first improbable; yet we have no problem associating Greek ideas of political and social organization with the founders, who read deeply in Greek.

Jefferson's ideas about essential masculinity and related sexual propriety, in fact, were probably closer to those of the ancient Greeks than they are to modern American norms. The Greeks he read often focused on men, women, and their appetites; they saw the pleasures of the world before them and discussed their options openly. And there was even Diogenes the Cynic, who bucked the trend by recommending regular masturbation.[8] Since early in the nineteenth century, the popular imagination has elevated the morals of the founding generation along with their wisdom and nonpartisan patriotism, and has maintained unreasonable expectations from these eighteenth-century men by recurrence to a decidedly puritanical code, which is entirely incorrect and ahistorical. Sin did not concern Jefferson's peers as much as it did the generations that came after them.

Aristotle was a widower who took a mistress and had children by her—she and they were included in his will. *The Politics* offers a prescription that was well known in the late eighteenth and early nineteenth centuries. He said: "[W]omen who have sexual intercourse at an early age are more likely to be dissolute. On the male side too it is held that if they have intercourse while the seed is just growing, it interferes with future growth. . . . The appropriate age for marriage is about the eighteenth year for girls and for men the thirty-seventh plus or minus." With adjustment of the male age downward a dozen years, the tenor of these remarks is similar to the prognostications of the eighteenth century's leading physicians and American society in the age of Jefferson. Aristotle's idea was that men and women would both reach the end of their child-producing years at around the same time. He stated that the robustness of the couples' children should be an additional consideration, and that a man past his midfifties "ought no longer to beget and openly acknowledge children. But for the sake of health or other such good reason intercourse may continue without secrecy."[9] For the record, the DNA tests conducted in 1998 genetically linked Thomas Jefferson with Sally Hemings's last son, Eston, who was born when President Jefferson was sixty-five.

It is worth speculating as to why, in his thirties, Jefferson repeatedly sought to impregnate his wife when she endured one difficult childbirth after another. The urge to produce sons was likely one important factor, if not the principal factor. Of the six children Patty Jefferson bore, the two to survive more than four years were both daughters. But did he not fear for Patty's life? Was her health not his first concern? Was social pressure—appearance—or the medical concession that women were put on Earth to bear children, more important to him? Did he feel at all guilty when she died in the wake of her sixth delivery? These questions cannot yet be answered with any degree of certainty. Nothing in the medical literature Jefferson owned addresses the issue either medically or ethically. Texts that treat pregnancy and birth speak to the physical comfort of the mother-to-be, and of surgical options and delivery methods; the postpartum period is only considered in terms of hastening recovery. Despite its poor record in saving mothers in distress, the medical profession maintained an unwarranted pose of confidence in its prescribed methods.

If the study of the nerves attempted to measure all that occurred mysteriously within the body that contributed to personality, skin and hair signified the outermost limit of physical humanness. The telltale skin, permeable organ of sensation between nerve endings and the hair, is, like the hair, both dead and alive, capable of growing and healing and transforming. Subject to natural processes, skin decays faster than hair. When it is alive, it protects the body; it also blushes and in other ways calls forth emotional expression. It contains nerve cells and sweat glands, which regulate heat and convey something (begging to be interpreted) about who we are. Skin is the part of us that most perceptibly comes into physical contact with another being; it is the quintessential barrier between the inside person and the outside person. Its tactile quality makes it a register of pleasure and pain—and that is how the neurologically oriented Jefferson perceived it, too. In his lifelong discourse on the pursuit of happiness he constantly viewed the issues and phenomena he ruminated on in the Epicurean terms of whether they contributed to tranquility or agitation, which he linked to bodily pleasure or pain.[10]

Then there is the related study of physiognomy, which in ancient Greece, where it first developed, and in the late eighteenth and early nineteenth centuries was viewed as an offshoot of science. Its foremost authority was the Swiss Johann Caspar Lavater (1741–1801), who read past smiles and frowns and emphasized instead permanent physical features such as a high forehead and the shape and size of the eyes, ears, and nose. Science was striving to unearth nature's secrets—and, of course, science was often overreaching. Lavater was convinced that boys inherited their firm bones and muscles from their fathers; girls took their delicate nerves from their mothers. He was just as persuaded that national physical characteristics were discernible and verifiable.[11]

Broadly speaking, Jefferson communicated his prejudices by identifying surfaces and then ascribing essential causal elements to them. In order to more fully understand his cultural chauvinism with regard to blacks or women, we need to appreciate the wider cultural phenomenon of communicating through surface appearances. In the early republic, one conveyed authenticity through public display. Formerly, aristocrats were easy to recognize, based on the clothes they wore: Lord Chesterfield had advised that gentlemen needed to dress so as to attract attention, for lack of any better measure of their pedigree. Jefferson presided over an ostensible change. He believed that the two political parties differed in terms of their members' nervous dispositions: stability-guarding Federalists continued to admire stately performances such as levees and balls, which served to separate them from the huddled masses, whereas unadorned Jeffersonian Republicans dressed down to make a statement against extravagance. At the same time, these men recognized each other as aristocrats who *could* put on airs by dressing up, if they chose to do so. The symbolic value of dressing down was perhaps less significant than Jefferson imagined. Nevertheless, this was one more standard by which he could differentiate between those of one ideology and those of another.

More meaningfully, there was no more profound keepsake of a loved one than a lock of hair: while their love letters were at some point burned (to keep them from prying eyes), Jefferson retained his wife's and one of their ill-fated infants' hair in a private drawer by his bedside for the last forty-four years of his life. Female hair was an important part of what a man found aesthetically desirable in his mate. Her hair, soft and pliant, was the emotive tie to shared memories that he reflected on and cherished; Jefferson's generation needed a physical reminder of the departed, whereas most today are satisfied to gaze at a framed photograph of the loved one.

Hair clothes the body. Dress, but especially the more intimate component of individuality, hair, symbolizes the physical person. Hair is at once corporeal and lifeless, of and not of the body, somewhere between the intimate and the unconcealed part of a person. In Jefferson's day, it positively radiated personhood and probably bore a sexual suggestiveness, even if not widely spoken of as such. The lock of Patty Jefferson's hair that he kept close stopped the clock for him, preserving materially the moment when she as a natural being was transformed into a personal memory. Her hair reminded him that he was a witness to a very visceral transformative event.[12]

The aesthetics of hair might also be relatable to Jefferson's hands-on concern with the natural world and his passion, as a landscape gardener, for grooming his immediate physical environment. No matter where he resided, he invariably sought to alter his living area by laying out gardens or adapting structures—achieving external growth and change, marking visible progress, labeling and cataloging his possessions were his goals as he assessed his happiness. The metaphor here is of an inviting natural adornment, growing upon and beautifying a surface. The irony lies in Jefferson's willfully crossing breeds in search of a superior plant in his garden, while anathematizing black-white unions in the public sphere; the first was wholesome progress, the second deviant activity. The word he and subsequent racist thinkers most often used to decry miscegenation was "mixture." There were some experiments that he was convinced nature proscribed, and he was not interested in the argument that abolitionists would advance: an "infusion" of Negro blood into the white would produce a more temperate people.[13]

Hair, like skin, was part of a conversation about irremovable inner attributes. When non-Caucasians were described, they were quite often diminished in capacity by referring to the nature of their hair: the beardlessness of the Asian and Native American, the "frizzled" (to use the Linnaean term), coarse, and unruly African look—all of which somehow equated to "indolent" behavior. Yet, as if to mark whites' confusion about these designations, Asians and Native Americans were seen as sexually obscure and Africans as sexually predatory. Untroubled by their skin pigmentation, natural odor, or other physiological attribute, Jefferson had to come to the defense of Native American males' virility in his *Notes on Virginia*. Only the Europeans' hair did not imply deficiency by these calculations; shaving was an eighteenth-century sign for advanced civilization. In Europe, and in Jefferson's mind, too, a long beard was associated with Jews, whose habits were ostensibly unappealing to the Christian majority. Thus, in a multitude of ways, hair was meant to define cultural evolution and human potential.[14]

Science, for Jefferson, was deterministic, and so his views on race and gender were limited by his classification as natural endowments what we regard as cultural prejudices. It was commonly argued in his time, drawing on the writings of the Scottish philosophe Lord Kames and others, that skin pigmentation was evidence of multiple creations, or polygenesis; thus, blacks could be seen as a separate race, closer to the recently discovered "orangutans" of the African jungle, and presumably inferior in many respects to light-skinned peoples. Jefferson's friend Dr. Benjamin Rush, an opponent of slavery, surmised that the color of Africans' skin was the result of a widespread leprosy outbreak sometime in the past.[15]

It is hard for today's reader to encounter the passages on race in *Notes on Virginia* and not see the text as a psycho-neurophysiological drama for its author. Skin color was not merely "skin deep" for him. It assumed such importance in Jefferson's mind that he allowed his imagination (in the guise of science) to conjure Gothic allusions. He was not satisfied to evaluate surface qualities but imputed psychic meaning to skin, which he justified by speculating on the distinctive operations of the African American's interior organs. By eliminating the boundary between surface and within, he assigned other kinds of values to people based on their skin: cleanliness, attractiveness, integrity, and purity—in short, indicators of health that could also be applied to moral judgment and capacity.

He desired to live in a well-ordered, sanitary place. There is no better evidence of this than the design of parallel walks and symmetrical pavilions that he borrowed from a schematic for a new hospital complex that he saw in France and implemented at the University of Virginia; it impressed him because it kept unhealthy people from infecting others and encouraged cleaner air circulation and the elimination of odors. It is significant that Jefferson remarked on the repulsion he felt with regard to slaves' bodily odors. Skin pigmentation was ineradicable; and so, for Jefferson, were the other characteristics that troubled him.[16]

As everyone knows who has read the oft-cited passages from *Notes on Virginia,* Jefferson believed Africans were less intelligent, less versatile, less imbued with "taste" than Europeans. Physical attributes were linked directly to mental ability. Black-white unions portended "degradation" of the species, and as I have argued elsewhere, his attraction to Sally Hemings is explained by two factors in his judgment: his treatment of the biracial Hemingses as family—albeit a subordinate parallel family lacking a public identity while enslaved at Monticello; and Sally Hemings's outer appearance. She was three-quarters white and was described by those who knew her as "nearly white," with long straight hair—it was not the telltale "woolly" or "frizzled" hair of the African. Jefferson could rationalize that any children she bore him would be accepted into white society, and thus no "degradation" would have taken place.[17]

The flip side of the coin was that put forward by Frances Wright, Lafayette's young friend, who accompanied the Revolutionary general on his 1824 visit to Monticello and engaged the then eighty-one-year-old Jefferson in a conversation about America's racial future. Merely a year and a half after Jefferson's death in 1826, she wrote: "Idle indeed is the assertion that the mixture of the races is not in nature. . . . the only question is whether it shall take place in good taste and good feeling and be made at once the means of sealing the tranquility, and perfecting the liberty of the country . . . or whether it shall proceed, as it now does, viciously and degradingly, mingling hatred and fear with the ties of blood—denied indeed, but stamped by nature herself upon the skin." Wright used some of the same vocabulary as Jefferson, denoting issues of "taste" and "good feeling," associating the goals of "liberty" and "tranquility"; but their understanding of the scientific basis (and thus intent) of nature could never be reconciled.[18]

It is possible that Jefferson's thinking on race represents, in fact, a paradigm shift. Traditionally, the philosophy of race and inheritance centered on bloodlines for the purpose of arranging desirable marriages and insuring the health of offspring. From the time of the Greeks to the American Revolution and beyond, aristocratic privilege was integrally linked with the bequest of blood, and bastardy was couched in a legal language associated with verified paternity and restrictions on the father's obligation. Jefferson did not reject this mode of thinking outright but argued its efficacy most notably in a series of exchanges with John Adams in 1813. He thoroughly understood how the laws of different states determined the number of combinations before an individual with an African bloodline could have the "taint" of blackness wiped clean. Yet he was the first to challenge "consanguinity," when, in the Declaration of Independence, he renounced his "British brethren" despite the consanguineous blood brotherhood that had bound the colonies to the motherland. So now, just as the science of the nerves had overtaken the former emphasis on "humours" within the body to describe illness and condition treatment, Jefferson's tendency to privilege skin over blood suggests a competing means of typing humans and a further move against the concept of traditional aristocracy, the effect of which was to expand the status of whites and expand opportunities for whites by recasting the standard for measuring social privilege. Michel Foucault has written of this moment of transition, as Western society moved from understanding "*a symbolics of blood*" to embracing "*an analytics of sexuality*."[19]

Jefferson wrote quintessentially about "harmony and affection" as social values without which republican society could not succeed. His First Inaugural Address builds to a crescendo with the line: "Let us, then, fellow citizens, unite with one heart and one mind. Let us restore to social intercourse that harmony and affection without which liberty and even life itself are but dreary things."[20] He was alluding to a state of body as well as a state of mind. Underlying Jefferson's political liberalism was a quality related to both the endowed moral sense and prevailing culture of sensibility, which was known in his generation as "fellow-feeling"—a mood sustained by neurophysiological balance.

Adam Smith, in his influential *The Theory of Moral Sentiments* (1759), explored the origins and character of "fellow-feeling" within the contexts of bodily constitution, conscience, and judgment. Smith stated that in the normal course of life human beings developed "moderated sensibility" drawing them to the misfortunes of others. It was a form of inward nerve-borne pain that could be productive and part of the quest for happiness in an inner contentment or "tranquillity." To accomplish this, one needed only to restrain excesses of passions, intrigue, cabal, faction, and fanaticism. These were the precise words Jefferson used to attack his Federalist critics, writing, for example, to his protégé Joseph C. Cabell: "There are fanatics both in religion and politics, who, without knowing me personally, have long been taught to consider me as a raw head and bloody bones." Political liberalism thus began with one's personal outlook, which was the height of manhood: "Our sensibility to the feelings of others, so far from being inconsistent with the manhood of self-command, is the very principle upon which that manhood is founded," Smith wrote. This was, at once, Jefferson's definition of manhood, and the core principle of his political ideology, which he felt Federalists were constitutionally averse to and thus neurologically damaged, deprived, or disadvantaged. When Henry S. Randall wrote his monumental biography of Jefferson in the 1850s, with the assistance of Jefferson's family, he promoted the Smithian image of his subject as a man who embodied fellow-feeling: "His look . . . fell benignantly and lovingly upon the weak, the simple, and the lowly, and they at once felt and returned the sympathy."[21]

Of the many adherents of "fellow-feeling," no one so effectively incorporated this concept as William Godwin (1756–1836), a religious skeptic and natural rights advocate whose similarity to Jefferson is extraordinary but has hardly been explored before. Godwin was as well known in the world as Jefferson in 1800; it would be fair to call Jefferson "America's Godwin," especially in the way each was singled out and targeted by conservative forces. They were democrats and humanists who spoke out against intellectual cowardice, using a similar, very visceral vocabulary. "I was born free," says Godwin's character Caleb Williams in the 1794 novel *Things as They Are; or, The Adventures of Caleb Williams.* "I was born healthy, vigorous and active, complete in all the lineaments and members of a human body. I was not born indeed to the possession of hereditary wealth; but I had a better inheritance, an enterprising mind, an inquisitive spirit, a liberal ambition." And Jefferson, shortly before he died: "[T]he mass of mankind has not been born with saddles on their backs, nor a favored few booted and spurred, ready to ride them legitimately, by the grace of God." The two writers, Godwin and Jefferson, used corporeal words as weapons in such a way that their political enemies considered them insurrectionists within the body politic. But for Godwin and Jefferson, it all depended on how one related natural endowments (in the vocabulary of bodily health) to social stability in the body politic. Political conservatives of Jefferson's era seemed less responsive to that vocabulary and that imagery.

For Godwin, as for Jefferson, the life of the mind could not be separated from the health of the body; nor the health of the body from finely tuned nerves. The fiction they responded to (selectively, because much fiction was disparaged for being merely provocative and not profound) allowed for characters to be physically emboldened through the exercise of reason, and weakened to the point of death from broken hearts. Godwin wove into his political writing as well as the plot of his widely read novels *Caleb Williams* and *Fleetwood; or, The New Man of Feeling* (1805) the healing power of sympathy. He also centered his plot on the power that the nerves held over human conduct. Of the novels that Jefferson recommended to his granddaughters and others, the only one authored by a male was Godwin's, which seems to prove his lifelong appreciation for Godwin's message.[22]

While virtue triumphed in *Caleb Williams,* which was the lesson young women were supposed to receive, the real world did not necessarily follow suit. Nerves were not always brought under control, and secret passions were not always fought off. Even the adherents of scientific rationalism might channel impure energies toward aggressive, destructive, or selfish ends. Power (whether social or political) reinforced the sense of entitlement.

His comfort as an executive in both the private and public spheres explains why gender roles had a legitimate scientific basis for Thomas Jefferson. While he did not subscribe to the strict dichotomy that "men were made to think and women were made to feel," he construed women as more vulnerable creatures than men, emotionally more susceptible and ill-equipped to engage in public competition with them. They could not be permitted to vote or hold public office, for the sake of their own bodies and minds as well as social harmony and political health. Just as he urged his strong, competent daughter to obey her temperamental husband, he did not take intellectualism in a woman to warrant a willful annulment of the social order; his friend and fellow signer of the Declaration of Independence Dr. Benjamin Rush was even more unrelenting on the subject when he wrote in the same vein to a woman about to be wed: "The subordination of your sex to ours is enforced by nature, by reason, and by revelation." A woman influenced by way of love and devotion—nature made her influence constitutionally passive. Concepts of the body were in this way integral to Jefferson's gendered construction of the harmonious nation.[23]

Yet Jefferson's politics did not find essential differences between upper- and lower-class white men. All were capable of meritorious achievement. Convinced of a "natural aristocracy" based on "virtue and talents," he did not see class as he saw race and gender.[24] He was a political subversive in the eyes of political conservatives; but he was a scientific conservative, unprepared to question inherited notions of human types.

It also matters that Jefferson was a materialist. He could not be convinced, without incontrovertible empirical evidence, that the human spirit survived physical death. His science explains why his political foes accused him of atheism. "I feel: therefore I exist," Jefferson wrote to John Adams in 1820, when both men were regularly contemplating their mortality. "Jesus taught nothing of [immateriality]. He told us indeed that 'God is a spirit,' but he has not defined what a spirit is, nor said that it is not *matter*." Newton had written that matter was not solid but came together when minute particles were attracted, and so Jefferson believed that personhood began with the stamp of physical birth. Morals were a part of that indelible stamp, too. What nature endowed could not be erased. What one did with that endowment (after accepting his or her acknowledged "natural" boundaries) determined whether an individual lived up to his or her potential.[25]

In spite of his commitment to the rational principles of natural law and science, Thomas Jefferson was not a cold-blooded thinker. His thousands of letters are nothing if not a campaign for intimacy with other individuals. So when we consider his encounters with skin and nerves, race and gender, we must not overemphasize the cerebral in his nature; he used the dominant medical vocabulary to justify a way of life, but he also left ample evidence to historical investigators that he lived and acted passionately. That is, he was governed by his imagination probably more than he was prepared to admit.

His intimate relationship with a female house servant was indelicately exposed in 1802 through satire, revealing, as satire is wont to do, that the highest in the land, no matter how chaste or wholesome in outward appearance, is at least as likely as the next man to indulge his desires, or act irrationally. Whatever Thomas Jefferson thought about his wife, Patty, or his concubine, Sally Hemings, his dietary and exercise regimen, his daily footbaths in cold water, and his painstaking record-keeping over the course of a lifetime strongly suggest that he paid close attention to his body and its urges.

Notes

1. The preceding reflects an engagement with Charles A. Miller, *Jefferson and Nature: An Interpretation* (Baltimore, 1988), and I. Bernard Cohen, *Science and the Founding Fathers: Science in the Political Thought of Jefferson, Franklin, Adams, and Madison* (New York, 1995) (quotation at 65). Additional material is drawn from Andrew Burstein, *Jefferson's Secrets: Death and Desire at Monticello* (New York, 2005).

2. TJ to Francis Adrian Van der Kemp, February 9, 1818, Thomas Jefferson Papers, Library of Congress, Washington, D.C. On Jefferson's neurophysiological vocabulary, see Burstein, *Jefferson's Secrets,* chap. 2–3, especially pp. 48–49, 56.

3. "Notes on the Letter of Christoph Daniel Ebeling," after October 15, 1795, in Jefferson, *Papers,* 28:508; TJ to Joel Barlow, May 3, 1802, Thomas Jefferson Papers, Library of Congress.

4. D. T. de Bienville, *Nymphomania, or, A Dissertation Concerning the Furor Uterinus . . . ,* trans. Edward Sloane Wilmot (London, 1775), 28–31, 108–10; John Aitken, *Principles of Midwifery, or Puerperal Medicine* (Edinburgh, 1785),

135; John Astruc, *A Treatise on All the Diseases Incident to Women* (London, 1743), 155, 160–61, 286–90 (quotations at 155, 286).

5. Luce Irigaray, *This Sex Which Is Not One,* translated by Catherine Porter with Carolyn Burke (Ithaca, N.Y., 1985); TJ to Martha Jefferson Randolph, April 4, 1790, and February 9, 1791, in *The Family Letters of Thomas Jefferson,* ed. Edwin Morris Betts and James Adam Bear Jr. (Columbia, Mo., 1966), 51, 71.

6. Dishonoring themselves, masturbating women reflected the fearful truth that, for both sexes, the sexual imagination could wreak havoc. At the other extreme were the cold or sterile females described in neurological terms as "languid and insensible," who "hate the Embraces of their Husbands or Gallants." It was assumed that their uteruses were "not permeable" owing to their density, so that "the Seed remains not long enough in its Cavity." For the quotations in this and the previous paragraph, see S. A. D. Tissot, *Onanism: or, A Treatise upon the Disorders Produced by Masturbation* (London, 1766), sections 7–8, esp. pp. 60–62, 75; Astruc, *Treatise on All the Diseases Incident to Women,* 336–37; and Roy Porter, *Flesh in the Age of Reason* (London, 2003), 235.

7. S. A. D. Tissot, *De la santé des gens de lettres* (Lausanne, Switzerland, 1775) (quotations at 103, 105–6, 239; my translation).

8. See especially James N. Davidson, *Courtesans and Fishcakes: The Consuming Passions of Classical Athens* (London, 1997), chap. 5.

9. Aristotle, *The Politics,* translated by T. A. Sinclair (Baltimore, 1962), book 7, chap. 16.

10. Ellen Lupton et al., *Skin: Surface, Substance and Design* (New York, 2002).

11. J. C. Lavater, *Essays on Physiognomy; for the Promotion of the Knowledge and the Love of Mankind* (Boston, 1794).

12. Christiane Holm, "Sentimental Cuts: Eighteenth-Century Mourning Jewelry with Hair," *Eighteenth-Century Studies* 38 (Fall 2004): 139–43.

13. Elise Lemire, *"Miscegenation": Making Race in America* (Philadelphia, 2002), 129–30. Writing to William Short near the end of his days, Jefferson gave one of the last of his comments with regard to emancipation and race mixing: "I consider that of expatriation to the governments of the W[est].I[ndies]. of their own colour as entirely practicable, and greatly preferable to the *mixture* [emphasis added] of colour here, to this I have great aversion." TJ to Short, January 18, 1826, Jefferson Papers, Library of Congress.

14. Angela Rosenthal, "Raising Hair," *Eighteenth-Century Studies* 38 (Fall 2004): 1–16; Amelia Rauser, "Hair, Authenticity, and the Self-Made Macaroni," *Eighteenth-Century Studies* 38 (Fall 2004): 101–17; Holm, "Sentimental Cuts."

15. Lemire, *"Miscegenation,"* 28; Porter, *Flesh in the Age of Reason,* 248. The remarkably well-informed Jefferson apparently did not know that orang-

utans were native only to Borneo and Sumatra. The Europeans who advanced this misperception must have meant another one of the great apes who did thrive in Africa, gorillas or chimpanzees. Chimps are, of course, the most humanlike.

16. William A. Cohen, "Deep Skin," in *Thinking the Limits of the Body*, ed. Jeffrey Jerome Cohen and Gail Weiss (Albany, N.Y., 2003), 63–82; Louis S. Greenbaum, "Thomas Jefferson, the Paris Hospitals, and the University of Virginia," *Eighteenth-Century Studies* 26 (Summer 1993): 607–26; Porter, *Flesh in the Age of Reason*, 249.

17. Burstein, *Jefferson's Secrets*, chap. 6.

18. See Catherine A. Holland, *The Body Politic: Foundings, Citizenship, and Difference in the American Political Imagination* (New York, 2001), 43–47 (quotation at 47).

19. TJ to Francis Gray, March 4, 1815, Jefferson Papers, Library of Congress; TJ to John Adams, October 28, 1813, in *The Adams-Jefferson Letters: The Complete Correspondence between Thomas Jefferson and Abigail and John Adams*, ed. Lester J. Cappon (1959; rept., Chapel Hill, N.C., 1987), 387–89; Michel Foucault, *The History of Sexuality*, vol. 1: *An Introduction* (New York, 1978), 147–48.

20. Thomas Jefferson, First Inaugural Address, in *The Portable Thomas Jefferson*, ed. Merrill D. Peterson (New York, 1975), 291.

21. Adam Smith, *The Theory of Moral Sentiments*, edited by D. D. Raphael and A. L. Macfie (Oxford, 1976), part 3, chap. 3, especially pp. 143–52; Jefferson to Cabell, February 26, 1818, in Malone, *Jefferson and His Time*, 6:275; Henry S. Randall, *Life of Thomas Jefferson*, 3 vols. (New York, 1858), 3:231–32.

22. On this paragraph and the previous one, see Burstein, *Jefferson's Secrets*, 105–10.

23. Benjamin Rush to Rebecca Smith, May 1792, in *Letters of Benjamin Rush*, 2 vols., ed. L. H. Butterfield (Princeton, N.J., 1951), 1:617. See also Eric T. Carlson et al., eds., *Benjamin Rush's Lectures on the Mind* (Philadelphia, 1981), 686–89, 695.

24. TJ to Adams, October 18, 1813, in Cappon, ed., *Adams-Jefferson Letters*, 388.

25. TJ to Adams, August 15, 1820, ibid., 567–68; Daniel J. Boorstin, *The Lost World of Thomas Jefferson* (New York, 1948), 112–19.

ANDREW J. O'SHAUGHNESSY

Afterword

The past decade has witnessed a resurgence of popular interest in the lives of the Founders with best-selling biographies by authors like David G. McCullough, Joseph J. Ellis, Ron Chernow, and Walter Isaacson. However, the celebratory tone of such books is rarely found in modern works on Thomas Jefferson. Indeed, in venerating his opponents and rivals, these biographers are often hostile in their treatment of Jefferson. The disparity is further widened by the iconoclastic scholarship on Jefferson that is expressed at its most extreme by the work of Conor Cruise O'Brien, who notoriously likened Jefferson to Pol Pot. As Peter S. Onuf notes in the first essay of this volume, it was inevitable that the hagiographical tradition of Dumas Malone would suffer in the wake of the civil rights movement and the growing evidence that Jefferson fathered at least one and probably all of Sally Hemings's children. Furthermore, Jefferson's posthumous reputation has traditionally been subject to vagaries and cycles, as has been so well demonstrated by Merrill D. Peterson and more recently by Francis D. Cogliano.

It is nevertheless ironic that Jefferson should be so diminished since he, more than even James Madison and certainly the Federalists, had an unwavering faith in the capacity of the people to govern themselves, and he embraced more readily than most of his illustrious contemporaries the post-Revolutionary changes in America. As Gordon S. Wood demonstrates in his *Radicalism of the*

American Revolution, the elite of Jefferson's generation became disillusioned by the more democratic demeanor of society in the late eighteenth and early nineteenth centuries. Jefferson's presidency appealed to this new ethos with its informality of style and absence of ostentation.

In this volume of essays of reappraisal by some of the foremost scholars of Jefferson, the authors variously express frustration with the current state of the scholarship and suggest the need for a major reevaluation of Jefferson that seeks to go beyond merely treating him as contradictory and hypocritical and rather places him in historical context and avoids the implicit anachronism of much of the current historiography. Onuf warns that Jefferson will continue to remain obscure as long as we continue to define him in relation to ourselves rather than in relation to his contemporaries. It is also of related interest that the authors in this volume do not even mention what seemed a relentless debate regarding the ideological influences on Jefferson. There is here much less emphasis on ideology and more attention to specific circumstances that influenced his behavior.

The Jefferson who emerges is less static than in most portrayals and is seen to have evolved and reacted to events. Eva Sheppard Wolf describes a traditional provincial member of the Virginia elite who reluctantly turned revolutionary and only gradually embraced the political ideas for which he is remembered. She notes several turning points in his career, placing particular importance on the severance of ties with Britain and the partisan politics of the 1790s. She writes of him adjusting to new realities and as being more concerned with the practice than the theory of politics. Peter J. Kastor demonstrates that Jefferson was far from thinking in terms of sea to shining sea in his treatment of the West. Indeed, in his Mississippi policy between 1801 and 1803, he expressly rejected the acquisition of territory in the Far West and even considered trading major portions of the Louisiana Purchase for territory on the Gulf Coast. Kastor finds that Jefferson's experience of policymaking in the West gradually transformed his thinking about Native Americans. Thomas E. Buckley makes a convincing case for the influence of the Reverend James Maury on Jefferson. As a child, Jefferson had lodged in the home of this remarkable individual. Buckley has a particularly fascinating account of Maury's attempt to baptize some black slaves before his white congregation.

These authors do not attempt to gloss over the current critical view of Jefferson. The issues they discuss are certainly the most controversial of his career rather than the more comfortable topics, such as his intellectual activities or his horticultural interests. They indeed contain necessary qualifications of our appreciation of his legacy. Kastor shows how Jefferson moved from proclaiming the possibility of Indians' incorporation to predicting their eventual extinction. Regardless of Jefferson's best initial intentions, the majority of Indians experienced his "principles as little more than systematized misery." Adam Rothman finds that Jefferson failed to acknowledge the political and economic interests arrayed against the emancipation of slavery and took comfort in the illusory concept of colonization. Like Barbara J. Fields, Rothman argues that Jefferson blamed race rather than racism. He himself was never able to imagine the possibility of a multiracial nation and full citizenship for African Americans.

Jefferson was far from transcending his time; indeed, Jan Ellen Lewis portrays him as remarkably conventional in his attitudes toward women. In the age of Mary Wollstonecraft, Jefferson was opposed to women engaging in politics and thought that they should confine themselves to the domestic sphere. He only modified his view in relation to female slaves, who he accepted might labor in the fields. He was dismayed by the salons and the political activities of women in Paris. Lewis believes that Jefferson's tenure as minister to France from 1784 to 1789 was one of only two periods in which he displayed real misogyny. The gendered order that he advocated suited his own needs, with his wife and later his daughters providing a domestic asylum from politics at Monticello. Andrew Burstein writes the most disconcerting essay in the volume by positing the possibility that Jefferson regarded his relationship to Sally Hemings in coldly scientific and physical terms in which a sexual outlet was necessary for good health and a balanced life. Burstein derives this insight from Jefferson's interest in the writings of the Swiss physician Samuel A. D. Tissot. Although any discussion of the Hemings-Jefferson relationship must be very speculative, Burstein raises an unpleasant possibility that would accord with Jefferson's failure to acknowledge his fathering one or all of the children of Sally Hemings.

Judging by the questions posed by members of the public to present-day interpreters at Monticello, the subject of religion vies with slavery as one that most often continues to elicit debate. Jefferson's letter to the Danbury Baptists, in which he speaks of a wall of separation, has been critical in the reinterpretation of church-state relations by the Supreme Court since the 1940s. It is central to the emotional debate about school prayer. Thomas E. Buckley concedes that Jefferson was more radical in his view on church-state relations than were his Virginia contemporaries like George Washington, Patrick Henry, and John Marshall. Jefferson was much influenced by Joseph Priestley and later moved toward Unitarianism. Buckley is nevertheless guarded about the idea of a complete separation, arguing that Jefferson never envisaged a government without religion. The separation he proposed was between church and state, not government and religion. Buckley, perhaps wisely, avoids discussing the implications of his conclusion for current policymaking.

This volume therefore does not attempt to completely rehabilitate Jefferson. It leaves the reader ambivalent, but it achieves the goal of the organizers of the conference that occasioned it and the challenge posed by Peter Onuf to better understand Jefferson. Thanks to the insights of this volume, Jefferson appears less of a sphinx. It should also be apparent that there is still much to do. Peter Kastor comments that the presidency of Jefferson remains strikingly understudied, possibly because the papers for this period have only just begun to be published by Princeton University Press. Jefferson's thinking and influence on nationalism are the subject of some of the most profound recent analysis in articles by Onuf and in a forthcoming book by Brian Douglas Steele. Only recently have historians begun to think again about Jefferson's foreign policy, with forthcoming studies by Francis D. Cogliano, James R. Sofka, and Leonard J. Sadosky. Adam Rothman notes that scholars have only recently begun to publish studies of the actual community of slaves at Monticello with the work of Annette Gordon-Reed, Lucia C. Stanton, and the archaeology department at Monticello. Jefferson's views of gender and his relationship with his daughters are current subjects of interest in works by Jan Ellen Lewis, Jon Kukla, Cynthia A. Kierner, Billy L. Wayson, Brian Douglas Steele, and Elizabeth V. Chew.

Jefferson scholarship has received a great boost from the Thomas Jefferson Foundation at Monticello, which among historic houses has devoted unparalleled resources to research with the establishment of the Robert H. Smith International Center for Jefferson Studies. The center funds fellowships for visiting scholars to Monticello; it has built the Jefferson Library with an online encyclopedia, a digital database, and a portal for searching for materials; it is publishing the retirement papers of Jefferson, which will halve the time due for the completion of the publication of the papers by the Princeton University Press; it has supported the archaeology department with the DAACS project (Digital Archaeological Archive of Comparative Slavery); it hosts an annual international conference abroad; it offers programs for all age groups; it hosts summer seminars for school teachers and has a research department that is much engaged in the larger scholarly community. As John B. Boles and Randal L. Hall write in their introduction to this volume, history is a continuing conversation between the past and present. If we concur with Peter Onuf that the legacy of Jefferson is inescapable for contemporary America, the conversation promises to remain especially vigorous and lively.

Selected Bibliography

WRITINGS OF JEFFERSON

Bear, James A., Jr., and Lucia C. Stanton, eds. *Jefferson's Memorandum Books: Accounts, with Legal Records and Miscellany, 1767–1826.* 2 vols. Princeton, N.J., 1997.

Betts, Edwin Morris, ed. *Thomas Jefferson's Farm Book, with Commentary and Relevant Extracts from Other Writings.* Princeton, N.J., 1953.

Boyd, Julian P., et al., eds. *The Papers of Thomas Jefferson.* 35 vols. to date, with 5 vols. in the Retirement Series. Princeton, N.J., 1950– .

Cappon, Lester J., ed. *The Adams-Jefferson Letters: The Complete Correspondence between Thomas Jefferson and Abigail and John Adams.* 2 vols. Chapel Hill, N.C., 1959.

Ford, Paul Leicester, ed. *The Works of Thomas Jefferson.* 12 vols. New York, 1904–5.

Jefferson, Thomas. *Notes on the State of Virginia.* Edited by William Peden. Chapel Hill, N.C., 1954.

Lipscomb, Andrew A., and Albert Ellery Bergh, eds. *The Writings of Thomas Jefferson.* 20 vols. Washington, D.C., 1903–4.

Peterson, Merrill D., ed. *The Portable Thomas Jefferson.* New York, 1975.

——, ed. *Thomas Jefferson: Writings.* New York, 1984.

Smith, James Morton, ed. *The Republic of Letters: The Correspondence between Thomas Jefferson and James Madison, 1776–1826.* 3 vols. New York, 1995.

GENERAL BIOGRAPHIES

Brodie, Fawn M. *Thomas Jefferson: An Intimate History.* New York, 1974.

Cunningham, Noble E. *In Pursuit of Reason: The Life of Thomas Jefferson.* Baton Rouge, La., 1987.

Hayes, Kevin J. *The Road to Monticello: The Life and Mind of Thomas Jefferson.* New York, 2008.

Kimball, Marie G. *Jefferson: The Road to Glory, 1743–1776.* New York, 1943.

——. *Jefferson: War and Peace, 1776 to 1784.* New York, 1947.

——. *Jefferson: The Scene of Europe, 1784–1789.* New York, 1950.

Malone, Dumas. *Jefferson and His Time.* 6 vols. Boston, 1948–81.

McLaughlin, Jack. *Jefferson and Monticello: The Biography of a Builder.* New York, 1998.

Peterson, Merrill D., ed. *Thomas Jefferson: A Reference Biography.* New York, 1986.

——. *Thomas Jefferson and the New Nation: A Biography.* New York, 1970.

Randall, Henry S. *The Life of Thomas Jefferson.* 3 vols. New York, 1858.

Randall, Willard Sterne. *Thomas Jefferson: A Life.* New York, 1993.

Schachner, Nathan. *Thomas Jefferson, A Biography.* New York, 1951.

INTERPRETATIVE BIOGRAPHIES / ESSAYS

Appleby, Joyce. *Thomas Jefferson.* New York, 2003.

Bailyn, Bernard. "Jefferson and the Ambiguities of Freedom." In *To Begin the World Anew: The Genius and Ambiguities of the American Founders,* by Bernard Bailyn, 37–59. New York, 2003.

Beran, Michael Knox. *Jefferson's Demons: Portrait of a Restless Mind.* New York, 2003.

Bernstein, Richard B. *Thomas Jefferson.* New York, 2003.

Binger, Carl. *Thomas Jefferson, a Well-Tempered Mind.* New York, 1970.

Boorstin, Daniel J. *The Lost World of Thomas Jefferson.* New York, 1948.

Burstein, Andrew. *The Inner Jefferson: Portrait of a Grieving Optimist.* Charlottesville, Va., 1995.

——. *Jefferson's Secrets: Death and Desire at Monticello.* New York, 2005.

Chinard, Gilbert. *Thomas Jefferson, the Apostle of Americanism.* Boston, 1929.

Cogliano, Francis D. *Thomas Jefferson: Reputation and Legacy.* Edinburgh, 2006.

Crawford, Alan Pell. *Twilight at Monticello: The Final Years of Thomas Jefferson.* New York, 2008.

Ellis, Joseph J. *American Sphinx: The Character of Thomas Jefferson.* New York, 1997.

Lehmann, Karl. *Thomas Jefferson, American Humanist.* New York, 1947.

Levy, Leonard. *Jefferson and Civil Liberties: The Darker Side.* Cambridge, Mass., 1963.

Nock, Albert Jay. *Jefferson.* New York, 1926.

Onuf, Peter S. *Jefferson's Empire: The Language of American Nationhood.* Charlottesville, Va., 2000.

——. *The Mind of Thomas Jefferson.* Charlottesville, Va., 2007.

Peterson, Merrill D. *The Jefferson Image in the American Mind.* New York, 1960.

Wilson, Douglas L. "Thomas Jefferson and the Character Issue." *Atlantic Monthly,* November 1992, 57–74.

Wood, Gordon S. *Revolutionary Characters: What Made the Founders Different.* New York, 2006.

COLLECTIONS OF ESSAYS

Ellis, Joseph J., et al. *Thomas Jefferson: Genius of Liberty.* Washington, D.C., 2000.

Gilreath, James, ed. *Thomas Jefferson and the Education of a Citizen.* Washington, D.C., 1999.

Onuf, Peter S., ed. *Jeffersonian Legacies.* Charlottesville, Va., 1993.

Shuffelton, Frank, ed. *The Cambridge Companion to Thomas Jefferson.* Cambridge, 2009.

JEFFERSON AND POLITICS/GOVERNMENT

Adams, Henry. *History of the United States of America during the Administrations of Thomas Jefferson.* Text selection and notes by Earl Harbert. 2 vols. in 1. New York, 1986.

Bailey, Jeremy D. *Thomas Jefferson and Executive Power.* New York, 2007.

Banning, Lance. *The Jeffersonian Persuasion: Evolution of a Party Ideology.* Ithaca, N.Y., 1978.

Ben-Atar, Doron S. *The Origins of Jeffersonian Commercial Policy and Diplomacy.* New York, 1993.

Cunningham, Noble E., Jr. *The Process of Government under Jefferson.* Princeton, N.J., 1978.

Ferling, John E. *Adams vs. Jefferson: The Tumultuous Election of 1800.* New York, 2004.

Fliegelman, Jay. *Declaring Independence: Jefferson, Natural Language, and the Culture of Performance.* Stanford, Calif., 1993.

Hatzenbuehler, Ronald L. *"I tremble for my country": Thomas Jefferson and the Virginia Gentry.* Gainesville, Fla., 2006.

Jayne, Allen. *Jefferson's Declaration of Independence: Origins, Philosophy, and Theology.* Lexington, Ky., 1998.

Johnstone, Robert M., Jr. *Jefferson and the Presidency: Leadership in the Young Republic.* Ithaca, N.Y., 1978.

Koch, Adrienne. *Jefferson and Madison: The Great Collaboration.* New York, 1950.

Maier, Pauline. *American Scripture: Making the Declaration of Independence.* New York, 1997.

O'Brien, Conor Cruise. *The Long Affair: Thomas Jefferson and the French Revolution, 1785–1800.* Chicago, 1996.

Matthews, Richard K. *The Radical Politics of Thomas Jefferson: A Revisionist View.* Lawrence, Kans., 1984.

Mayer, David N. *The Constitutional Thought of Thomas Jefferson.* Charlottesville, Va., 1994.

Pasley, Jeffrey L. "Politics and the Misadventures of Thomas Jefferson's Modern Reputation: A Review Essay." *Journal of Southern History* 72 (November 2006): 871–908.

Rahe, Paul A. "Thomas Jefferson's Machiavellian Political Science." *Review of Politics* 57 (Summer 1995): 449–81.

Sheldon, Garrett Ward. *The Political Philosophy of Thomas Jefferson.* Baltimore, 1991.

Sloan, Herbert E. *Principle and Interest: Thomas Jefferson and the Problem of Debt.* New York, 1995.

Steele, Brian. "Thomas Jefferson, Coercion, and the Limits of Harmonious Union." *Journal of Southern History* 74 (November 2008): 823–54.

Tucker, Robert W., and David C. Hendrickson. *Empire of Liberty: The Statecraft of Thomas Jefferson.* New York, 1990.

Waldstreicher, David. "Why Thomas Jefferson and African Americans Wore Their Politics on Their Sleeves: Dress and Mobilization between American Revolutions." In *Beyond the Founders: New Approaches to the Political History of the Early American Republic,* edited by Jeffrey L. Pasley, Andrew W. Robertson, and David Waldstreicher, 79–103. Chapel Hill, N.C., 2004.

Wills, Garry. *Inventing America: Jefferson's Declaration of Independence.* New York, 1978.

Wiltse, Charles Maurice. *The Jeffersonian Tradition in American Democracy.* Chapel Hill, N.C., 1935.

Yarbrough, Jean M. *American Virtues: Thomas Jefferson on the Character of a Free People.* Lawrence, Kans., 1998.

Jefferson and the West / Native Americans

Ambrose, Stephen E. *Undaunted Courage: Meriwether Lewis, Thomas Jefferson, and the Opening of the American West.* New York, 1996.

Carlson, Laurie M. *Seduced by the West: Jefferson's America and the Lure of the Land beyond the Mississippi.* Chicago, 2003.

Engeman, Thomas S., ed. *Thomas Jefferson and the Politics of Nature.* Notre Dame, Ind., 2000.

Jackson, Donald, ed. *Letters of the Lewis and Clark Expedition, with Related Documents, 1783–1854.* 2nd ed. 2 vols. Urbana, Ill., 1978.

———. *Thomas Jefferson and the Stony Mountains: Exploring the West from Monticello.* Urbana, Ill., 1981.

Kaplan, Lawrence S. *Thomas Jefferson: Westward the Course of Empire.* Wilmington, Del., 1999.

Kastor, Peter J. *The Nation's Crucible: The Louisiana Purchase and the Creation of America.* New Haven, Conn., 2004.

Kennedy, Roger G. *Mr. Jefferson's Lost Cause: Land, Farmers, Slavery, and the Louisiana Purchase.* New York, 2003.

Kukla, Jon. *A Wilderness So Immense: The Louisiana Purchase and the Destiny of America.* New York, 2003.

Miller, Charles A. *Jefferson and Nature: An Interpretation.* Baltimore, 1988.

Ronda, James P. "Jefferson and the Imperial West." *Journal of the West* 31 (July 1992): 13–19.

——. *Jefferson's West: A Journey with Lewis and Clark.* Charlottesville, Va., 2000.

——, ed. *Thomas Jefferson and the Changing West: From Conquest to Conservation.* Albuquerque, N.M., 1997.

Sheehan, Bernard W. *Seeds of Extinction: Jeffersonian Philanthropy and the American Indian.* Chapel Hill, N.C., 1973.

Wallace, Anthony F. C. *Jefferson and the Indians: The Tragic Fate of the First Americans.* Cambridge, Mass., 1999.

JEFFERSON: WOMEN, GENDER, AND FAMILY

Betts, Edwin Morris, and James Adam Bear Jr., eds. *The Family Letters of Thomas Jefferson.* Columbia, Mo., 1966.

Boykin, Edward, ed. *To the Girls and Boys, Being the Delightful Little-Known Letters of Thomas Jefferson to and from his Children and Grandchildren.* New York, 1964.

Bullock, Helen Duprey. *My Head and My Heart: A Little History of Thomas Jefferson and Maria Cosway.* New York, 1945.

Kaminski, John P., ed. *Jefferson in Love: The Love Letters between Thomas Jefferson and Maria Cosway.* Madison, Wis., 1999.

Kukla, Jon. *Mr. Jefferson's Women.* New York, 2007.

Lewis, Jan. *The Pursuit of Happiness: Family and Values in Jefferson's Virginia.* Cambridge, 1983.

Lockridge, Kenneth A. *On the Sources of Patriarchal Rage: The Commonplace Books of William Byrd and Thomas Jefferson and the Gendering of Power in the Eighteenth Century.* New York, 1992.

Randolph, Sarah N. *The Domestic Life of Thomas Jefferson . . .* New York, 1871.

Steele, Brian. "Thomas Jefferson's Gender Frontier." *Journal of American History* 95 (June 2008): 17–42.

JEFFERSON: SLAVERY AND RACE

Finkelman, Paul. *Slavery and the Founders: Race and Liberty in the Age of Jefferson.* Armonk, N.Y., 1996.

Gordon-Reed, Annette. *The Hemingses of Monticello: An American Family.* New York, 2008.

——. *Thomas Jefferson and Sally Hemings: An American Controversy.* Charlottesville, Va., 1997.

Heath, Barbara J. *Hidden Lives: The Archaeology of Slave Life at Thomas Jefferson's Poplar Forest.* Charlottesville, Va., 1999.

Helo, Ari, and Peter S. Onuf. "Jefferson, Morality, and the Problem of Slavery." *William and Mary Quarterly,* 3rd ser., 60 (July 2003): 583–614.

Lewis, Jan Ellen, and Peter S. Onuf, eds. *Sally Hemings and Thomas Jefferson: History, Memory, and Civic Culture.* Charlottesville, Va., 1999.

Matthewson, Tim. "Jefferson and Haiti." *Journal of Southern History* 61 (May 1995): 209–48.

Miller, John Chester. *The Wolf by the Ears: Thomas Jefferson and Slavery.* New York, 1977.

Oakes, James. "Why Slaves Can't Read: The Political Significance of Jefferson's Racism." In *Thomas Jefferson and the Education of a Citizen,* edited by James Gilreath, 177–92. Washington, D.C., 1999.

Onuf, Peter S. " 'To Declare Them a Free and Independent People': Race, Slavery, and National Identity in Jefferson's Thought." *Journal of the Early Republic* 18 (Spring 1998): 1–46.

Reed, B. Bernetiae. *The Slave Families of Thomas Jefferson: A Pictorial Study Book with an Interpretation of His Farm Book in Genealogy Charts.* 2 vols. Greensboro, N.C., 2007.

Rothman, Adam. *Slave Country: American Expansion and the Origins of the Deep South.* Cambridge, Mass., 2005.

Stanton, Lucia. *Slavery at Monticello.* Charlottesville, Va., 1996.

Waldstreicher, David. "Why Thomas Jefferson and African Americans Wore Their Politics on Their Sleeves: Dress and Mobilization between American Revolutions." In *Beyond the Founders: New Approaches to the Political History of the Early American Republic,* edited by Jeffrey L. Pasley, Andrew W. Robertson, and David Waldstreicher, 79–103. Chapel Hill, N.C., 2004.

Walker, Clarence E. *Mongrel Nation: The America Begotten by Thomas Jefferson and Sally Hemings.* Charlottesville, Va., 2009.

Wolf, Eva Sheppard. *Race and Liberty in the New Nation: Emancipation in Virginia from the Revolution to Nat Turner's Rebellion.* Baton Rouge, La., 2006.

JEFFERSON AND RELIGION

Adams, Dickinson W., ed. *Jefferson's Extracts from the Gospels: "The Philosophy of Jesus" and "The Life and Morals of Jesus."* Princeton, N.J., 1983.

Buckley, Thomas E., S.J. *Church and State in Revolutionary Virginia, 1776–1787.* Charlottesville, Va., 1977.

——. "Reflections on a Wall." *William and Mary Quarterly,* 3rd ser., 56 (October 1999): 795–800.

Dreisbach, Daniel L. *Thomas Jefferson and the Wall of Separation between Church and State.* New York, 2002.
Gaustad, Edwin S. *Sworn on the Altar of God: A Religious Biography of Thomas Jefferson.* Grand Rapids, Mich., 1996.
Hutson, James H. "Thomas Jefferson's Letter to the Danbury Baptists: A Controversy Rejoined." *William and Mary Quarterly,* 3rd ser., 56 (October 1999): 775–90.
Sheridan, Eugene R. *Jefferson and Religion.* Charlottesville, Va., 1998.
——. "Liberty and Virtue: Religion and Republicanism in Jeffersonian Thought." In *Thomas Jefferson and the Education of a Citizen,* edited by James Gilreath, 242–63. Washington, D.C., 1999.
Sanford, Charles B. *The Religious Life of Thomas Jefferson.* Charlottesville, Va., 1984.

Jefferson: Renaissance Man of the World
Adams, William Howard, ed. *The Eye of Thomas Jefferson.* Washington, D.C., 1976.
——, ed. *Jefferson and the Arts: An Extended View.* Washington, D.C., 1976.
——. *Jefferson's Monticello.* New York, 1983.
——. *The Paris Years of Thomas Jefferson.* New Haven, 1997.
Bedini, Silvio. *Thomas Jefferson and His Copying Machines.* Charlottesville, Va., 1984.
——. *Thomas Jefferson, Statesman of Science.* New York, 1990.
Cripe, Helen. *Thomas Jefferson and Music.* Charlottesville, Va., 1974.
Dewey, Frank L. *Thomas Jefferson, Lawyer.* Charlottesville, Va., 1986.
Dumbauld, Edward. *Thomas Jefferson, American Tourist . . .* Norman, Okla., 1946.
Gabler, James M. *Passions: The Wines and Travels of Thomas Jefferson.* Baltimore, 1995.
Hellenbrand, Harold. *The Unfinished Revolution: Education and Politics in the Thought of Thomas Jefferson.* Newark, Del., 1990.
Howard, Hugh. *Thomas Jefferson, Architect: The Built Legacy of Our Third President.* New York, 2003.
Kelsall, Malcolm. *Jefferson and the Iconography of Romanticism: Folk, Land, Culture, and the Romantic Nation.* New York, 1999.
McDonald, Robert M. S. *Thomas Jefferson's Military Academy: Founding West Point.* Charlottesville, Va., 2004.
Nichols, Frederick Doveton, and Ralph E. Griswold. *Thomas Jefferson, Landscape Architect.* Charlottesville, Va., 1978.
Peterson, Merrill D., ed. *Visitors to Monticello.* Charlottesville, Va., 1989.
Rice, Howard C., Jr. *Thomas Jefferson's Paris.* Princeton, N.J., 1976.

Shackelford, George Green. *Thomas Jefferson's Travels in Europe, 1784–1789*. Baltimore, 1995.

Stein, Susan. *The Worlds of Thomas Jefferson at Monticello*. New York, 1993.

Wagoner, Jennings L. *Jefferson and Education*. Charlottesville, Va., 2004.

Wilson, Douglas L., and Lucia Stanton, eds. *Jefferson Abroad*. New York, 1999.

Wilson, Richard Guy, ed. *Thomas Jefferson's Academical Village: The Creation of an Architectural Masterpiece*. Rev. ed. Charlottesville, Va., 2009.

Contributors

JOHN B. BOLES is the William Pettus Hobby Professor of History at Rice University and editor of the *Journal of Southern History.*

THOMAS E. BUCKLEY, S.J., is Professor of Modern Christian History at the Jesuit School of Theology of Santa Clara University at Berkeley.

ANDREW BURSTEIN is the Charles Phelps Manship Professor of History at Louisiana State University.

RANDAL L. HALL is Managing Editor of the *Journal of Southern History* and Adjunct Associate Professor of History at Rice University.

PETER J. KASTOR is Associate Professor of History and American Culture Studies at Washington University at St. Louis.

JAN ELLEN LEWIS is Associate Dean of Faculty and Professor of History at Rutgers University at Newark.

PETER S. ONUF is Thomas Jefferson Memorial Foundation Professor of History at the University of Virginia.

ANDREW J. O'SHAUGHNESSY is Saunders Director of the Robert H. Smith International Center for Jefferson Studies.

ADAM ROTHMAN is Associate Professor of History at Georgetown University.

EVA SHEPPARD WOLF is Associate Professor of History at San Francisco State University.

Index